UNDER THIS ROOF

The White House and the Presidency—
21 Presidents, 21 Rooms, 21 Inside Stories

PAUL BRANDUS

Guilford, Connecticut

An imprint of The Rowman & Littlefield Publishing Group, Inc.
4501 Forbes Blvd., Ste. 200
Lanham, MD 20706
www.rowman.com

Distributed by NATIONAL BOOK NETWORK

British Library Cataloguing in Publication Information Available

Library of Congress Cataloging-in-Publication Data

Brandus, Paul.
  Under this roof / Paul Brandus. — 1st edition.
     pages cm
  Includes bibliographical references and index.
  ISBN 978-1-4930-0834-6 (hardcover) — ISBN 978-1-4930-1931-1 (e-book) — ISBN 978-1-4930-3359-1 (pbk. : alk. paper) 1. White House (Washington, D.C.) 2. Presidents—United States—History. 3. Washington (D.C.)—Buildings, structures, etc. I. Title.
  F204.W5B736 2015
  975.3—dc23

                                    2015020568

♾™ The paper used in this publication meets the minimum requirements of American National Standard for Information Sciences—Permanence of Paper for Printed Library Materials, ANSI/NISO Z39.48-1992.

Printed in the United States of America

For Kathryn and Julia, the two great loves of my life

And to my wonderful parents, Gene and Rosemary,
for a lifetime of love and support

Contents

PREFACE

We Americans like to think of our country as a young one, and set against the long sweep of history, 240 years is indeed the proverbial blink of an eye. Yet most are surprised to learn that the White House is one of the oldest continuous residences for a head of state in the world. Buckingham Palace didn't became home to the British monarchy until 1837, and the emperor of Japan first moved into Tokyo's Imperial Palace in 1869. Even Moscow's Kremlin, for centuries home to the czars, only regained its head-of-state status when Vladimir Lenin's Bolsheviks moved the Russian capital back from Saint Petersburg in 1918. By that time, the White House had been home to the president of the United States for 118 years.

It's this sense of history that envelopes you when you enter the White House grounds. Walk through the Northwest Gate, stroll into this magnificent architectural gem and it hits you: This is where Thomas Jefferson and Abraham Lincoln walked. In the Diplomatic Reception Room: Franklin D. Roosevelt gave his fireside chats, right here! In the East Room, I've stood on the spot where Lincoln and John F. Kennedy's coffins lay and felt a chill run down my spine. On the South Lawn, I have seen Marine One land and leave countless times and it never fails to impress. And no matter your political leanings, meeting the president of the United States—any president—is always a great privilege.

The White House is today perhaps the most famous building in the world. For more than two centuries—through triumph and tragedy, war and peace—what has transpired here, in the northwest quadrant of America's capital city, reflects the story of the United States and its rapid rise from an exuberant but weak and disorganized new nation to global colossus. It is the ultimate symbol of the nation itself, a place of power and grandeur that has awed emperors and kings, prime ministers and popes, tycoons and movie stars, not to mention the millions of ordinary tourists who have walked its halls.

But to the forty-two men and their families who have lived here since November 1, 1800, when John Adams moved in, the "Executive Mansion," "President's Palace," or "President's House" (all three names have been used to describe the White House) is also something more mundane: a place to kick back, walk the dog, or fix a peanut butter and jelly sandwich. In other words, home. That's what this book is all about. I hope you enjoy reading it as much as I have enjoyed writing it.

CHAPTER ONE

John Adams: A Benediction for the Future

The State Dining Room

On October 13, 1800, a Monday, the president of the United States, John Adams, climbed into his weather-beaten coach in Quincy, Massachusetts, and headed south.[1] It was never easy leaving his beloved farm, but it was moving day; he was traveling to his new home in the capital city of Washington, in the District of Columbia, some 450 miles away. It was a new home in a new city, in a new nation in a new century of extraordinary promise.

There was every reason for optimism, but as his carriage bounced up and down the dirt roads, the president was likely in a gloomy mood. He was up for reelection, and his campaign against what had been a lifelong friend, Virginia's Thomas Jefferson, had descended into a mud-splattered brawl, tarred by viciousness and slander on both sides.

Though both towering figures of their time and one-time allies, the foreign policy of President Adams, a member of the Federalist Party, had come under increasing criticism from his own Vice President Jefferson—a leader of the Democratic-Republican Party. To tamp down the criticism, Adams signed into law the Alien and Sedition Acts of 1798, giving him, among other things, the power to

John Adams was the first President to live in the White House. His benediction is today carved into the mantle of the State Dining Room: "I pray Heaven to bestow the best of blessings on this house, and on all that shall hereafter inhabit it. May none but honest and wise men ever rule under this roof!" NATIONAL ARCHIVES

The White House as it looked when John Adams moved in on November 1, 1800. This original design, by the Irish architect James Hoban, was modeled after the Leinster House in Dublin, Ireland. The original White House did not include the north and south porticos. LIBRARY OF CONGRESS

silence his political opposition. Opponents of the president were fined and/or tossed in jail; many newspapers were shut down. The Jefferson camp framed this all as a blatant attack on the First Amendment and called Adams a mad power monger. Adams's supporters depicted Jefferson as a "coward" and anti-Christian.

The candidates in those days generally did not campaign, as it was considered beneath the dignity of someone running for so esteemed an office. Such high-mindedness certainly didn't apply to the newspapers, which—Sedition Act or not—let loose daily with merciless barrages attacking the other side. The New England states—Adams's home turf—would certainly back him, while Jefferson would do equally well in the South. That left the vast area in between, the middle Atlantic region, up for grabs. But Adams also knew that in May Jefferson's Democratic-Republican Party had won control of the legislature of the nation's biggest state, New York, along with its twelve electoral votes. That October, as he watched the autumn countryside roll past on his way to Washington, the president understood that his prospects for reelection were uncertain at best.

But troubled as he was by his shaky political standing, Adams may have been even more preoccupied with personal tragedy. The president had learned two years before that Charles, his second-born son, was an alcoholic, had been cheating on his wife, and was penniless. The revelations were obviously devastating to the president and his wife, Abigail. The first lady maintained hope that her son would recover, but Adams washed his hands in the matter. He painfully renounced Charles and swore to never see him again. He kept that promise, declining to stop as the presidential carriage rolled through East Chester, New York.[2] Charles, who was described by his father as a "beast,"[3] would be dead within seven weeks at age thirty.

This was the president's mind-set—a man beset with personal and political problems—as he traveled from his lifelong home to what would be a temporary abode of just four months. From a simple saltbox structure to the grandest home in all the land, known in his day as the President's House but to the world today as the White House.

The cornerstone of the mansion that would become the White House had been laid eight years before to the day: Saturday, October 13, 1792. A newspaper report said a polished brass plate was pressed into a layer of wet mortar, which had been spread across a foundation stone. The brass plate was inscribed:

> *This first stone of the President's House was laid the 13th day of October 1792, and in the seventeenth year of the independence of the United States of America.*
>
> *George Washington, President*
> *Thomas Johnson,*
> *Doctor Stewart,*
> *Daniel Carroll,*
> *Commissioners*
> *James Hoban, Architect*
> *Collen Williamson, Master Mason* [4]

A stone was placed on top of this, and Williamson nudged it into place. President Washington, tending to the nation's business in Philadelphia, was not present but was the recipient of at least one toast given that night during a celebratory dinner at the Fountain Inn, a fancy establishment in the Georgetown section of the young city.[5] The building they honored that day would be, by design, a place of power. But not too much power.

Washington was impressed with the mansion's original design, which was submitted during a contest by an Irishman by the name of James Hoban. Hoban proposed that the mansion have two stories and a raised basement; it was later decided to eliminate the basement. Official government business would be conducted on the first floor, the "state floor," with the president's family living upstairs.[6] But Washington ordered the mansion's overall size increased by one-fifth and that its exterior be adorned with intricate carvings.[7 8]

Construction proceeded slowly. Using sandstone from Aquia Creek quarry south of Mount Vernon as the principal raw material, workers generally labored from April to October each year. But after eight years and an estimated $232,372 in expenditures[9] (equivalent to $72 million in today's dollars), the mansion was still far from complete by the time its first occupant moved in. The sandstone itself seemed an odd choice, given how porous it was; workers sealed the blocks with a white-colored paint that was mixed with salt, ground rice, and glue.

Even after years of work, the mansion was in such a state during the summer of 1800, just months before Adams was due to arrive, that Oliver Wolcott Jr., who had been Washington's last treasury secretary and Adams's first, wrote in a letter to his wife that: "I cannot but consider our Presidents as very unfortunate men if they must live in this dwelling. It must be cold and damp in winter. . . . It was built to be looked at by visitors and strangers, and will render its occupants an object of ridicule with some and pity with others."[10]

Adams himself had a good idea of what to expect. He had toured the President's House on June 4, when he first visited Washington. He took a room in Tunnicliffe's City Hotel (also conveniently a tavern) on Capitol Hill. The president quickly learned that the new Federal City, where hogs and cattle ran free in the filthy, ramshackle streets, was quite uncouth. As David McCullough notes in his biography of Adams, the president "could rightfully have fumed over the heat, the mosquitoes, the squalid shacks of the work crews . . . there was no city as yet, only a rather shabby village and great stretches of tree stumps, stubble and swamp. There were no schools, not a single church."[11]

It might have been an affront to the president's patrician ways, which had been reinforced by diplomatic stints in Paris and London, but it apparently was not. From Tunnicliffe's he wrote Abigail on June 13:

I like the seat of government very well and shall sleep or lie awake next winter in the President's house. . . . [Secretary of State] Mr Marshall and [Secretary of War] Mr Lodge with me at Tunnicliff's City Hotel very near the capitol. The establishment of the public offices in this place has given it the air of the seat of government and all things seem to go on well.[12]

"The air of the seat of government" seems exaggerated, given that Washington was home to perhaps eight thousand people in 1800, and only 125 federal workers. The only government building that had been finished was the Treasury Building, which stood at what is today 15th and Pennsylvania Avenue NW, right next to the still-uncompleted President's House. The city was really nothing more than a sleepy little hamlet, rather staid and quite removed from bustling and colorful Philadelphia, where Adams lived during the first three years of his presidency.

But if nothing else, John Adams, the so-called "Atlas of Independence," was a man of the future. Like George Washington and Pierre Charles L'Enfant, the architect and civil engineer who was designing the layout of the new capital, the president saw grandeur in the making, a glorious city. So when he first laid eyes on the President's Mansion in June, he saw beyond what it was to many—a muddy, disheveled construction site—to what it would eventually become: an imposing edifice, meant to reflect the power and prestige of its occupant: the president of the United States.

Nevertheless, Adams was displeased with the pace of construction, and with some work that had already been done. He ordered composition reliefs featuring nude figures removed from mantelpieces and that a bell system be installed so he could summon servants as needed. The president had also ordered wallpaper and the planting of a vegetable garden on the southern side of the mansion. He told three commissioners (bureaucrats) overseeing the project—Capitol architect Dr. William Thornton, Virginia politician Alexander White, and Gustavus Scott, a businessman—that these, and other changes, could not possibly be completed by November 1st, his scheduled move-in date.[13]

As the summer of 1800 yielded to fall and the mansion awaited the arrival of the president, workers scurried about making last-minute preparations. By law, the federal government was to occupy Washington no later than Saturday, November 1st. Though it was known that Adams was en route, no one was sure when he would show up. As the date neared, their activity became more frantic.

On November 1st, Commissioners Thornton and White were still making a last-minute inspection. Thornton's wife alerted the men that she saw, through a window at a nearby silversmith's shop, the president's coach approaching the south entrance. It was a "chariot" and four horses, "no retinue, only one servant in horseback."[14] It was 1:00 p.m. Nineteen days after leaving his Massachusetts farm, the President of the United States had arrived at the President's House.[15]

As his carriage pulled up to the south door, Adams—accompanied by his nephew William "Billy" Shaw and John Briesler, a servant from Quincy—saw an imposing building that looked very much like it does today. It ran 168 feet east to west and eighty-five feet north to south. The walls rose forty-five feet.[16] For the next sixty years it was bigger than any building in the United States. The president may have noticed that "chimneys, indeed for the most part its parapet, reached higher than the highest trees."[17] In short, it was massive, dominating all within its periphery.

Not that the surroundings were much. A small kitchen garden had been planted, but not the more extensive private gardens the president ordered five months before. The overall impression Adams likely had, notes historian Gilbert Gude, was that "the muddy landscape of the President's House was just as deplorable as the rest of the city."[18] Adams certainly saw "workman's shanties, supply huts, and old kilns strewn about the grounds." For a young nation with grand aspirations, it may have seemed an inauspicious symbol.[19]

Stepping down from his carriage, Adams saw that a temporary wooden porch had been constructed on the south side, running around the bow of the mansion. This led into the Oval Drawing Room (known today as the Blue Room). Inside, the president found his new home dusty and smoky; every available fireplace—there were thirty-nine at the time—crackled and glowed. They were lit not so much to ward off the autumn chill but to hurry the drying of still-wet plaster (mixed with hog and horse hair) on the building's walls. The rooms likely reeked of beer (a key ingredient in wallpaper paste), lead paint, and varnish, and the floors of unfinished mahogany.[20] Adams no doubt got a good whiff of it all.

Because the president entered by the south door, he initially missed the fine work that had been done to the mansion's exterior on the north side. The north door, framed by four Ionic columns, was topped by an exquisite transom of garlands, leaves, roses, acorns, ribbons, and bows, all intricately carved by a group of Scottish stonemasons. Such decoration was considered passé in Scotland itself, but rich carvings like these were what George Washington wanted. When Adams eventually saw them—as visitors today can—it was evident that Mr. Washington got his way.[21]

Bureaucrats (known as "commissioners") who were appointed to oversee the construction of the house frequently interfered with the architect Hoban, often prompting Washington, who had bonded with the genial Irishman, to step in to sweep their sometimes petty intrusions aside. A blunt "I require it" from the president was usually all it took to silence them.[22]

The White House that Adams entered was quite sturdy, thanks to another of Washington's desires. He insisted from the beginning that it would be made of stone so that federal architecture in the new capital city would be sound and strong, like the great buildings of Europe.

And strong it was. The walls were lined with two feet of brick, each measuring nine inches wide, four and a half inches tall, and two and a half inches thick. Interior partitions were all brick as well. It was stronger than his own home down the Potomac at Mount Vernon, Virginia, which was constructed from wood that had been beveled to simulate stone blocks and then painted with crushed sandstone to strengthen the exterior.[23]

The mansion had thirty-six rooms, only half of which were plastered. Main rooms had been wallpapered, including the oval drawing room on the main floor (today the Blue Room) and the oval room on the second floor above it, which Hoban intended as a ladies' salon (today the Yellow Oval Room). His design called for the construction of three staircases, but only one had been built, and that was for servants, a narrow, twisting path that ran from basement to attic.[24]

Since only half the rooms were finished, certainly less than half were furnished, and even then it was a shabby assortment of French, English, and some American pieces. Adams eyed their "worn damask, peeling gilt and scarred mahogany,"[25] and given the vast size of the mansion, even rooms that were said to be furnished probably appeared rather spartan.

But despite the mansion's unfinished state, the president still found much to impress. For starters, there was the sheer size of the place. "A wagon and team could have passed easily down the transverse halls," wrote the historian William Seale, "and the parlors, although among the smaller rooms, were very large and a full 18 feet tall."[26] Adams would also see that while some windows were glazed, others had no glass at all, just iron bars installed to guard against intruders.

Then there were the ceilings, which soared as high as twenty-two feet in the mansion's biggest room, the Public Audience Chamber (today known as the East Room). The walls, still moist, were like a vast palette awaiting the artist's brush. They were, for the most part, bare.

But in the oval drawing room, one grand piece of art had been hung: the "Lansdowne portrait," a full-length painting of George Washington by Gilbert Stuart. Stuart painted the eight-foot, five-inch masterpiece in 1796 and sold it to the government for the princely sum of $800,[27] and in the summer of 1800 it had been carefully transported from Philadelphia and mounted with screws. Adams surely admired the work, which shows Washington at age sixty-four in a black velvet suit, right arm outstretched, celebrating the ratification of the Jay Treaty, which diffused tensions between the United States and Britain after America won her independence.[28]

In Washington's left hand, held against his hip, is a dress sword. On the table are two books: *Federalist*—likely a reference to *The Federalist Papers*—and *Journal of Congress*—the *Congressional Record*. Books under the table symbolize Washington's command of the Continental Army and presidency of the Constitutional Convention. The rule of law is symbolized by a pen and paper on the table. Like the father of our country himself, the painting was larger than life, and although George Washington never lived in the White House, he—or at least Stuart's depiction—would play a prominent role in the building's very near future.[29]

The mansion's floors had been allocated prior to the president's arrival. His office was on the second floor, with a view of the South Lawn that on this first day was less than grand. Next to this, through a pocket door, was the presidential bedroom. Housekeeping was on the second floor; kitchen, laundry, and housekeeping rooms were on the basement level (today the ground floor). The oval room that is today known as the Diplomatic Reception Room was the housekeeper's room, which had built-in cabinets.[30]

The biggest room in the mansion then, as now, was the Public Audience Chamber (today's East Room), which was unfinished. Several rooms on the second floor and ground floors were used for storage. What is today the Red Room was used, as architect Hoban envisioned, as a breakfast room, furnished with tables, mahogany chairs, and two easy chairs.[31] His inspection of his new home complete, the president spent the rest of that first afternoon meeting with a variety of callers. He usually tended to official business until sunset, which on that day would have been shortly after 5:00 p.m. He ate supper, and then, holding a single candle, climbed the winding staircase—intended for servants—to his bedchamber on the top floor. As his footsteps echoed across the dim, damp halls, Adams found his new home to be very much like the nation he led: quite unfinished, but brimming with potential. Fireplaces continued to hiss and spit, fed through the night by a watchman.[32][33]

John Adams's stay in the President's House would be brief. As he suspected, the election of 1800, which began on October 31 and ended on December 3, resulted in a Jefferson victory—a reversal of their bitter 1796 match.

The president's only consolation was that Abigail had by now joined him in Washington, where they shivered together in their vast, chilly abode. "It is habitable," she wrote a friend, "by fires in every part, thirteen of which we are obliged to keep daily, or sleep in wet and damp spaces."[34]

Abigail soon became known for hanging wet laundry in the Public Audience Chamber, which was to remain a raw and unfinished space for several more years. In December, the president and first lady received another dreadful but expected bit of news: Their beloved son Charles had died. The first and only winter Adams and Abigail would spend in the President's House truly was their winter of discontent.

On March 4, 1801—Inauguration Day—the defeated Adams made his way out of the President's House before dawn, departing in the same low-key manner in which he had arrived. Eager to return to Massachusetts to join Abigail, who had departed nineteen days before, the president would not attend the swearing-in of his successor and rival.[35] The first president of the United States to live in what is today known as the White House, Adams would never return, not even a quarter-century later when, to his immense satisfaction, his oldest son, John Quincy, became the sixth president of the United States.

But the spirit of John Adams endures. More than a century later, President Franklin Delano Roosevelt learned of a letter that Adams wrote to Abigail on the morning of November 2, 1800—his first full day in the President's

House. The letter was brief, just 256 words, and it began with Adams addressing the first lady as "My dearest friend." He told her "The Building is in a State to be habitable. And now we wish for your Company . . ."

Roosevelt was particularly moved by thirty-two words, so much so that he ordered them carved into a mantle in the State Dining Room.[36] Every president since has no doubt read the words, which were written in the form of a benediction, and reflect the hopes of every American:

> *I pray to heaven to bestow the best of Blessings on this House and all that shall hereafter inhabit it. . . . May none but honest and wise men ever rule under this roof.*

CHAPTER TWO

Thomas Jefferson:
The Lewis & Clark Expedition

The President's Library

ARCHITECT. INVENTOR. SCIENTIST. SCHOLAR. A READER OF FIVE LAN-
guages. These attributes seemingly just scratch the surface when describing
Thomas Jefferson. Many presidents have had a range of eclectic interests, but
none so broad and deep. Well before the term was first coined, he was a true
Renaissance man. Perhaps another president, John F. Kennedy, put it best
when he welcomed forty-nine Nobel laureates to a 1962 dinner: "I think
this is the most extraordinary collection of talent, of human knowledge, that
has ever been gathered at the White House—with the possible exception of
when Thomas Jefferson dined alone."[1]

It should come as no surprise, then, that Jefferson surrounded himself
with like-minded brilliance. Indeed, his administration featured a constel-
lation of talent, notably Secretary of State James Madison—known as the
"Father of the Constitution" and the author of the Bill of Rights, Albert
Gallatin as treasury secretary, and Henry Dearborn, who served as secretary
of war.

Yet in terms of sheer impact on American history, perhaps the most
important person our third president would invite into his administration
was a somewhat shy but tough and resourceful young man—just twenty-
seven years old—with no Cabinet rank at all. He would be closer to Jefferson
than anyone, both literally and figuratively, living in the mansion's biggest
room—the East Room—all by himself, in a temporary space built from nothing more than a cheap wooden room divider and heavy sailcloth. It was his
relationship with the president, whose own office was just down the hall, that
would change the young nation forever. His name was Meriwether Lewis.

For a man who fought so hard to win the presidency—losing in 1796 to his Federalist rival John Adams but exacting his revenge four years later—Thomas Jefferson was in no hurry to live in the President's House itself. He spent the first fifteen days of his presidency living in Conrad & McMunn's tavern on Capitol Hill (on the present site of the Longworth House Office Building), living simply in two rooms: one for personal use and the other for business. He took his meals in the dining room, sitting at a communal table alongside other guests.[2]

Jefferson's nonchalance about moving into the President's House was rooted in his republican preference for simplicity, and an accompanying disdain for anything that reeked of strong, central authority—a central philosophy of the now-vanquished Adams. Even in its partially completed state, Jefferson thought the mansion too imposing, too fancy, and too monarch-like for his taste, incompatible with a man who had authored America's Declaration of Independence from an overbearing English king.

At first, Thomas Jefferson refused to live in the White House, which he considered too grand. He relented—and made it grander, adding east and west pavilions—the beginning of today's East and West Wings.
LIBRARY OF CONGRESS

In short, "The place was a monument to the Federalist point of view and Thomas Jefferson counted it important to cut the palace down to size."[3] But the architect and designer in Jefferson would get the best of him; he had to admit that he was intrigued by the mansion, its symbolism, and the promise it conveyed. During the design competition for it a decade earlier, Jefferson—then George Washington's

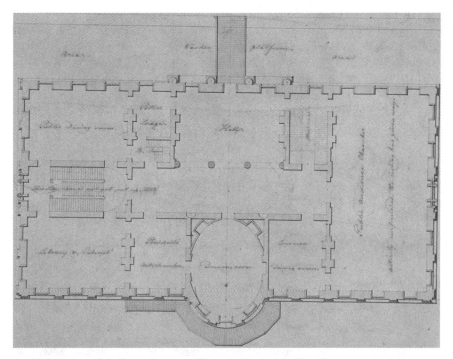

An 1803 plan of Jefferson's State Floor. Jefferson's office/library in the lower left. Meriwether Lewis lived down the hall on the southern side of the Public Audience Chamber—today's East Room. LIBRARY OF CONGRESS

secretary of state—had even submitted an anonymous entry, one of at least six known submissions before Thomas Hoban's winning entry was selected.[45]

But in 1801, with Adams preparing to leave the mansion after a mere four months, Jefferson realized he would be the first president of the United States to live in the mansion for an extended period. He also knew that the home, with its vast interior spaces and grounds, remained quite unfinished and raw. It was an irresistible opportunity for the president-architect to truly shape both the mansion and its surroundings as he saw fit.

Jefferson inspected the President's House within a week of being inaugurated, believed to be the first time he had ever set foot inside. On entering he would discover a building that, while far from complete, was much further along than it was when Adams encountered the pungent aroma of wet plaster, lead paint, and varnish just four months earlier.[6] He likely agreed that the mansion was as a newspaper had described it: "big enough

Thomas Jefferson's office in the southwest corner of the White House, which is today part of the State Dining Room. In this Peter Waddell painting, the president consults with his secretary, Meriwether Lewis, who would later lead the Lewis and Clark expedition. Lewis lived down the hall in the East Room. Jefferson's pet bird, Dick, often flew about and sometimes ate from the president's lips. PETER WADDELL FOR THE WHITE HOUSE HISTORICAL ASSOCIATION

for two emperors, one pope and the grand lama in the bargain."[7] In January, Hoban had completed the second of three staircases, this one near the entrance hall on the north side of the mansion. But the third had yet to be built; Hoban planned to install it in the west end of the transverse hall. In its place, the new president found a hole, illuminated during portions of the afternoon by shafts of light that streamed in through a "great half-round lunette window."[8]

Jefferson saw that the mansion's biggest room, the vast Public Audience Chamber—used by Abigail Adams to hang dripping wet laundry[9]—still lacked plaster walls and a ceiling. And there were no water closets, just an outhouse known as a privy. Aside from the fact that rain and snow made it uncomfortable, it was undignified for the president of the United States—particularly a fastidious man like Jefferson—to be seen scurrying back and forth between his home and an outdoor commode. One of his first acts as president, therefore, was to have two proper water closets installed on the upper floor of the mansion where he would live, one on the western end of the house, the other on the eastern end. An order went to a "Mr. Dorsey" on Third Street in Philadelphia for "Water closets . . . of superior construction, which are prepared so as to be cleansed constantly by a Pipe throwing Water through them at command from a reservoir above."[10] By "above," Jefferson meant the attic, where the reservoirs, made of tin, collected rainwater.[11]

Even so, Jefferson's water closets lacked running water, a luxury that wouldn't appear until the administration of Andrew Jackson nearly three decades later.[12] Jefferson also had coal-burning fixtures installed in fireplaces; he knew that coal burned more slowly than the wood Adams relied on, making it more efficient and freeing up servants for other tasks.[13]

Curiously, given his belief that the President's House was too grandiose, the president expanded it. Borrowing a page from Monticello, his mountaintop plantation near Charlottesville, Virginia, Jefferson ordered one-story extensions added to the President's House, on the east and west sides of the mansion, respectively; these became known, appropriately enough, as the East and West Wings. They would be used, among other things, for servants' quarters, woodsheds, and a wine cellar.[14] Drawings, most in Jefferson's hand, indicate a larger desire to extend the mansion's wings to federal buildings on each side of it.[15]

And while Adams considered the south side of the President's House to be its principal entrance, Jefferson didn't. He cared little for the aesthetically unappealing wooden stairs and platform leading into the mansion and ordered them torn down. He considered the north door, framed by four Ionic columns and topped by a Palladian window surrounded by beautiful stone carvings of flowers, leaves, acorns, ribbons, and bows, to be more suitable.[16] When visiting dignitaries arrived through this door and entered the Entrance Hall, the room directly before them (today's Blue Room) would be a drawing room, just as Hoban had intended. Jefferson may have lost the competition to design the President's House to Hoban, but there can be little doubt that as he settled in, the architect of Monticello came to increasingly admire his rival's magnificent creation, even as he improved upon it and made it his own.

A widower since the death of his wife, Martha, in 1782, Jefferson recognized the need for someone who could help run the President's House. And he knew exactly whom he wanted. On February 23, 1801, nine days before he was to be sworn in, the president-elect wrote Meriwether Lewis a letter, saying he needed a secretary "not only to aid in the private concerns of the household, but also to contribute to the mass of information which it is interesting for the administration to acquire."[17]

Lewis was an Army captain who also hailed from Virginia. Within days of learning that he had been elected president, Jefferson sent a letter to General James Wilkinson, commanding general of the US Army, asking him to locate Lewis. The president-elect said he sought Lewis because of "a personal acquaintance with him, owing from his being of my neighborhood."[18]

By "neighborhood" Jefferson meant the central Piedmont region of Virginia, where Lewis was born in 1774, some ten miles west of Monticello. There were blood ties as well: Two of Jefferson's siblings had married into the Lewis family, and Lewis's uncle, Nicholas, helped run Jefferson's farms while he served as ambassador to France between 1785 and 1789.[19]

In an 1804 letter to a former secretary, Jefferson described the broad portfolio that Lewis had been given—astonishing in retrospect for such a young man whom Jefferson knew only casually and had never worked with before:

> *The office is more in the nature of that of an Aid [sic] de camp, than a mere Secretary. The writing is not considerable, because I write my own letters & copy them in a press. The care of our company, execution of some commissions in the town occasionally, messages to Congress, occasional conferences and explanations with particular members, with the offices, & inhabitants of the place here it cannot so well be done in writing, constitute the chief business.*[20]

But Jefferson had another reason for wanting Lewis. The young Army officer possessed "a knolege [sic] of the Western country, of the army & it's [sic] situation," which Jefferson considered invaluable.[21][22] The "Western" country in 1801 generally extended to the Mississippi and Ohio Rivers and the western edge of Pennsylvania. He predicted that Lewis, who would be provided with a servant and a horse, would find the job an "easier office" than being in the Army, and that it "would make you know & be known to characters of influence in the affairs of our country, and give you the advantage of their wisdom." The president-elect sweetened the pot further, assuring Lewis that he could also retain his officer's rank and be eligible for further promotion. [23]

A chance to escape a dreary Army base and work alongside the president of the United States? Unable to resist such an offer, Lewis accepted immediately and "with pleasure."[24]

Jefferson, wanting the trusted Virginian nearby at all times, invited Lewis to live in the President's House itself. He ordered carpenters to build two rooms in the vast Public Audience Chamber for Lewis's personal use. At the time, it was being used for storage, and Lewis soon had, on the southern end of the room, an office and a smaller room for a bedchamber.[25] There was more than enough room for Lewis in the cavernous space, which measured 2,844 square feet and featured ceilings that soared twenty-two feet.

Then, as now, proximity is power in Washington: The closer one is to the president, the more powerful the person is perceived to be, and likely is. Meriwether Lewis quickly became known as one of the most influential people in the Jefferson administration, a man who literally was just down the hall from the president's office.

That the president's office itself was on the ground floor was another change from Adams's short-lived tenure in the mansion. It was the room Adams had used for levees (receptions for visitors) and today is the State Dining Room. But for Thomas Jefferson it was his office—and thus for eight years the focal point of his presidency. "Tall and generously proportioned, the office had fireplaces east and west, and was flooded with daylight through tall south and west windows." Jefferson presumably appreciated the unimpeded view out the southern window, which offered a sweeping vista down the Potomac River all the way to the port of Alexandria.[26]

A private man, Jefferson granted relatively few people access to his inner sanctum—a privilege largely reserved for his Cabinet and for Lewis. There was at least one outsider though, who gradually worked her way into this exclusive club—Margaret Bayard Smith, a prominent journalist. The careful notes she took offer wonderful insight into President Jefferson's private office: "In the centre was a long table, with drawers on each side . . . around the walls were maps, globes, charts, &c."[27]

The tables were covered with green baize (a cloth or felt), and there were library steps for reaching tall bookshelves. The presidential chairs were painted black and gold, and the mahogany floor was largely bare.[28] There was one contrast with the rest of the mansion. Although he had replaced log-burning fireplaces elsewhere, he kept two of them in his private work-space. The office as a whole, which measured thirty-eight feet by twenty feet, with an eighteen-foot ceiling, was referred to as the "cabinet" or "library."[29] Next to this was a small sitting room, and beyond this, in an easterly direction, was the oval drawing room—today known as the Blue Room. It was here that the most prominent piece of art in the President's House—then as now—was first hung: Gilbert Stuart's larger-than-life portrait of George Washington.[30]

Jefferson often mixed business and pleasure. One drawer in his "library" was stuffed with gardening tools; there were plants and flowers—mostly roses and geraniums—on one window sill, and suspended from above was a birdcage. Jefferson owned a mockingbird named Dick and let it fly around the room. Smith says Dick "was the constant companion of his solitary and studious hours," and often perched on Jefferson's shoulder or ate "food from his lips."[31] It is easy to visualize the president, engrossed in work, surrounded by greenery, warmed by two crackling log fires, and serenaded by the warble of his beloved bird.

Although he enjoyed socializing, Jefferson lived a rather isolated existence in the President's House. His solitude was such that he extended an open invitation to Treasury Secretary Gallatin and his wife to have dinner each night. It would be "a real favor," he said.[32] But for health reasons ("the city is rather sickly"), Gallatin told the president, they moved farther away, to Capitol Hill. Regardless, the president—who ate just two meals a day—rarely dined alone; Lewis, naturally, was a frequent companion.

That Jefferson and his young protégé enjoyed each other's good fellowship was obvious to many observers. In addition to being a regular at the presidential dinner table, Lewis often joined Jefferson at church; the seat to the president's left was always reserved for him.

In general, the two men lived "like two mice in a church," Jefferson once said.[33]

It is not that Jefferson was lonely or unhappy. "We find this a very agreeable country residence," he noted. "Good society, and enough of it, and free from the noise, the heat, the stench, and the bustle of a close built town."[34] Comfortable in his own skin, surrounded by his beloved books, plants, and his singing mockingbird, he delighted in solitude and the opportunity it gave him to read and think.

Visitors to Monticello these days are usually surprised, when they see Thomas Jefferson's grave, that his headstone—written by the man himself—only mentions three of his many towering achievements: "Author of the Declaration of American Independence, Of the Statute of Virginia for Religious Freedom and Father of the University of Virginia."

It may seem incredible to some that Jefferson deliberately chose to omit the eight years he served as president of the United States. But this should not be overly surprising given his fundamental aversion to what the presidency itself represented—a strong, single authority figure at the heart of the government. But it can be argued that another of Jefferson's accomplishments—and certainly the greatest of his presidency—should have been included: his audacious purchase, in 1803, of the Louisiana Territory from Napoleon and his decision to have Lewis explore it.

Even before the United States was able to purchase the territory, Jefferson had dreamed of acquiring at least a portion of it, and talked about it frequently with Lewis. During the summer of 1802, in the president's office, Lewis's office down the hall, and at Monticello, they conversed "about little else" other than Alexander Mackenzie, a Scottish explorer who had traveled over much of the territory, and written about it in a book called *Voyages from Montreal, on the River St. Lawrence, Through the Continent of North America, to the Frozen Pacific Ocean.* Unwieldy title aside, and despite the fact that it was probably ghostwritten, the book was a useful rendering of much of the Louisiana Territory itself, and the president and Lewis "devoured it."[35]

But Mackenzie's mission seemed insufficient to the two men. The Scotsman was only in search of little more than an economically efficient route for the fur trade. He took few notes on flora and fauna, potential mineral deposits, or Indian life. Lewis, the rugged outdoorsman and Army officer, knowledgeable about botany and wildlife, knew he could do better. As for Jefferson, he worried that the British—or someone else—would carve a commercial path to the West Coast ahead of America; both he and Lewis were determined to prevent this from happening.[36]

At some point in the latter half of 1802—there is no documentation on exactly when or where—the president told Lewis he was being given command of an expedition to the Pacific. The order was as presumptuous as it was bold, given that America at that point neither owned the Louisiana Territory nor had any prospect of buying it. Jefferson evidently consulted no one else about the wisdom or folly of such an undertaking and gave no consideration to anyone other than Lewis for the mission; Lewis was going to do it, and that was all there was to it.

Why Lewis? Jefferson later explained:

It was impossible to find a character who to a compleat [sic] science in botany, natural history, mineralogy & astronomy, joined the firmness of constitution & character, prudence, habits adapted to the woods, & a familiarity with the Indian manners & character, requisite for this undertaking. All the latter qualifications Capt. Lewis has.[37]

Jefferson knew this because Lewis had access to the president's extensive collection of books and maps at both Monticello and in the president's office in the mansion; the two talked incessantly about them. Some of the president's advisors failed to share Jefferson's confidence in Lewis, considering him uneducated and a bit of a hothead. But knowing of Lewis's voracious reading habits, inquisitiveness, and eagerness to learn, Jefferson knew better. History would ultimately validate the president's judgment.[38]

Jefferson's intense interest in the Louisiana Territory was not limited to botany, wildlife, or astronomy. He also saw the territory, controlled by a European power sitting on America's doorstep, in national security terms. When he entered office in 1801, the area was controlled by Spain, a fading colonial power that had no substantive military presence in North America. But Britain had commercial interests in upper Louisiana; the Russians, connected to the continent through their vast holdings in Alaska, did business near the mouth of the Columbia River, and the French, who once owned Louisiana, had expressed renewed interest in the territory.

The presence of any of these powers on America's doorstep, Jefferson believed, was an unacceptable security and commercial threat. It was imperative that the United States be the unchallenged master of the North American continent, which in his mind was meant to be an "Empire of Liberty," settled by a people "speaking the same language, governed in similar forms and by similar laws."[39]

It was Napoleon's France that soon emerged as Jefferson's principal worry. Shortly after taking office, he learned of a treaty the French had made with Spain, returning control of the Louisiana Territory to Paris. The president was alarmed: "There is on the globe one single spot, the possessor of which is our natural and habitual enemy. It is New Orleans, through which the produce of three-eighths of our territory must pass to enter market." Jefferson told a British diplomat that "the occupation of this country by France" would likely lead to eventual hostilities. "The day that France takes possession of New Orleans . . . we must marry ourselves to the British fleet and nation."[40]

The president dispatched fellow Virginian James Monroe, the former governor of the commonwealth, to Paris, who, along with Ambassador to France Robert Livingston, was to inquire about buying New Orleans and Western Florida (which stretched along the Gulf Coast of what are today Alabama and Mississippi).[41] At some point soon after, Jefferson informed Lewis of the possibility that the United States might take ownership of this territory, and instructed him to prepare a journey of exploration.

As it happened, Napoleon, focused on the possibility of war with England, saw Louisiana as a far-off and expensive burden that he could not afford to maintain. On April 11, 1803, he told his finance minister that he was renouncing the territory. That same day the French foreign minister, Talleyrand, stunned Monroe and Livingston by asking if the United States wanted to buy not just New Orleans and West Florida but the entire Louisiana Territory itself—all 828,000 square miles of it. It was the size of the entire United States itself.[42]

On April 30, the two Americans, on their own, negotiated a treaty to purchase it for $15 million.[43] It would not be possible to name another real estate transaction of such consequence that was concluded so smoothly and quickly. It is a rich irony that Jefferson, a man who in principle opposed strong executive authority, would oversee and conclude such a stupendous deal on his own. Federalists in New England who disliked Jefferson were particularly critical; but even their recriminations withered away in the face of the enormous benefit the territory would bring to the nation at large.

Word of the deal reached the President's House on the evening of July 3, a Sunday.[44] Reading the letter from Monroe and Livingston, Jefferson was as stunned as he was thrilled, though the dispatch lacked one key detail—the price. Jefferson had nothing to worry about: The $15 million worked out to about three cents per acre. It was a steal. "This removes from us the greatest source of danger to our peace," he wrote.[45] A friend, General Horatio Gates, wrote that it was "the greatest and most beneficial event that has taken place since the Declaration of Independence."[46] Meriwether Lewis prepared to depart immediately.

The president wasted no time in announcing the stupendous news. The American people would first hear of the Louisiana Purchase the very next day—the Fourth of July—twenty-seven years to the day after Jefferson's Declaration of Independence was adopted by the Continental Congress, formally severing ties between the thirteen colonies and Great Britain. Now the public learned that the United States had just *doubled* in size, expanding across the Mississippi River, north into the Dakota Territory, and up and down the spine of the Continental Divide. All told, the Louisiana Purchase encompassed what would become all or part of fifteen future states. It was a stunning achievement for both Jefferson and the young nation.

It made for a particularly glorious Fourth. Jefferson appeared on the north steps of the President's House for all to see, and then invited the public inside to shake hands. He then joined a party in progress, probably in the Oval Reception Room (today's Blue Room), where the Louisiana news was the main topic of excitement. Ironically, one man wasn't there. Meriwether Lewis had slipped away, probably out the south entrance. He would leave the next day for St. Louis to join his handpicked colleague, William Clark.[47] Together they would journey into the Louisiana Territory—and the history books—chronicling, with their "Corps of Discovery," one of America's greatest adventures.

The president wrote his departed aide, describing "the journey which you are about to undertake for the discovery of the course and source of the Mississippi, and of the most convenient water communication from thence to the Pacific."[48] Their voyage would represent the culmination of a long-standing dream of Jefferson's, the high-water mark of his presidency, and one of the most monumental chapters in American history. As he dispatched the letter, one wonders whether the president felt a twinge of envy.

CHAPTER THREE

James and Dolley Madison:
The Burning of the White House

The Queen's Sitting Room, State Dining Room

IT WAS A BLAZING HOT DAY WITH SKIN-SOAKING HUMIDITY AS DOLLEY Madison anxiously peered through her spyglass. "Mrs. President"—as first ladies were called two centuries ago—was on the very top floor, the northeast corner of the President's House, part of what is today known as the Queen's Sitting Room. The small, sparsely decorated chamber was used by Mrs. Madison as a respite from official duties. The room contained a settee on one wall, a modest writing desk on the other, and a small, round table that displayed family bric-a-brac. A fireplace stood in one corner, giving the room an odd five-walled appearance.

But there was no respite on this day, Wednesday, August 24, 1814. Mrs. Madison was looking for her husband James—the president of the United States—who, she knew, was six miles to the northeast in the Maryland tobacco town of Bladensburg, overseeing a last-ditch effort to keep British troops from storming the new capital city.

At noon, she put her spyglass down and dashed off a note to her sister:

James Madison, a protégé of Jefferson, almost always wore black and a grim expression. He looked like a "schoolmaster dressed for a funeral." LIBRARY OF CONGRESS

Since sunrise I have been turning my spy-glass in every direction, and watching with unwearied anxiety, hoping to discern the approach of my dear husband and his friends; but alas! I can descry only groups of military wandering in all directions, as if there was a lack of arms or spirit to fight for their own firesides![1]

No sitting commander in chief had ever visited an active battlefront, and as she continually scanned the horizon, Mrs. Madison feared for her husband's life. Warned of the "very threatening" British advance, the president had rushed to the front the day before.[2]

Their final conversation on the 23rd had been ominous. "He inquired anxiously whether I had the courage and firmness to remain in the Presidential house till his return," she wrote her sister, "and on my assurance that I had no fear but for him and success of our army, he left me. . . ."[3]

Neither president nor first lady could have possibly fathomed what the day would bring. Within hours, both would be forced to run for their lives, uncertain of the whereabouts or safety of the other. They would never sleep in the President's House again, which, along with another great symbol of American democracy—the still-unfinished Capitol—would soon be reduced to a "most magnificent ruin."[4] The day would go down as one of the darkest, most humiliating days in American history.

❦

That it would come to this was inconceivable five and a half years before, when Madison took the oath of office. Inauguration Day—March 4, 1809—was windy and brisk, and America was at peace, though increasing British provocations against its former colonies hinted of troubles ahead. Outgoing president Thomas Jefferson attended his successor and protégé's swearing-in at the Capitol; in his first moments as a regular citizen, Jefferson even went back to the President's House with President and Mrs. Madison to receive well-wishers. The transition of power had been a friendly one—a stark contrast to 1801, when John Adams, bitter over his failure to win reelection, left town on an early-morning coach hours ahead of Jefferson's inaugural.[5]

The Madisons inherited a President's House that had advanced considerably during the Jefferson era, yet was still unfinished. The Public Audience Chamber (today the East Room) still had yet to be plastered over. Several upstairs bedrooms also remained works in progress.[6]

Jefferson, republican that he was, made sure that the mansion was open to all as he preferred—in contrast to architect Benjamin Latrobe's advice to close it and keep the "troublesome multitudes"[7] away. That the Madisons would maintain this tradition of openness was never in doubt. In fact, they would expand it.

While Jefferson retreated socially as his presidency wore on, James and Dolley Madison, far more welcoming—especially Dolley—flung open the doors to their new home. Now that they were America's First Couple—he was fifty-seven, she was forty—Washingtonians clamored to land in their orbit. Shrewd to the capital's ways, the Madisons eagerly took advantage of the public's interest in them. The new president saw the President's House in advantageous terms, a place where others would come to him and, on his home turf, be politically seduced.[8]

Even before moving in, the president-elect put architect Latrobe to work. A stable and a coach house that

With her beauty and charm, Dolley Madison made the White House the focal point of Washington society; her entertaining was on par with anything that the high society doyennes of New York or Philadelphia had to offer.
LIBRARY OF CONGRESS

Jefferson had begun were completed. Gardens were spruced up, and a pair of large stone eagles, purchased from a Philadelphia shop, were placed at an entrance on the north side of the mansion.[9]

Inside, beyond the view of passersby, there were major changes. The President's House was generally quite pleasant during the summer, thanks to the thick plaster walls that kept Washington's brutal heat from seeping in. During the winter, those same walls offered a buffer against howling winds. But when temperatures dropped, towering windows—fourteen feet high and five feet wide—and tall ceilings made heating difficult. The mansion's fireplaces, big and deep, were aesthetically pleasing, yet threw off little heat. Often a person standing directly before a hearth would roast on one side while freezing on the other. Were it not for the dense walls, deep carpets, and thick

As British troops neared the White House, Dolley Madison directed that a Gilbert Stuart portrait of George Washington be removed from the State Dining Room. It proudly hangs today in the East Room. THE MONTPELIER FOUNDATION

curtains in every room, many a First Family would have shivered through the winter.[10]

In 1810, Latrobe, best known for designing the US Capitol building, installed a "Pettibone" furnace for the Madisons. It was probably situated in the southwest corner of the basement, where the present-day medical office is located. Through a series of air chambers (called "kettles") and ducts ("clay pipes"), it forced hot air from the basement toward upper floors. It was, in essence, a central heating system. The mansion's prior occupants would have been jealous indeed.[11]

The Madisons also made changes of their own. The biggest was to turn Jefferson's office at the western end of the mansion's ground floor into the State Dining Room. In turn, a space across the hall that had been Jefferson's bedroom was transformed into two offices, one for the president and the other for his personal secretary, Edward Coles.[12]

At the other end of the ground floor, the rooms in the vast Public Audience Chamber where Meriwether Lewis lived and worked were expanded and turned into a room for Cabinet meetings and for Coles's bedroom. What had been Jefferson's dining room became a reception area for guests, while Jefferson's sitting room became Mrs. Madison's parlor.[13] Only one room on the ground floor remained as it was—the oval salon (also called the "Elliptical Salon"), which became the main drawing room.[14] It was here that the Gilbert Stuart portrait of Washington (soon to play such a prominent role in the history of both the Madison administration and the President's House itself) was first hung[15] before being moved to the State Dining Room.

The burning of the White House by British troops reduced the mansion to a charred shell. President and Mrs. Madison lived in a nearby home for the remainder of his administration. LIBRARY OF CONGRESS

The oval salon became Mrs. Madison's personal project. When she asked architect Latrobe to hang red velvet curtains, he was privately appalled: "Oh the terrible velvet curtains. Their effect will ruin me entirely, so brilliant they will be."[16] But he was an eager supplicant and did as he was told. "I consider it my duty," he wrote, "to follow her directions in all things relative to the Pr. House."[17] The room immediately to the west, today's Red Room, was a "sunflower yellow" that enthralled visitors; one noted its "blazing splendor."[18]

The overall refurbishment was worth every penny of the $26,000 that Congress had approved,[19] the Madisons thought. They wanted the salons in which they entertained to be on par with anything that the high society doyennes of New York or Philadelphia had to offer, and they certainly were.[20] Ironically, it was also meant to mirror a drawing room in high society London, a distinction lost on British troops, who would soon reduce it to ashes.

Dolley Madison, regarded even two centuries later as one of America's greatest first ladies, was also one of its most glamorous. Thanks to her friend, the journalist Margaret Bayard Smith (whose husband happened to own the *National Intelligencer*, America's first national newspaper), Mrs. President's clothes, her parties, even her pets got the kind of coverage reserved for movie stars today. She was a trendsetter before such a term existed.[21]

Her first social stamp on the President's House was to bring back weekly receptions (called "levees"), first held by Martha Washington and briefly by Abigail Adams (Jefferson, a widower, preferred small dinner parties to large gatherings; the first of them was held on March 30, 1809).[22]

Beautiful, charming, unassuming, and sought after by seemingly everyone, Dolley worked her parties skillfully, laughing and putting her guests at ease[23]—personally filling glasses with red wine, whiskey, or rum punch. Plates of ham, beef, and crab, bowls of turtle soup, and sweets were abundant; the first lady even served a new delicacy called ice cream, which was served in hot pastry shells.[24] Entertainment was varied, including regular appearances by the Marine Band ("the President's Own"), which first made its debut on behalf of John Adams on New Year's Day 1801. Mrs. Madison also purchased a piano for the then-exorbitant sum of $450, which produced music that was of "superior tone in strength and sweetness."[25]

The levees, which were usually held on Wednesday, soon became known as "crushes," a reflection of the passion Dolley Madison had for life and the social whirl. However, the first lady didn't enjoy the rough and tumble world of politics; that was her husband's domain. As she charmed all, the president, less sociable and more awkward, could usually be seen off in one corner having a serious chat with a few visitors, waiting for certain guests "like a spider in his web."[26] Almost always dressed in black and wearing a grim expression, he looked, one visitor observed, like a "schoolmaster dressed for a funeral."[27]

War with Britain, long brewing, finally erupted in 1812. On June 1, Madison sent Congress a message outlining American grievances, and there were many. Since the 1790s, Britain—which had been at war with France for years—had periodically seized American sailors in French ports and forced them to serve in the Royal Navy. Britain had also imposed trade blockades on American shipping and had stirred up trouble inland by supporting Indian tribes that were opposed to America's westward expansion. All of this, Madison told lawmakers, undermined US sovereignty. Without explicitly asking for war, he made his opinion clear enough:

> *Whether the United States shall continue passive under these . . . accumulating wrongs, or, opposing force to force in defense of their national rights, shall commit a just cause into the hands of the Almighty Disposer of Events, . . . is a solemn question which the Constitution wisely confides to the legislative department of the Government. In recommending it to their early deliberations I am happy in the assurance that the decision will be worthy the enlightened and patriotic councils of a virtuous, a free, and a powerful nation.*[28]

Congress got the message. After four days of debate, the House voted 79 to 49 to declare war, the Senate 19 to 13. Madison formally signed a Declaration of War on June 18, and the War of 1812—sometimes called America's Second War of Independence—was on.[29]

The Americans quickly went on the offensive. After several failed attempts to invade southern Canada, US troops succeeded, in April 1813, in seizing York—today called Toronto. The Americans engaged in not a small amount of plundering; some troops set fire to Parliament and other key government buildings.[30] The British were outraged and called for revenge against the Yankee invaders.

But because Britain was also fighting Napoleon's France, it paid little attention to its former colonies an ocean away. This changed in April 1814 when the Napoleonic Empire collapsed for good. "Now that the tyrant Bonaparte has been consigned to infamy," the *London Times* seethed on April 15, "there is no public feeling in this country stronger than that of indignation against the Americans." Redcoats were put on ships and off they sailed across the Atlantic. Finally, Britain, the world's most powerful nation, would unleash the full fury of its military on its upstart American cousins.[31]

On July 17, George Cockburn, the Royal Navy rear admiral who was hated and feared by the Americans—who compared him to Attila the Hun for his viciousness[32]—submitted to his superiors a secret plan to capture the city of Washington. Cockburn said it would force the United States to divert troops from Canada, but he had an even bigger objective in mind. Taking the capital city would possibly cause the US government itself to collapse, and there wasn't anything that "Jemmy," as the admiral contemptuously called President Madison, could do about it. The plan was approved.[33]

As the broiling summer of 1814 began, the Madisons continued to entertain; few concessions had been made to the fact that the enemy was drawing near. Convening a series of meetings in the East Room (as the Public Audience Chamber was now generally referred to) Madison and his Cabinet debated what the British were up to. It was decided that Baltimore, an important port city with significant military value, was the primary enemy objective.

But what about Washington? Secretary of War John Armstrong told the president that a British attack on the capital was highly unlikely. A transplanted New Yorker, Armstrong was contemptuous of Washington, with its unsightly clusters of buildings and surrounding swamps and meadows. Overlooking the symbolic value of the city, he called it nothing more than a "sheep walk" of no military value. "What the devil will they do here?" he said. "No! No! Baltimore is the place, sir. That is of much more consequence."[34]

That a senior officer of the government—the secretary of war no less—deemed the nation's capital so unworthy of defending says much about how small and undeveloped Washington was in 1814. Secretary of State James Monroe, meanwhile, didn't think the British were even capable of mounting an attack on the capital.[35] Such an attempt, he wrote a friend, had "little prospect of success."[36]

Yet the president was worried. Convinced that the British were quite capable of being vindictive, he wisely did not discount the symbolic value of the nation's capital to the invaders and realized the city was highly vulnerable to an attack. On July 4th, he gave Gen. James Winder command of the newly created Tenth Military District, which covered Maryland, northern Virginia, and the District of Columbia itself. Winder quickly issued a blunt warning: "The door of Washington is wide open and cannot be shut with the few troops under my command."[37]

The warning was more than mere hyperbole. The federal government's lack of preparation meant that by August 1814, there were just five hundred troops, an untrained militia, and a few gunboats able to defend the city. This as a great armada of Royal Navy ships—fifty-one in all—had gathered in Chesapeake Bay. They carried one thousand crack British marines and thirty-five hundred combat-hardened army veterans—the finest that King George III had to offer.[38] The fleet would split in two, with half the ships proceeding north toward Baltimore, the rest into the Potomac and Patuxent Rivers, toward the capital.[39]

On Monday, August 22, Monroe, who had secretly rushed to an observation point on the Patuxent, thirty-five miles southeast of the capital, sent a dispatch to the president: "The enemy are in full march for Washington," he warned.[40]

The principal road into Washington ran through Bladensburg, Maryland, a small tobacco town about six miles east of the city. It was here that the Americans would make their stand. "A motley throng made up of militia, regulars, volunteers, sailors, generals, secretaries" rushed to the front.[41] The president himself would join them.[42]

Madison's decision to travel to the front was a reflection of his bravery. He was no military expert and knew it, but had convinced himself that his presence would be a morale booster for the largely unprepared force struggling to fight off the invaders.

But for a man whose contributions to American democracy had been so towering, Madison as commander in chief was less than inspiring. Standing just 5'4"—the shortest American president—and possessing a soft-spoken, shy demeanor, he appeared on the battlefield as "timid, doubtful, and hesitating . . . [a president who] could not add to the confidence or effectiveness of either officers or troops."[43]

Armstrong and Monroe had accompanied the president to the front. But instead of huddling with them and his commanders and taking charge of the desperate situation, Madison apparently spent much of his time scribbling notes to his wife. The battle went badly. Finally, when it was clear that the situation on the battlefield had become untenable, Madison, who had nearly been captured at one point, said, "Come, Armstrong, come Monroe, let us go, and leave it to the commanding general!"[44]

The president of the United States fled. It was humiliation of the highest order, and as the sixty-three-year-old commander in chief raced west, away from the roar of the cannons, away from the volleys of rifle fire, away from the screams of the wounded and dying, he surely knew that Washington itself now lay in mortal danger. The man who had not only written much of the Constitution but taken an oath to "preserve, protect and defend" it, had failed.

Still perched in the Queen's Sitting Room, still in the dark about her husband's fate, Dolley Madison put down her spyglass and dashed off another note to her sister: "Will you believe it, my sister, we have had a battle or skirmish near Bladensburg, and I am still here within sound of the cannon! Mr. Madison comes not. May God protect him!"[45]

From her distance—just six miles—the cannons were just a dull thump, but their sound was unmistakable to everyone in the city. Panic was everywhere. Most able-bodied men who could handle a musket had gone to the front, leaving women, children, and servants behind. The streets began to fill as clumps of people began to flee west, hauling whatever their horses could bear.

At least on two occasions the mayor of the District of Columbia, James Blake, urged Mrs. Madison to leave the President's House and seek safety elsewhere. She refused. "I am determined not to go myself until I see Mr. Madison safe, so that he can accompany me, as I hear of much hostility toward him," she wrote. "Disaffection stalks around us. My friends and acquaintances are all gone.[46]

Determined to maintain appearances, the first lady ordered dinner prepared. It was to be served, as usual, at 3:00 p.m. Paul Jennings, the fifteen-year-old slave who was the Madisons' servant, arranged thirty-eight place settings on the long table in the dining room. War or no war, Mrs. Madison would have a grand feast. "As usual, I brought up the ale, cider and wine, and placed them all in coolers, as all the Cabinet and several military gentlemen and strangers were expected," he wrote.[47] As Jennings worked, the distant rumble of cannons continued, and he knew that the commander in chief was in the thick of it. Jennings feared for the president's safety.

Yet Mrs. Madison, despite her outward calm, was making preparations to flee just in case. Keeping her cool and working quickly, she stuffed government papers that she deemed valuable into a trunk. She also folded up the brilliant red velvet curtains that had hung in the oval drawing room, a few pieces of silverware, books, and a small bronze clock. Into the trunks it all went.[48]

The situation was so dire that at one point, Jean-Pierre Sioussat, the head of the household staff who was supervising the dinner, approached Mrs. Madison. There were two cannons at the front gates of the President's House. French John (as the Parisian emigré Sioussat was commonly known) offered to spike them with explosives and lay a trail of gunpowder as a long fuse. If necessary, he told the first lady, he would ignite them at just the right moment and blow the approaching redcoats up.[49]

But Dolley Madison, a Quaker who opposed war, said this would be unfair. If war had to be fought, it should be done in a fair manner. "To the last proposition I positively object," she later told her sister. The first lady thanked Sioussat for his loyalty. He went back to preparing supper; she resumed packing.[50]

"I am accordingly ready," she wrote. "I have pressed as many Cabinet papers into trunks as to fill one carriage; our private property must be sacrificed, as it is impossible to procure wagons for its transportation."[51]

As the minutes wore on, Mrs. Madison, back on her top floor vantage point, and with her spyglass, saw the growing stream of people headed west, away from the front. As the noisy, sweaty caravan fled in the searing heat, the growing sense of fear was palpable. Yet the first lady remained determined to stay. (She did, however, send her pet parrot, Uncle Willy, to the French consulate for safekeeping.[52])

Through the maelstrom a man on horseback appeared. Riding fast, he entered the grounds of the President's House. Observers thought it must be a messenger with something momentous to report, given his sense of urgency.

The rider was James Smith, the freedman servant to President Madison. As he galloped onto the North Lawn, he began waving his hat and yelling "Clear out! Clear out! General Armstrong has ordered a retreat!"[53]

Everyone within earshot heeded Smith's panicked tone. Jennings stopped setting the long dinner table and ran to the North Portico. "All was then confusion," he wrote.[54] Upstairs, Smith's cry reached the first lady. Whatever fear she had successfully masked was now unleashed.

A friend of the First Family, Charles Carroll, the owner of a Georgetown home called Bellevue (since 1932 known as Dumbarton House), directed his carriage to the north door of the mansion. With the thud of cannon fire in the distance and panic in the streets rising, he urged the first lady to get in his carriage immediately. But Dolley Madison still wasn't ready to go. As the wagon bearing trunks she had packed pulled away, she went back inside, motioning for Carroll, the Irish gardener Tom Magraw, and Sioussat to follow. Turning right, hurrying down the great hallway, they entered the State Dining Room. The long table groaned under the weight of the supper that had been set by Jennings.[55]

Mrs. Madison pointed to the Gilbert Stuart portrait of George Washington; she said she would not leave until it had been saved. "Save that picture," she ordered. "If it is not possible, then destroy it. Under no circumstances, allow it to fall into the hands of the British."[56]

Sioussat and Magraw thought they could just pull the eight-by-five-foot painting down. But the heavy gilt frame, which in turn held a light wooden frame over which the canvas was stretched, was bolted to the wall. As Dolley's sister Anna Payne Cutts frantically implored her to get in Carroll's carriage and leave, Sioussat and Magraw took a hatchet and smashed the heavy outer frame. Sioussat then pulled a small knife from his pocket and carefully cut the painting out (it was still in a lesser frame called a stretcher) and gently laid it on the floor.[57]

It was then given to two businessmen friends of the Madisons who had rushed to the President's House that afternoon to help—Jacob Barker and Robert De Peyster. They later removed the canvas itself and took it away to a nearby farmhouse for safekeeping.[58] One painting that was left behind: a small portrait of Mrs. Madison herself, which would soon be taken by the British as a war souvenir.[59]

With the British closing in and the most prominent piece of art to grace the President's House safely removed, Dolley Madison felt she could finally leave. Along with her sister and several others, she hopped into Carroll's carriage, and off they sped to Bellevue. It was about 3:30 p.m.[60]

Had Dolley Madison waited perhaps half an hour longer, she might have been reunited with her husband. The president's arrival was as dramatic as it was disconcerting. Soaked in sweat and covered in dust from the long horseback ride, Madison returned not knowing what to expect or whether he would see his wife. Accompanied by Attorney General Richard Rush and others, he entered, probably through the north entrance. Almost everyone was gone. The mansion's interior, cooled by the thick plaster walls, must have felt comfortable to the president, who within moments found himself where his wife had been less than an hour before. They found supper on the table, still warm—and the Washington painting, in its light wooden frame, on the floor.[61]

The president, plopping himself down in a chair, poured himself a glass of wine and discussed the day's dramatic events. Even as the city around him continued to flee, Madison sat, contemplating his next move. He debated meeting Mrs. Madison in Georgetown, but with the British drawing closer, sent word that the first lady and her party were to meet him at a foundry northwest of the city, along the Potomac.[62]

Before leaving the President's House for the final time, Madison took one last look around. He never recorded his thoughts as he quickly surveyed what had been,[63] for fourteen glorious years, the home of the president of the United States. Perhaps he was ruing the bad advice he received from Monroe and Armstrong—that Washington was an unlikely enemy target—and how little he had done to fortify the city's defenses, despite being at war for more than two years. As commander in chief, he had failed on a grand scale.

The president mounted his horse and headed northwest out of the city. Minutes later, Barker and De Peyster loaded the Washington portrait onto a cart and fled as well.[64] What might George Washington—the hero of Valley Forge, the Father of His Country, the very embodiment of American liberty—have thought of such an undignified retreat from the city which so proudly bore his name?

What happened next—the destruction of the President's House by British troops—is quite well known. What has been forgotten over the past two centuries, though, is that even before the invaders arrived, several local residents beat them to it. "A rabble," Jennings wrote, "taking advantage of the confusion, ran all over the President's House, and stole lots of silver and whatever they could lay their hands on."[65]

British forces approached the now deserted and partially ransacked President's House about 10:30 p.m. There were 150 sailors, commanded by Cockburn and Major General Robert Ross.[66] They were in no hurry; the prize was theirs. Using torches to guide them in the dark, the conquerors toured the mansion. Attracted by the aroma of food, the hungry redcoats entered the State Dining Room and eyed the feast that had been set for the Madisons. Officers sat down and helped themselves. Drinking the president's wine, ale and cider, a series of toasts were made. One was "to Jemmy's health."[67]

Their stomachs now full, their thirst slaked, the British engaged in a bit of plundering of their own. Entering the president's bedroom, Cockburn took one of Madison's tri-cornered hats, while another officer put on one of his clean shirts. A portrait of Dolley Madison, which the first lady had declined to save earlier, was taken down. Someone else turned a tablecloth into a rucksack, stuffed it full of silver and plates, and hauled it away.[68]

Finally, Cockburn gave the order to burn the building down. Windows were smashed. Furniture, carpets, and some of the drapes Dolley Madison had so carefully selected were piled together and doused in lamp oil and coal taken from a neighboring tavern. About 12:30 in the morning on August 25, sailors outside hurled flaming torches through the smashed-out windows.[69] "Our sailors," wrote one British officer, "were artists at work."[70] Within minutes, James Hoban's magnificent creation, home to three of the first four presidents of the United States, was fully engulfed.

Mahogany floors hissed and cracked as they burned. The few windows that hadn't been smashed shattered as the inferno spread.[71] Bright tongues of fire soared into the night sky, glowing embers floating down over a wide swath of the city. One witness, a Mrs. Thornton, wrote: "The spectators stood in awful silence, the city was light and the heavens redden'd with the blaze!"[72] Never in the history of the young republic had there been a more shameful spectacle.

President and Mrs. Madison would never meet that night. The first lady stopped at the home of a friend in Virginia; the president, accompanied by Attorney General Rush and John Mason, commander of the District of Columbia militia, arrived around midnight at the nearby home of Reverend John Maffitt.[73] Behind them, just a few miles down the Potomac, the great fires ignited by the enemy were clearly visible, "some burning slowly, others with bursts of flame and sparks mounting high up in the dark horizon," Rush wrote. "This can never be forgotten by me."[74] The fires burned until a fierce storm—which possibly included one or more tornadoes[75]—tore through the city. Torrential rains doused the flames but inflicted, along with powerful winds, still more damage on the beleaguered city. "Great God, Madam!" Cockburn asked a woman. "Is this the kind of storm to which you are accustomed in this infernal country?"

"No, sir," she informed the admiral. "This is a special interposition of Providence to drive our enemies from our city."[76]

Their work finished, the British did withdraw. In their wake, the President's House, the Capitol, the Treasury Building, and the State and War departments, along with other federal buildings, had been laid to waste.

On August 27th, three days after the city fell, the reunited Madisons ventured into town. If James Madison's retreat from his home and his city had been humiliating, it likely paled in comparison to his return. Looting had broken out. Merchants gouged fellow residents, tripling prices of necessities like firewood and hay. The president, now the subject of scorn and contempt, quietly took it all in.

Graffiti blaming him for the destruction of the nation's capital began to appear. One said that George Washington had founded the city after a seven-year war with England; "James Madison lost it after a two-year war." "James Madison is a rascal, a coward, and a fool," said another.[77] Newspaper editorials around the country would be no less harsh in their criticism of the president.

The Madisons found the President's House a charred, smoldering wreck, its sandstone walls streaked with ugly black scorch marks. They quickly discovered that nothing was salvageable beyond a few pots and pans and a big cooking range, all made from iron. For months, any mention of the British would reportedly cause the first lady to cry; the president himself was "shaken and woe-begone . . . as if his heart was broken,"[78] an acquaintance said. Their home destroyed, the Madisons moved into Octagon House, the former home of the French ambassador at 18th Street and New York Avenue NW.

The nation's capital had been moved from Philadelphia in 1800 in part for security reasons: Congress had been attacked in 1783 by four hundred soldiers of the Continental Army.[79] Ironically, one of the biggest proponents of relocating the capital to a new location had been Madison himself. Now, with Washington exposed as vulnerable, there was new talk about moving the capital yet again—perhaps west, behind the safety of the Shenandoah or Allegheny Mountains. Cincinnati, in the new state of Ohio, was one suggestion.[80] Such talk was quickly squashed, however, with both a defiant President Madison and Congress deciding that the federal city would stay right where it was.

Two months after the fire, a report to Congress determined that the walls of both the Capitol and the President's House remained sound, and, with not inconsiderable repairs, both buildings could be rebuilt.[81] Several banks in the District of Columbia, anxious to keep the federal government in their city, offered to lend the government $500,000, at an interest rate of 6 percent.[82] In February 1815, Congress approved the loan. It was less than what was needed, but enough to get going.[83] The nation's capital, built from scratch not even a generation earlier, would rise again—this time literally from the ashes. But it would be too late for James and Dolley Madison; they would never live in the President's House again.

CHAPTER FOUR

James Monroe: The Monroe Doctrine

The Oval Room

THAT THE UNITED STATES HAD BEEN ATTACKED AND THE NATION'S CAPI-
tal ravaged by invasion in 1814 was tragically ironic. One goal of Thomas Jefferson's Louisiana Purchase, concluded a decade before, was to enhance the
nation's security by expanding westward. Such a move, it was thought, would
eliminate, or at least degrade, any
designs that European powers like
Spain, France, Britain, and Russia
had on North America. But the
British invaders had arrived from
the east, by sea. America paid a
grievous price, losing its most
valuable symbols of democracy—
the Capitol building and White
House—on one terrible summer
night.

In 1816, the man who bore
part of the blame for that humiliation—James Monroe—was
elected as the fifth president of
the United States. Just two years
before, as James Madison's secretary of state, he had at first
downplayed the possibility of
an attack on Washington, advis-
ing Madison that it was highly
unlikely to occur.

Only one person in American history has
been a governor, senator, secretary of
state, secretary of war—and president:
James Monroe. LIBRARY OF CONGRESS

The Monroes moved into the rebuilt White House, vacant for more than three years after the British attack, on September 17, 1817. This drawing shows the north entrance of the mansion as it appeared then. LIBRARY OF CONGRESS

But it did occur, and as a result Monroe, for the first seven months of his presidency, was forced to live in a modest rowhouse at 2017 I Street NW as the President's House—two blocks south and four blocks east—was rebuilt.[1] That the young nation had been so vulnerable to attack from a faraway foreign power would leave a lasting impression on the fifth president. The lasting achievement of his eight years in office would be the creation of a policy to discourage future European intervention, and expansion, in the Western Hemisphere, which the United States declared as within its sphere of influence. A quarter-century after he left office, and nineteen years after his death, this policy would be dubbed the "Monroe Doctrine," which for more than a century would be a key pillar of American foreign policy.

No man has ascended to the presidency with the kind of qualifications that James Monroe brought to the job. Nineteen presidents had previously been governors. Sixteen were senators. Six served as secretary of state. Just two were secretary of war (now defense). Not only did James Monroe serve with distinction in all four roles—the only president to do so—he was also the only man in American history to serve as secretary of state and secretary of war at the same time.[2] Monroe was also ambassador to both France—where he helped negotiate the Louisiana Purchase—and Great Britain.

It was the most glittering of résumés, and Monroe, the last of America's Founding Fathers to become president, used this extensive experience to guide the United States in the years following the war. The conflict with Britain had secured American independence once and for all, and Monroe worked to burnish the nation's reputation as a growing power on the world stage. To that end, he stabilized relations with America's two-time enemy, resolving disputes that carried over from the war, including the establishment of what is today the world's longest international border, running between the United States and Canada.

Aside from being exceptionally prepared to serve as president, James Monroe looked every inch as one. Standing an even six feet tall, the fifth president and the fourth from Virginia, Monroe was born in what is today Westmoreland County—the birthplace of George Washington and his predecessor, James Madison. Monroe even looked like Washington, those who had the honor of knowing both men observed.[3]

Washington himself admired Monroe tremendously. The general, who was also commander in chief of the Continental Army, led Monroe, then a teenaged officer, in several key battles of the Revolutionary War. During the Battle of Trenton on December 26, 1776, just hours after Washington's famous crossing of the Delaware River, Monroe was shot in the shoulder. An artery was severed and he nearly bled to death on the battlefield.[4] For this and other displays of bravery, Monroe earned a promotion to captain and still greater respect from his superiors.

In fact, George Washington, who wrote few letters of recommendation, wrote one on Monroe's behalf in 1778 when his protégé wished to return to Virginia to assume his own field command:

> *... it is with pleasure I take occasion to express to you the high opinion I have of his worth. . . . he has in every instance, maintained the reputation of a brave, active and sensible officer ... if an event of this kind could take place, it would give me particular pleasure; as the esteem I have for him,*

and a regard for his merit, conspire to make me earnestly wish to see him provided for in some handsome way.[5]

A gushing letter of recommendation from the father of his country: What young man wouldn't be thrilled to have that? It was more than enough to have Monroe, just twenty-one, appointed colonel in the Virginia infantry. He soon began a friendship with another towering figure of the Revolution, Thomas Jefferson, who, in the afterglow of his Declaration of Independence, had been elected governor of Virginia. Jefferson sent him to North Carolina to gather intelligence on British forces. When the war ended the next year with the British surrender at Yorktown, Virginia, Jefferson urged Monroe to study law, which Monroe did at the College of William and Mary. This crucial bit of advice would set the young man on his path to political greatness.[6]

Monroe ascended to the presidency at a rather fortuitous moment in American history. The War of 1812 was over, and despite being dangerously unprepared and suffering terrible damage, the nation survived. Sandwiched between the Revolutionary and Civil Wars, the conflict has been forgotten by many Americans. But the War of 1812, which can be regarded as America's second War of Independence, secured the nation's future once and for all.[7]

Inventions like Robert Fulton's steamboat and John Woods's plough, which made farming infinitely easier, helped the postwar economy grow quickly. Construction was just beginning on a 363-mile canal, which would link Lake Erie with the Hudson River. Even more mundane improvements were making life easier. A kitchen device featuring a metal sieve began to make inroads in the marketplace: It was called the coffee pot.[8]

In short, America was free, at peace, and prospering. A Boston newspaper called it an "era of good feelings."[9] The prosperity would not last—the nation was hit by a crippling depression in 1819—but it does describe the early stage of the Monroe years accurately.

Inaugurated in March 1817, Monroe was unhappy that he and his wife, Elizabeth, could not live in the White House right away. He pushed Col. Samuel Lane, commissioner of public buildings, to speed up its reconstruction: "You ought to be especially forward in procuring all the materials, requisite for every part of the work . . . it would be particularly to be regretted if the want of labourers or of materials should retard the progress for a single day." The president demanded to move in by November of 1817.[10]

His impatience was less than justified. The original construction of the White House had taken eight years; by the time Monroe took office, the rebuilding was barely in its second year. Still, the man overseeing the actual work, James Hoban—the White House's original architect had been hired again—scrambled to make the mansion minimally habitable for the new president and first lady.

Agreeing to a salary of $1,600 a year—a considerable sum in that era—Hoban began work in the spring of 1815. Surveying the destruction, he echoed the conclusion of others after the previous fall, that the mansion's shell—which was all that remained from the inferno—was structurally sound. This was not only testament to the quality of the mansion's construction two decades earlier but also meant that its restoration would proceed faster than first thought.[11]

But Hoban soon realized he was wrong. The walls were, in fact, in poor shape. Heavy rains that followed the fire had caused the hot stones to crack, necessitating their replacement.[12] For sandstone to rebuild the walls, he reopened Virginia's Aquia Creek quarry, used between 1792 and 1800, and used a second quarry at Seneca, Maryland.[13] In the spring of 1816, much of the mansion's outer shell was torn down. New walls were quickly put up. Less than a year later, in February 1817, Hoban reported that the new exterior of the mansion was complete.

He had the roof raised and temporarily covered with shingles (the permanent roof would be constructed of copper), giving cover for his rapidly growing workforce. By summer, there were some 190 stonecutters, carpenters, and general laborers on the job, perhaps a third of them slaves.[14]

The accelerated effort bore fruit. "The President, James Monroe, returned last Wednesday" (September 17, 1817), Secretary of State John Quincy Adams wrote in his diary three days later. "He is in the President's House, which is so far restored from the effects of the British visit in 1814, that it is now for the first time habitable."[15] It was a remarkable effort. The first time he built the President's House, it had taken the better part of a decade. Now Hoban and his team—many of the same men from the original construction—had finished in less than three.[16] [17]

The Monroes found a mansion similar to what John Adams had encountered seventeen years before: the unappealing aroma of wet plaster, slowly drying from the heat of fireplaces. Floors, this time made of pine, were still raw and yellow, unpainted or, in the case of formal rooms on the ground floor, uncovered by carpet or oilcloth. Fireplaces lacked mantels, glazing remained incomplete around soaring window frames, and most woodwork, while primed, awaited the painter's brush.[18]

But on the second floor, private quarters for the president and first lady had been prepared (though some spaces like the Oval Room remained boarded up), and a kitchen to support them downstairs was ready to go, as were a wash-house, meat house, and other rooms for support staff. Monroe, not one to let perfect be the enemy of the good, thought it sufficient enough, though he was "apprehensive of the effects of the fresh painting and plastering."[19] A few things, however, were quite different from the Adams move-in. On both the front and rear of the mansion, unsheltered porches had been built, the first step in what would eventually be the North and South Porticoes.[20] And parts of the stone walls that had not been torn down during the mansion's rebuilding had been quickly covered in white lead paint, hiding the ugly black scorch marks and cracks made when the British set the mansion on fire.[21]

That the commander in chief was now back where he belonged—in the President's House—was a powerfully symbolic moment for the American people. It reflected resiliency and purpose, and the Monroes were determined to make their new home—the people's house—reflect this pride. On January 1, 1818, the First Couple ushered in the new year with an open house, and from noon until 3:00 p.m., the citizenry paid their respects.[22] The leading newspaper of the day, the *National Intelligencer*, wrote: "It was gratifying to be able once more to salute the President of the United States with the compliments of the season in his appropriate residence."[23]

Something else was in its appropriate residence as well. Before the president and Mrs. Monroe arrived, the portrait of George Washington—the Gilbert Stuart masterpiece that Dolley Madison had ordered saved in the frantic hours before the British burned the President's House down—was once again hung; it has graced the walls of the mansion ever since.

Since just two formal furnishings survived the fire of 1814—a silver candelabra saved by a slave named Rhodes and the famous Washington portrait—it fell upon James and Elizabeth Monroe to redecorate the new mansion from

43

scratch. Between that point and the Civil War, most of the decor in the mansion can be traced to them. Monroe, who had been ambassador to France under President Washington, deployed agents in Paris who soon began sending back ninety-three crates[24] of Napoleonic-era objects. There was silverware, porcelain urns, bronze clocks, and a dazzling plateau, also bronze, for a dining room table. But of this vast treasure trove, there were two highlights. Monroe's shoppers found a gilded bronze and crystal chandelier that held thirty candles. Often said to belong to Napoleon himself, it was now gathering dust in a warehouse. Across the Atlantic it went, and for the next three decades hung in the Blue Room.[25] There was also gilded beechwood furniture by the designer Pierre Antoine Bellange. His pieces, covered with their distinctive crimson silk and highlighted with golden eagles,[26] would become famous to all nearly a century and a half later when Jacqueline Kennedy took Americans on a TV tour of the White House.

There were two problems with this French shopping spree. Most of the items purchased wound up filling just two rooms where the Monroes planned to entertain—the Oval (Blue) Room and the State Dining Room at the far end of the central hallway.[27] The second problem was the cost. In an early example of federal budget-busting, the tab for all this was $18,429.26, plus $1,286.82 in shipping charges—significantly beyond the $12,000 that had originally been allotted. In fact, just $20,000 had been appropriated by Congress for furnishing the entire mansion.[28] Lawmakers would soon approve an additional $30,000; the Monroes, not shy about living well, would spend it quickly.[29]

The East and West Wings were also rebuilt to Thomas Jefferson's original design, which featured the now famous colonnades (open-columned walkways) running in straight lines from each side of the mansion. Monroe took it a step further, ordering a stable to be built at the western end. This meant extending the colonnade by sixty feet. But instead of extending it in a straight line, the president asked that the new colonnade run south. This ninety-degree turn framed what is today the Rose Garden, and at the end of the walkway, the site of where the Oval Office would be constructed eleven decades later.[30]

The President's House also saw an increase in security. An iron fence was constructed on the north side of the mansion; gates sported heavy locks. At the president's request, a guard was posted in the entrance hall adjacent to the north entrance, with firearms nearby should they be needed.[31]

As hosts, President and Mrs. Monroe seemed the opposite of their predecessors. While Elizabeth Monroe, according to one newspaper account, was "an elegant, accomplished woman" who "possesses a charming mind of dignity of manners which peculiarly fit her elevated station,"[32] she was seen as more aloof than the gregarious Dolley Madison. Unlike Mrs. Madison—who, to be fair, set a standard as hostess that few, if any, other first ladies would be able to match—Elizabeth Monroe, who was "never giddy and not adept at small talk," did not place a big priority on being sociable. She abandoned Mrs. Madison's popular practice of calling on the wives of diplomats and new lawmakers. She also ended the regular series of open houses that had made Mrs. Madison so popular and sought after. And she attended few dinner parties at the White House itself, prompting most women to stay home in response.[33] As a substitute, the Monroes' daughter Eliza often filled in, but her rude and snobbish behavior seemed to have done more harm than good. In fairness, it should also be mentioned that Elizabeth Monroe was in poor health for much of her husband's administration and would, in fact, pass away at the age of sixty-two in 1830—a year before her husband.[34]

The president himself entertained mostly for political purposes. He thought that too much hobnobbing and glad-handing—even with lawmakers and diplomats—had the effect of diluting the power and aura of the presidency. He made a deliberate effort to maintain a certain remoteness.[35] In this respect, he was very much like his mentor, George Washington, who throughout his life was cautious about extending friendship easily. Monroe exuded warmth, but seemingly behind a veneer of reserve. Said one woman at Monroe's last New Year's reception at the President's House in 1825: "He is tall and well formed. His dress plain and in the old style. . . . His manner was quiet and dignified. From the frank, honest expression of his eye . . . I think he well deserves the encomium passed upon him by the great Jefferson, who said, 'Monroe was so honest that if you turned his soul inside out there would not be a spot on it.'"[36] This too could pass for a description of Mr. Washington himself.

❧

For all his accomplishments and lofty positions he had held prior to the presidency, Monroe's time in office seemed rather placid by comparison. By 1823—halfway through his second term—he had achieved relatively little.[37] His presidency, in fact, had been largely defined by the Panic of 1819, the first peacetime depression to hit the United States since its founding.[38] Since this was the first economic downturn of its kind, neither the president nor lawmakers were sure how to respond. As both dithered, the crisis would grind on into 1823.[39] As presidents always are, Monroe was criticized for not doing enough to stop it. He surely did not, as he believed that the Bank of the United States (a precursor of sorts to the current day Federal Reserve) and the states themselves had more power to influence the economy than he did.

The president did feel, of course, that he could influence foreign policy. The war with Britain may have ended in 1814, and America's relations with the mother country had since warmed, but there were certainly no guarantees of future amity.

While US-British ties were now on friendlier footing, Europe in general was cause for concern. The continent was in disarray, the president told Congress in his first annual message (today known as the State of the Union) in 1817.[40] Spain was a particular worry, the president noted. Spanish colonies in the Western Hemisphere were restive and clamoring for independence; Monroe feared Spain might try to reassert its authority. France, even in its weakened post-Napoleonic era, was a concern as well.[41]

Monroe and his secretary of state—and soon-to-be-successor—John Quincy Adams were also worried about Russia. Czar Alexander I, whose vast Eurasian empire extended into Alaska (first settled by Russians in 1741) and down the Pacific coast to what is today Bodega Bay, California, just north of San Francisco,[42] had declared that any territory north of the 51st parallel would be off-limits to non-Russians. The Russians also made territorial claims on the Pacific Ocean, saying that waters within 100 miles of the coast were to be considered off-limits as well.[43]

This was both an economic and a security threat to the United States, Monroe and Adams quickly concluded. They rejected the czar's claim, with Adams telling his Russian counterpart that the United States would defend the principle that the "American continents are no longer subjects of any new European colonial establishments."[44] It was probably the first formal utterance of what would eventually be known as the Monroe Doctrine.

The president had actually been entertaining such a policy for some time. In 1818, Britain, trying to protect lucrative Latin-American trade ties, warned the French and Russians to stay away. The next year Monroe appealed to Britain to join with the United States in recognizing the independence of Argentina, but London declined.[45] But now, in the fall of 1823, it was the British who did the asking, urging Monroe to join them in condemning any European attempt to meddle in Latin America, and ruling it off-limits to future colonization.[46] The president, prodded by his two immediate predecessors—Jefferson and Madison—weighed the idea of responding favorably to the British idea.[47] Jefferson, now eighty years old, told Monroe that it was the most "momentous" issue offered for his "contemplation since independence."[48]

The British request was itself telling. Prior to the War of 1812, Britain certainly would not have deigned to seek America's counsel or assistance on world affairs. But in the near-decade since, Napoleon had been vanquished and America had once again thwarted London's ambitions; there was a growing sense that the United States was beginning to step, albeit gingerly, onto the world stage as a legitimate power.[49]

While Jefferson and Madison urged Monroe to accept the British offer, his secretary of state had a different idea: Why not issue a unilateral declaration? "It would be more candid as well as more dignified," Adams said, "to avow our principles explicitly to France and Russia than to come in as a cockboat in the wake of a British man-of-war."[50]

Monroe sided with Adams. In his annual message to Congress on December 2, 1823, the president declared:

> *As a principle in which the rights and interest of the United States are involved, that the American continents, by the free and independent condition which they have assumed and maintain, are henceforth not to be considered as the subjects for future colonization by any European powers.*[51]

To those European powers, Monroe then issued what can be considered a threat:

"...We should consider any attempt on their part to extend their system to any portion of this hemisphere as dangerous to our peace and safety...."[52]

The dramatic pronouncement—which would not be known as the Monroe Doctrine until 1850[53]—reflected what the British themselves seemed to have sensed: that the United States, now secure, free, and apparently incapable of being challenged by any European power, "intended to stand on her own two feet in the community of nations."[54]

CHAPTER FIVE

Andrew Jackson: The Nullification Crisis

The East Room

ASK JUST ABOUT ANYONE WHEN THE CIVIL WAR BEGAN, AND THE ANSWER IS likely to be December 20, 1860, when South Carolina seceded from the Union, or April 12, 1861, when Confederate forces shelled the Union garrison at Fort Sumter, South Carolina. But it could also be argued that America's bloodiest war—a war that took the lives of more than one in fifty Americans in just four years—actually began three decades earlier, also in South Carolina.

A trade tariff, passed by Congress on May 19, 1828, and signed by President John Quincy Adams, raised the price of manufactured goods, a boon to companies in northern states, but a tremendous liability for southern states, which did not possess the North's manufacturing base—and thus had to pay more for the North's goods. The tariff also made it harder for a key trade partner, Britain, to pay for the only southern product it imported: cotton. Thus the 1828 tariff greatly benefitted and protected northern states but was financially damaging to the South. It was soon dubbed the "Tariff of Abominations" by its southern detractors for its harmful effects on the antebellum southern economy.[1]

In 1832, after four years of being crippled economically by the tariff, a movement erupted in South Carolina to nullify it. Led, ironically, by John C. Calhoun, vice president under Adams when the tariff was passed—he also served as VP under Adams's successor, Andrew Jackson—the movement was based on the belief that states' rights could not be usurped by the federal government; thus a national tariff passed by Congress could be voided by any state which sought to do so. Extending this argument further, many in the South believed that if the federal government could tax the South against its will, it could do other things against the South's will as well—namely, end slavery.[2]

But Andrew Jackson, though a southerner himself (born and raised in Tennessee), had a different view. While initially believing in limited government and states' rights—key planks of his 1828 election campaign—his views would evolve after winning the presidency. While acknowledging that the tariff was painful to the southern states, Jackson firmly believed that no state had the right to nullify any individual federal law.

The simmering dispute between Jackson and his vice president boiled over in a dramatic and public way on April 13, 1830, when both men attended the annual Jefferson Day dinner. A host of the gala, South Carolina senator Robert Hayne made a toast in which he called for greater states' rights.[3] President Jackson then rose. Ignoring Hayne and staring directly at Calhoun, he made a toast of his own: "Our federal Union: It *must* be preserved!"—a public rebuke from president to vice president. After a dramatic silence, a pale and shaken Calhoun rose. Raising his glass, he answered: "The Union: Next to our Liberty, the most dear!"[4]

Andrew Jackson's joy at winning the election of 1828 was short-lived: His wife of 34 years, Rachel, died soon afterwards. Her passing cast a dark shadow over the new president, who held a grudge over opponents—including the vanquished President John Quincy Adams, who had slandered her. LIBRARY OF CONGRESS

With that, the early battle lines between North and South were drawn. Not over slavery, another simmering issue that would soon boil over, but money and states' rights. The Nullification Crisis would be one of the defining issues of Andrew Jackson's tumultuous eight years as president of the United States.

Nearly suffocated during a wild inaugural party at the White House, Jackson—
"Old Hickory"—had to be evacuated through a window by frantic aides. To clear
the mansion, servants lured partygoers outside with free liquor. Note the South
Portico, added in 1823. The North Portico was completed in 1829, Jackson's
first year in office. LIBRARY OF CONGRESS

With the possible exception of Zachary Taylor or Theodore Roosevelt, no
tougher man would occupy the White House than Andrew Jackson. Nick-
names like "Old Hickory" and "Sharp Knife"[5] (applied by American Indians
for his ruthless relocation of them to lands west of the Mississippi) reflected
his hardy, tough-as-nails character. A war hero who once killed a man with
his bare hands, a participant in at least five duels in his life (likely apocryphal
estimates range as high as one hundred), he was shot in 1806, with a bullet
lodging next to his heart.[6] He survived, but would be in chronic pain for the
rest of his life.

Seven years later—by then a hero of the War of 1812—he was shot in
the arm during a Tennessee street fight. It was a hideous wound, and doctors wanted to amputate. But bleeding profusely and ruining two mattresses,
Jackson mustered enough strength to say, "I'll keep my arm."[7]

Yet the most painful wound Jackson would ever endure was the loss
in December 1828—just days after his election to the presidency—of his
wife of thirty-four years, Rachel Donelson Robards Jackson.[8] Her passing

cast a dark shadow over Jackson. The president-elect wore a black armband in mourning for months; despite the grave responsibilities of his new job, he retreated into seclusion, deep in grief.[9] A friend said that Jackson seemed to look "twenty years older in a night," after her passing.[10]

At the same time, his wife's death flooded Jackson's mind with bad memories of enemies who had slandered the couple with charges of adultery and bigamy.[11] The pain was deep, and Jackson, furious, was not one to forget. He held a grudge against, among others, President Adams, whose campaign had done some of the slandering. After the nasty campaign, in which the incumbent was crushed, Adams sent cordial notes to Jackson in an attempt to mend fences. Jackson ignored them.[12] Like his father, who left town before Thomas Jef-

Jackson lived for decades with a bullet lodged close to his heart, after being shot in an 1806 duel. He later nearly lost his arm in a Tennessee street fight. He is shown here in a rare photo, taken just months before his death in 1845.
LIBRARY OF CONGRESS

ferson's inaugural twenty years before, John Quincy Adams would not attend his successor's swearing-in.[13]

Old Hickory's supporters viewed him as a true man of the people. As his carriage made the short trek from Capitol Hill to the President's House after the swearing-in, they brandished anything they could find that was made out of the wood: bridles, stirrups, and clubs—their tribute to Old Hickory. Rarely, if ever, had the capital city seen such exuberance. It nearly killed the new president, in fact, just hours into the job.

During an inaugural party at the mansion, things quickly got out of hand when a "rabble mob" swarmed the premises in search of food, drink, and a look at the new president. At one point, the sixty-one-year-old Jackson found himself pinned against a wall. He began to gasp for air. Aides fought their way through the mob and, locking arms, hustled the president through a window, onto the South Portico, and into a coach. He was taken to his suite at Gadsby's Hotel, where he had lived since February 11th.[14] To lure the mob from the mansion, servants offered liquor and punch on the lawn.[15] The president would move into the White House one week later, giving servants time to clean up the mess, which included broken glass and china, and carpeting and "damask satin-covered chairs" which had been soiled by "boots heavy with mud."[16]

Prior to the inaugural, the commissioner of public buildings in the District of Columbia, Charles Bulfinch—best known for overseeing the first completion of the US Capitol building—was asked to report on the condition of the White House. Surprisingly, though it had been painstakingly rebuilt just a decade earlier under the careful eye of Hoban, Bulfinch concluded that the mansion was shabby and run-down. Several rooms remained in various stages of disrepair, most notably the East Room, which had been incomplete even before the fire of 1814 and remained so more than fourteen years later.[17]

The "man of the people" living in such decrepit quarters? The new president found this unacceptable. One of his first tasks upon moving into the mansion was to complete the East Room once and for all. He dispatched his friend William Lewis (mayor of the District of Columbia) to Philadelphia, where he selected everything that was needed for the sprawling room's twenty-eight hundred square feet.[18]

The room soon became—for the first time in the three-decade history of the White House—a bold, vibrant, showcase. A Philadelphia vendor, the French-born Louis Veron, was chosen by a Jackson aide to oversee the design job. Lemon yellow wallpaper with cloth border was hung. Windows were draped in thick royal blue curtains with yellow draperies. Perched on top were gilt eagle cornices. There were 498 yards of carpeting, colored in fawn, blue, and yellow and trimmed in red.[19]

The ceiling, which had accumulated years' worth of soot from the room's four fireplaces, was whitewashed until it gleamed. And, as was customary in the nineteenth century, the room was dotted with twenty spittoons[20]—each sitting atop a square of oilcloth in case the spitter missed. Wood paneling and decorative wooden beams were installed. The vast room also featured four sofas, twenty-four armchairs, and a silver service bought from a Russian minister, which alone cost $4,308.[21]

Hovering above all of this had been three rather plain-looking iron chandeliers that held some twelve candles each. These were not good enough for the biggest room in his house, Jackson decided, and down they came, to be replaced by three much bigger, grander chandeliers, each with eighteen oil peg lamps.[22] During the day, sunlight streaming through hundreds of pieces of glass in each cast rainbows throughout the room; at night, each set off a lustrous glow. Jackson upped the wattage still further with wall and table lamps. All of this magnificent light was reflected in giant mirrors atop the room's four fireplaces. When the president entered, often wrapped in his trademark blue cape, he passed beneath a halo of gold stars and rays from the sun, which adorned the wallpaper above.[23] The overall effect, an aide noted, was one of "thundering grandeur."[24] For the first time in White House history, the East Room had finally become what Hoban had always envisioned it to be: a magnificent and dignified gathering place for moments of triumph, tragedy—and everything in between. The now lavish room reflected Jackson's newly acquired taste for the comfortable life, a seemingly incongruous development for the rough-and-tumble general turned statesman. The president lived and worked on the second floor, claiming the bedroom in the southwest corner as his own; a family parlor and his own sitting room were adjacent. Next to this was the Oval Room, which, as always, dominated the second floor. It became a parlor for the president's hostess, his niece Emily Donelson. Here she would greet visiting ladies and hold dinner parties. It became known as the "Circular Green Room" because of its green walls.[25]

Next to this were three rooms that composed the president's offices. The first room was used by Jackson to receive guests. Next to this—in what is today the Lincoln Bedroom—was the president's private office. Maps were tacked onto wallpaper; a rubber oilcloth—painted in a tile or carpet pattern—covered the floor. Silk curtains adorned the room's two windows, crowned by gilded-eagle cornices purchased by the president himself. An iron heater (called a "Russia stove") stood in a sandbox, with a pipe protruding through a board covering a fireplace opening.[26]

The room was dominated by a holdover from the Jefferson era: the long table, covered in green felt, that Jefferson used in his own office downstairs. There were numerous cabinets and bookcases. Near the fireplace, Jackson kept a rocking chair, which helped ease his lifelong discomfort from wounds, which were compounded by rheumatism as he aged. One visitor recalled seeing him in the big rocker, with "the look of pain fixed on his thin face."[27]

Splendid as the upgrades to the mansion's interior were, the most noticeable and long-lasting changes to the President's Mansion were on the exterior. In 1829–30, the first two years of the Jackson era, construction was completed on the North Portico—the front side facing Pennsylvania Avenue. It was the realization of Thomas Jefferson and James Hoban's unfulfilled vision, and to this day, the gracious extension, supported by Ionic columns nearly sixty feet high and topped with rose petals,[28] remains the principal entrance to the great home.[29] Along with the South Portico, which had been built in 1824, during the final year of James Monroe's presidency, the mansion now measured 152 feet wide, slightly shy of its 168-foot length.[30]

The mansion also took a huge technological leap forward during the Jackson era, getting running water for the first time. Hoban first proposed this in 1816, during the rebuilding after the 1814 fire. Surprisingly, the idea was rejected for being too visionary. But not for Jackson. The president thought the system he inherited—where water was brought up from a well in a breezeway between the mansion and West Wing and distributed through the house by buckets—quite antiquated.[31]

In the summer of 1833, while Jackson was vacationing at the Hermitage, Mayor Lewis began work on a massive project to bring running water to the President's House. The federal government happened to own a water reservoir on Franklin Square, a few blocks north of the mansion (today bordered by 13th and 14th Streets NW and I and K Streets NW).[32]

A pipe made from hollowed-out tree trunks was installed, running aboveground down the middle of 14th Street, cutting over to New York Avenue, then south on what is today Madison Place to the White House itself, where the water ran into a pond five or six feet deep that had been dug just east of the mansion. Along the half-mile route (the entire distance from Franklin Square was slightly sloped, so the water flowed easily) algae was filtered out by white sand.[33]

From the pond, water was pumped into the mansion itself manually. A pump house was built—which resembled a steeple and included a clock—operated by a full-time "pump-keeper." He would turn a wheel that pushed water through a pipe, which ran into the White House basement (where laundry was done) and into a brick-floored bathing room in the East Wing. When President Jackson wished to bathe, he would come here, a valve would be opened, and the water would flow. This proved to be such a success that Jackson ordered the water system expanded to his private quarters on the second floor of the mansion in 1835.[34]

The president and his family could now have running water in sinks, an enormous convenience at the time. But there was still no bathtub in the family quarters—there wouldn't be one for another eighteen years; President Jackson and his next six successors still had to troop down to the East Wing for a soak.

And aesthetics weren't that important in this part of the house: Water pipes were generally exposed, and no effort was made to conceal them.[35] For all the stateliness the mansion projected to the outside world, in its more obscure corners it was often anything but.

The trade tariff of 1828 that so incensed much of the South was not an isolated act. Congress had first passed a protective tariff in 1816, and increased its rates eight years later. Thus decades before the first shots were fired at Fort Sumter, these protectionist measures, implemented over a dozen years, can be seen as a serious wedge between North and South.[36] The tariff of 1828 only widened this divide, and affected southerners quickly pinned their hopes on the possibility that the new president, a southerner himself, would do something about it.

But Jackson did not. Thus the tense exchange between the president and Vice President Calhoun at the April 1830 gala became a defining moment, one that sparked genuine fear for the country's future. Former secretary of war William Crawford, who attended the dinner, seemed to speak for many when he wrote: "I seriously apprehend a civil war if something is not done to conciliate the discontents which prevail at this time and for aught that I can see will increase."[37]

On July 26, 1831, Calhoun provoked the president further by issuing what came to be known as the Fort Hill Address, in which he argued that the Union could only survive if states had the right to nullify any law that was not part of the Constitution. He said the Constitution could be amended later to include any law; but in the interim, states should have the power to decide which national laws to obey or dismiss.[38]

It was a constitutional crisis the likes of which the young nation had never experienced. One can imagine Jackson, swaying back and forth in his second floor rocking chair, seething in anger as logs in the nearby fireplace hissed and crackled. Convinced he was right, the president took comfort in receiving support from James Madison, the author of much of the Constitution. One of the few Founding Fathers still alive, the fourth president had written a few months earlier to say that Calhoun and the "nullies" (as Jackson contemptuously called them) were not only wrong, but dangerous. Nullification, Madison said, would result in "a final rupture and dissolution of the Union." It "must be shuddered at by every friend to his country, to liberty, to the happiness of man."[39]

The split with Calhoun was reason enough for Jackson to choose another running mate for his 1832 reelection bid: former secretary of state Martin Van Buren. From this point, events slid quickly downhill. In the middle of the presidential election, which lasted from November 2nd to December 5th, South Carolina lawmakers passed an ordinance saying that the newly lowered tariff was null and void and would not be honored after February 1, 1833. With the ordinance came a blunt warning: If the president attempted to use force, then South Carolina would secede from the Union.[40]

An outraged Jackson accused South Carolina's nullies of treason. He vowed to lead an army of ten thousand into the Palmetto State and "crush and hang" them. The president got Congress to pass a bill allowing him to use force. However, wishing to avoid war, Jackson urged that the offensive tariff be lowered again.

With the prospect of federal troops moving into South Carolina appearing increasingly likely, the president got assistance from an unlikely ally: Henry Clay, the Kentucky senator whom Jackson had just beaten in the 1832 election. Walking a fine line between federal demands and those of the nullies, Clay crafted what came to be known as the Compromise Tariff of 1833. Congress approved, and the bill arrived on the president's desk on the same day as its authorization to send US troops to South Carolina. Calhoun, by now known by many in the South as the first president of the Confederacy,[41] accepted Clay's terms on behalf of his nullification colleagues, and the crisis faded. It is quite likely that Calhoun was also influenced by Jackson's threat to hang him; Calhoun knew that those who underestimated Andrew Jackson did so at their peril. Old Hickory was a man who meant what he said, Calhoun knew, and the former vice president of the United States had no desire to sway from the hangman's noose.[42]

"Nullification is dead," Jackson declared. But he knew that the rift between North and South had not healed and wouldn't without some larger action.[43] In a letter dated May 1, 1833, he predicted, "the next pretext will be the Negro or slavery question."[44] He was right.

The North-South chasm would widen over the next twenty-eight years, defying attempts by the next eight presidents to do anything about it. Six days after Jackson made his prediction, he would appoint a twenty-four-year-old man in Illinois to be postmaster for the small town of New Salem. His name was Abraham Lincoln.[45]

CHAPTER SIX

John Tyler: Ten Funerals and a Wedding

The East Room

"Tippecanoe and Tyler Too!" was the campaign slogan in 1840 that thrust William Henry Harrison into the presidency, and John Tyler into the vice presidency. But Harrison's tenure would be quite short-lived. Three weeks after his inaugural—a cold, wet, raw day in which the sixty-eight-year-old president not only refused to wear a coat or hat, but stood in the damp chill to deliver a two-hour inaugural address—he came down with a bad cold. It quickly worsened into pneumonia, and despite the best efforts of doctors, Harrison died, at half past midnight, on April 4th. He had been president of the United States for just thirty days—by far the shortest tenure of any chief executive before or since.

Within hours, black bunting, the universal sign of mourning, appeared on buildings and private homes across Washington. One young reporter, Nathaniel Parker Willis, wrote a poem to the deceased president:

> What! Soared the old eagle to die at the Sun?
> Lies he stiff with spread wings at the goal he has won!
> Death, Death in the White House? Oh never before
> Trod his skeleton foot on the President's floor.[1]

The death of Harrison—the first of eight presidents to die in office—established a series of precedents for such occasions. His coffin was taken to the East Room, the largest room in the mansion, for public and private viewing. The focal point of the nation's grief—the President's House itself—was draped in black. When the late commander-in-chief left the mansion for the final time, his remains would be borne by horse-drawn carriage.

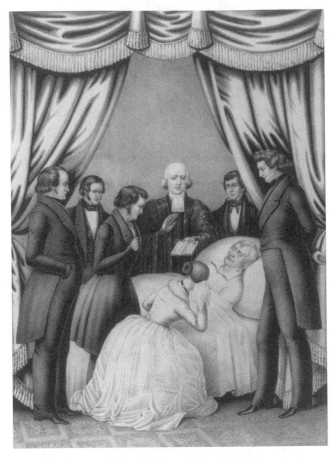

Prior to Ronald Reagan, William Henry Harrison was, at sixty-eight, the oldest man elected president; his death a month later sparked a crisis over presidential succession. The room in which he died later became the site of Abraham Lincoln's autopsy and is today a private dining room for First Families. LIBRARY OF CONGRESS

Harrison's body was probably embalmed, though the records only show that it was shaved and dressed, and covered with a "winding sheet." A mahogany coffin was delivered to the mansion. Its exterior was upholstered with black silk velvet and sunbursts, with a rosette in the center of each. The rim of both the coffin and the lid were trimmed in gold lace.[2]

This coffin fit inside a larger walnut coffin, which was then placed in a giant third coffin made of lead. All three coffins had a glass window built into the lid, so mourners could see, through the triple panes, the face of the chief executive who had died before having a chance to make his mark. As if all this wasn't enough, the third coffin was then covered with an elaborately decorated outer case. But at the funeral itself, only the innermost casing, the mahogany coffin, would be displayed to the public.[3]

John Tyler, the first of eight vice presidents to succeed to the presidency, also became the first sitting president to marry. He was fifty-four; Julia Gardiner was just twenty-four. LIBRARY OF CONGRESS

The first funeral for a sitting president was arranged by Alexander Hunter, a prominent Washington merchant, who seems to have used royal funerals as a template. He expanded the black bunting at the White House, overseeing its hanging among the columns of the North Portico and windows. Inside, it adorned chandeliers and mirrors in state rooms on the ground floor.[4]

In the East Room itself, Harrison's coffin was placed in the center of the vast room, on a table draped in heavy black shroud, trimmed in silver and gold lace. A centerpiece of wax flowers—further decorated by crossed swords and a rolled-up copy of the Constitution—sat atop the casket.

A reporter for the preeminent newspaper of the day, the *National Intelligencer*, wrote: "The great East Room of the President's House—that room in which I had seen a thousand gay and joyful faces glowing in the light of ponderous chandeliers, radiating the light of a hundred burners, was now the scene of death!"[5]

As Washington and the nation plunged into grief with the passing of President Harrison, a very different drama was playing out behind closed doors.

Who would succeed him? The line of succession in 1841 was uncertain. As Harrison lay in his deathbed slipping away, he had tried to make his wishes clear. "Sir, I wish you to understand the true principles of the government. I wish them carried out. I ask nothing more." Moments later, he breathed his last. Though these final words were spoken to his doctor, N. W. Worthington, it was generally assumed that they concerned his vice president, John Tyler.[6]

This is certainly what Tyler immediately assumed when he learned of Harrison's death. Leaving his home in Williamsburg, Virginia, he rushed back to Washington by horse and steamboat, and proceeded immediately to the Executive Mansion to pay his respects to the dead president and his family. To maintain the continuity of the government, Tyler, convinced that he was now president of the United States, began working out of the late president's office. It was a reasonable assumption, given that Article II, section I of the Constitution, which deals with presidential succession, states:

> *In case of the removal of the President from office, or of his death, resignation, or inability to discharge the powers and duties of the said office, the same shall devolve on the Vice President, . . . and [the Vice President] shall act accordingly, until the disability be removed, or a President shall be elected.*

But upon closer examination, the wording was vague. What did "the same" mean? Tyler thought it meant the presidency itself. Others thought it meant the mere duties of the office. In other words, when a president dies in office, would the vice president become the president, legally and officially, or just an *acting* president? The Founding Fathers also failed to stipulate whether the vice president would serve the remainder of the president's term, until the next election or only temporarily, until an emergency election could be organized and held.

It was a loophole to end all loopholes, and immediately became the subject of fierce debate with the late president's Cabinet, whose members were less than enamored with "Tyler too." It was their belief that Tyler was nothing more than a caretaker president. A decade after the crisis over nullification, America was plunged into yet another constitutional dilemma. The freely elected president of the United States lay dead in the East Room, and his own Cabinet and vice president differed over who would succeed him.

Tyler, quickly dispensing with such concerns, asserted himself as president. He began holding official dinners and levees at the President's House. Letters which were addressed to him as anything other than the president were returned unopened. John Tyler, unequivocally and without reservation, was the president of the United States—at least in his mind.

The Harrison-appointed Cabinet disagreed. Meeting with "His Accidency," as Tyler was referred to by critics, its members informed Tyler that he was not the president, just an "acting president," and that any decisions he wished to make would first have to be approved by them. Secretary of State Daniel Webster made it clear: "Our custom and proceeding was that all measures whatever, however, relating to the administration, were brought before the Cabinet, and their settlement was decided by a majority—each member, and the president, having one vote."[7]

There was silence as the Cabinet waited for Tyler's response. Blunt and dismissive, it changed the course of American history:

I beg your pardon, gentlemen. I am sure I am very glad to have in my Cabinet such able statesmen as you have proved yourself to be, and I shall be pleased to avail myself of your counsel and advice, but I can never consent to being dictated to as to what I shall or shall not do. I, as president, will be responsible for my administration. I hope to have your co-operation in carrying out its measures; so long as you see fit to do this, I shall be glad to have you with me—when you think otherwise, your resignations will be accepted.[8]

Tyler wasn't bluffing. A states' rights president, he believed that the Constitution placed narrow parameters around what the federal government could and could not do. This led to a series of vetoes of bills passed by his own Whig party in Congress—including one that would have started a new national bank of the United States.[9] As the vetoes mounted, the Whigs rebelled against who they thought had been their president.

At one point, a mob believed to consist of angry Whigs marched to the President's House, where they threw rocks, fired guns, and hung Tyler in effigy. It was probably the most violent demonstration to ever occur at the mansion, and as the melee continued, First Lady Letitia Tyler lay in her bed shaking and crying in fear.[10]

A few weeks later, Whig anger boiled over among the Cabinet itself. On the afternoon of September 11, 1841, Tyler accepted five Cabinet resignations, one after the other. As the day drew to a close, only one Cabinet member remained: Webster—the same man who earlier had stiffly informed Tyler that the Cabinet would not be submissive to him. But now, Webster had a change of heart.

"Where am I to go, Mr. President?"

"You must decide that for yourself, Mr. Webster," Tyler replied.

"If you leave it up to me, Mr. President, I will stay where I am."

Tyler stood up, extended his hand, and said warmly—and perhaps with some mixture of relief and vindication—"give me your hand in that."[11]

The crisis was finally resolved: John Tyler was the president of the United States without further debate or equivocation. His stubborn insistence that the vice president, upon the death of a sitting president, became the president himself—with all the power and authority the title conveyed—became known as the Tyler Precedent. It would serve as the blueprint for presidential succession for more than one hundred years, until codified by the 25th amendment to the Constitution in 1967.

With the question of succession firmly behind him, Tyler and First Lady Letitia Christian Tyler settled in at the President's House. They inherited a mansion that both structurally and aesthetically was in good shape. Martin Van Buren, who preceded Harrison, had been given $6,000 by Congress to buy new furniture—as long it was made in America. Tyler tried to get additional funds when he became president, but a stingy Congress refused him. Records show Tyler purchased a white marble table for $100—big money in those days—and a porcelain oil lamp for a hallway. The president also made a few small purchases for his office on the second floor, notably desks and tables, with pigeonholes for the increasing amount of presidential paperwork.

Perhaps the only thing the Tylers weren't particularly fond of in their new home was the lighting. Rooms in the President's House in 1841 were illuminated by candles and lamps fueled by lard oil. Made from pork fat, they emitted a foul aroma that some found "sour and obnoxious." Big rooms on the ground floor, like the East Room, were spared such a foul treat, since they were illuminated by large candle-burning chandeliers.[12]

Unfortunately, the odor from the lamps wafted about the upstairs bedrooms. The long dark winter, when the need for lighting was at its greatest, must have been unpleasant. One can imagine the president of the United

States, on a cold winter's night, shuffling over to his bedroom window and cracking it open to get some fresh, albeit frigid, air.

There was plenty of socializing in the Tyler White House, but not with Letitia Tyler. After suffering a stroke in 1838, she was largely bedridden and rarely appeared in public with her husband. Records show just one public appearance at an official event as first lady, the February 1842 marriage of daughter Elizabeth.[13] But the president didn't lack for a hostess: a twenty-four-year-old daughter-in-law, Priscilla Cooper Tyler, filled that role with grace and charm. At East Room receptions, she would enter on the president's arm, resplendent in her lush silk gowns and elegant headdresses."[14] There were also monthly levees, which were attended by as many as a thousand guests. The president also opened the mansion to visitors on New Year's Day and the Fourth of July.

Behind the scenes, though, Leticia Tyler wielded considerable influence. She was deeply involved in managing the presidential household and overseeing social events that she refused to attend. The first lady even displayed something that would come in handy for many a successor: media savvy. Apparently she read piles of newspapers and advised family members, likely including the president himself, on how to cultivate the proper public image.

Then tragedy struck. On September 10, 1842, the first lady died at age fifty-one. After three decades of marriage, John Tyler was a widower. The man who ascended to the presidency upon the first death of a sitting president now had the sad distinction of being the first sitting president to suffer the loss of a wife.[15] [16] Seventeen months after Harrison's death, the White House was again draped in black, and a coffin lay in the center of the East Room. The death of Leticia Tyler devastated the president. He escorted her remains home to Virginia on a steamboat.

— ⁓ —

The president would not remain a widower for long. At a reception just five months after his wife's death, he met Julia Gardiner, a ravishing twenty-three-year-old New York socialite. New in town, Gardiner quickly found herself being chased by everyone from a Supreme Court justice and high-ranking naval officer to several members of Congress. But Gardiner, clearly drawn to powerful men, had her eyes on the president—and vice versa. Tyler didn't seem bothered that a mourning period of at least a year was customary following the passing of a spouse; the president's family, anxious about how this might look in public, kept the budding romance under wraps as best they could.

On February 28, 1844, she accompanied the president on a Potomac River cruise he had arranged on the naval frigate USS *Princeton*. The crowd on board included several Cabinet members, former First Lady Dolley Madison, and Gardiner's father. It was a chilly day. To entertain guests, a cannon—called the Peacemaker—had been fired several times during the cruise. Then, as the president, Gardiner, and others warmed themselves inside, others gathered on deck to watch the Peacemaker fired again. This time it exploded, killing eight people, including Secretary of State Abel Upshur, Secretary of the Navy Thomas Gilmer—and Julia Gardiner's father, David. Twenty others were injured. Julia fainted and was carried off the ship in the president's arms.[17]

The bodies were taken to the East Room, which for the third time in less than three years, was decked in black for a funeral—eight of them. A dispatch from the *National Intelligencer* on March 4th reflected the shock and grief: "in that vast apartment so often the scene of brilliant festivity—so often echoing the strains of joyous music and the mingled voices of the gay—now converted, by the act of God, into a sepulchral chamber, cold and silent as the grave." Following the funeral, the coffins were borne through the streets—by now a familiar, sad sight to Washingtonians—to the city's Congressional Cemetery.

The shared tragedy cemented the relationship between the president and Julia Gardiner. They were soon engaged and married in June. The new first lady was just twenty-four years old.

The presence of such a gorgeous, outgoing, and young first lady changed the tenor of the Tyler White House. Julia Tyler not only kept up her husband's pace of entertaining, but livened things up. With the urging of Dolley Madison—now seventy-five—she introduced the waltz, a dance that was all the rage in New York, and soon couples were gliding across the East Room. Because it involved men putting their arm around a woman's waist, the waltz was seen as morally questionable by more conservative-minded folks.

Julia Tyler introduced something else as well. She instructed the Marine Band that whenever the president entered the room for an official event, it was to play a song called "Hail to the Chief":

Hail to the Chief we have chosen for the nation,
Hail to the Chief! We salute him, one and all.
Hail to the Chief, as we pledge cooperation
In proud fulfillment of a great, noble call.
Yours is the aim to make this grand country grander,
This you will do, that's our strong, firm belief.
Hail to the one we selected as commander,
Hail to the President! Hail to the Chief!

Not that there was any doubt about John Tyler's authority in 1844, but for a man whose ascension to power occurred under such a cloud of uncertainty, the song—simple yet stirring—conveyed great power. For him, and for all chief executives who followed, "Hail to the Chief," which derives from an 1810 poem by the Scottish writer Sir Walter Scott, would indelibly be associated with the president of the United States.

CHAPTER SEVEN

James K. Polk: Five Presidents, One War

The President's Office

When President James Knox Polk walked into his office on the second floor of the Executive Mansion for the first time in March of 1845, he found a huge map of North America—nearly six feet square—on the wall. It consisted of several sections that were glued onto a linen background, varnished, and hung between two horizontal poles.[1]

Probably hung by Andrew Jackson or Martin Van Buren, the right half of the map depicted the United States as it was up to that point. But it was the left half that no doubt intrigued the new president. It showed a vast expanse of land—wide open and, Polk thought, ripe for the taking—stretching all the way to the Pacific. The new president wanted the nation to expand. This reflected a view that many Americans held in the 1840s: that they were a special people and the United States a special nation that was justified—if not entitled—to grow. The philosophy came to be known as Manifest Destiny.

During the campaign of 1844, Polk had pledged to secure two prizes on that map: California, which was controlled by Mexico, and, by settling a border dispute with Britain, the vast Oregon Territory. Polk would make good on both pledges, their fulfillment representing not just two of the central accomplishments of his presidency but a defining chapter of the American story itself. The United States would expand by more than a million square miles during the Polk years—more than during any other presidency, eclipsing even Thomas Jefferson's Louisiana Purchase.[2] Under James Polk, the United States became a true continental power.

In addition to acquiring California and the Oregon Territory, Polk had two other big goals when he arrived in the White House: to cut trade tariffs and to reestablish an independent US Treasury. Considering that he had pledged to serve just one term, it was an ambitious agenda. Just forty-nine

The first known photograph of the White House, taken in 1846, during the administration of James K. Polk. LIBRARY OF CONGRESS

when he moved into the Executive Mansion—the youngest president ever at the time[3]—he was a self-proclaimed lame duck from day one.

But this sense of urgency and unrelenting focus on his objectives did not take away from Polk's interest in his new home. Both the president and the new first lady, Sarah, found the White House—which hadn't had a face-lift since the Jackson years a decade before—in need of an overhaul. With $14,000 allocated by Congress for repairs, maintenance, and new furniture,[4] the Polks brought in William W. Corcoran, a prominent Washington banker and art collector, to oversee the job.

Corcoran traveled to New York frequently and it was there he purchased numerous items, including forty-two chairs covered in purple velvet, which would grace the State Dining Room until 1882. The Polks also splurged on a rococo French dinner and dessert service. The plates and bowls—lavishly decorated with red, white, and blue shields and emblazoned with the national motto "E Pluribus Unum"—were rather fancy, not in keeping with the image of a man who generally preferred to keep things simple and unpretentious.[5]

"No President who performs his duty faithfully and conscientiously can have any leisure," Polk wrote. The workaholic commander in chief died three months after his one very consequential term was over. LIBRARY OF CONGRESS

The Polks also made one change that has lasted to this day. The room on the State Floor that was adjacent to the State Dining Room, which had been the Yellow Drawing Room (and before that, a breakfast room) was redone in red, and has been known since as the Red Room.[6] Working with

Corcoran, Sarah Polk furnished the room with French antiques. Chairs and sofas, carved from mahogany and rosewood, were upholstered in silk velvet. Carpets, deep crimson, featured flowers and leaves, while gold-leafs, tassels, and fringe adorned sumptuous wallpaper.[7]

The overall effect, which had a Versailles-like ostentatiousness to it,[8] was illuminated by coal-powered gas lighting, a new convenience in the 1840s. The room, measuring twenty-eight feet by twenty-two and a half feet, was used frequently by the president and first lady; it was later enjoyed by Mary Lincoln; 120 years after that, Nancy Reagan said it was probably her favorite room in the entire White House.

The idea to light the Executive Mansion by gas was inspired by its successful use on Capitol Hill, where gas represented an improvement over the often-careless use of candles by lawmakers and their staffs. It was decided that pipes would be extended, underground, from the Capitol's power plant to the mansion, one and a half miles to the west. When pipes reached the mansion, space in the walls was gouged out for them, and gas flow was controlled by a series of "thumbscrew cocks."[9]

The Jackson-era chandeliers in the East Room were modified, as were lights in the Red and Green Rooms. But Mrs. Polk, no fan of gas lighting, drew the line in her favorite room, the Blue Room, insisting that it remain lit by candles. Criticized for this, the first lady had the last laugh. At the first major reception illuminated by gas, the lights suddenly went out, plunging every room on the State Floor into darkness—except the Blue Room. Guests crowded into the room, where Mrs. Polk stood, vindicated in the warm glow of the candles she preferred.[10]

The Industrial Revolution, which brought efficiencies and comforts that Americans previously could scarcely imagine, brought additional changes to the Executive Mansion. In the spring of 1840, during the last year of President Martin Van Buren's administration, a hot-air heating system had been installed in the basement furnace room, in what is today the Diplomatic Reception Room. It was a self-contained coal-burning system consisting of an iron firebox, which was enclosed in an outer shell of plastered brick, where the air was warmed. Like the earlier Pettibone furnace installed for James Madison, it was a gravity system, built on the premise that hot air rises. Air ducts ran from both the outer shell and the room itself (which grew quite warm) through the floors and walls to the rooms above. It brought warmth to the State Floor and the great transverse hall, but not to the private quarters on the second floor. Residents of the second floor—the Van Burens, the

Harrisons, and the Tylers—still relied on fireplaces, fed by never-diminished stacks of wood.[11]

The heating system was expanded in 1845 and 1846.[12] Workers converted the furnace to a water-based system, in which water-filled copper coils could be maintained at near boiling temperatures. Air ducts were extended to the second floor, allowing warm moist air—much more pleasant than the prior, stale air—to heat the president's office and the First Couple's private quarters down the hall.[13] It was a dramatic improvement, and would endure for nearly two decades, through the presidency of Abraham Lincoln.

President Polk's focus on his job, his iron-willed determination to achieve his goals before leaving office, was so intense that he rarely took any time off. In his annual message to Congress in 1848, he said, "No President who performs his duty faithfully and conscientiously can have any leisure."[14] And in what might not have been much of an exaggeration, he wrote: "I am the hardest working man in the country."[15] Polk meant it. During his four years in office, he left Washington on overnight trips only four times for a total of about six weeks—much of which was work related.[16]

Among the president's travels: a day trip to visit George Washington's home at Mount Vernon and another to visit the nearby mansion of Francis Blair, a prominent Washington journalist.[17] He did take a six-day break in August 1846, when he, Sarah Polk, a niece, three friends, and two servants stayed at a cottage near a beach in Virginia. The president apparently felt the need to justify even this rare respite: "My long confinement to my office," he wrote, "has considerably enfeebled me & tendered some recreation necessary . . . no public interest will, I think, suffer by my absence for a few [days]." But even this one short trip could not be fully enjoyed—he was felled for two days by a high fever.

He visited his alma mater, the University of North Carolina at Chapel Hill, in 1847, and in August 1848 took a ten-day break at spas in Pennsylvania and West Virginia. It wasn't a full vacation, however, given that Mrs. Polk stayed at the White House to entertain.

But confining himself to Washington wasn't enough for Polk; the president rarely ventured far from the White House itself. Each day he took a short morning walk and a longer evening stroll. He attended church every Sunday and enjoyed an occasional horseback ride, but that was about it. No president before or since was so completely tethered to the White House as James Polk.

"He was an obsessed workaholic, a perfectionist, a micromanager"[18] with an "obsessive desire to control every aspect of the executive branch."[19] The president "seems to have trusted no one, and this led him to make excessive demands upon himself."[20] He was his own political strategist and chief lobbyist, personally talking to scores of lawmakers who came to visit him. He was involved in scheduling all White House events and insisted on writing all of his speeches himself. His desire for control extended deep into the federal bureaucracy, where he was involved in the far-flung minutiae of even lower-level employees.[21] It all stemmed from "his congenital affinity for the martyrdom of duty."[22] The president alluded to this in his diary:

> *The public have no idea of the constant accumulation of business requiring the President's attention. No President who performs his duty faithfully and conscientiously can have any leisure. If he entrusts the details and smaller matters to subordinates constant errors will occur. I prefer to supervise the whole operations of the Government myself . . . and this makes my duties very great.[23]*

He "almost resented amusement of any kind as idle"[24] and saw socializing as a means to a political end. Visitors quickly came to realize that an evening with James and Sarah Polk was not necessarily geared toward relaxation and enjoyment. Stiff conversations about politics typically dominated. The president worked the room like the politician he was, twisting arms and pushing his legislative agenda. To liven things up, the first lady always made sure there was a band, the occasional singer, and once, a juggler.

Despite the attempts at entertainment, visitors chafed at Mrs. Polk's puritanical style. She served no refreshments, and even banned card-playing and dancing. [25] The absence of alcohol may have been influenced by religious views, but there was a more pragmatic reason as well: Downing whiskey for breakfast was common in the nineteenth century, and as the imbibing continued throughout the day, Mrs. Polk likely grew to dislike the effect it had on men, with its ability to loosen both tongues and inhibitions. Whatever the reason, once it became apparent that White House receptions would be dry, she became known as "Sahara Sarah."[26][27] As for her refusal to serve food, the first lady pointed out that she and the president—who footed the bill for such events—were trying to live within their means, which in those days was a quite exorbitant $25,000 salary. But the ban on dancing seemed downright perplexing.

"Oh, Mrs. Polk, why will you not let us dance?" one group of young ladies once asked the first lady.

"Would you dance in so public a place as this?" Mrs. Polk responded. "I would not. To dance in these rooms would be undignified, and it would be respectful neither to the *house* nor to the *office*."[28]

Not only that, Mrs. Polk informed her young guests, prominent lawmakers and diplomats were probably engaged in serious discussions on weighty matters at that very moment in the room next door. Such a juxtaposition of frivolity and gravity would be inappropriate, she argued, though the first lady might really have felt threatened by the presence of young, beautiful women twirling about on the dance floor. Mrs. Polk sometimes invited guests to gather around a piano in the Red Room and sing Methodist hymns such as "How Tedious and Tasteless" and "Come, Humble Sinner." The President's House under Sarah Polk was considerably duller than in years past.[29]

Her decision to ban hard liquor could have been offset by warmth and charm, but here, too, she appears to have fallen short. "She also preferred the company of men"[30] to women, what with their focus on—as she saw it—lesser matters. Both men and women learned to be guarded in her presence. Once a guest, making nothing more than casual chitchat, said "Madam, you have a very genteel assemblage tonight." The first lady's chilly response: "I have never seen it otherwise."[31][32] Though he tried to enjoy these evenings, the president, when lured away from his work by the first lady, often thought his time was "unprofitably spent." Constantly aware of his one-term pledge, and so focused on his work, Polk felt that if he spent too much time at a social event, he would get up even earlier the next morning to make up for it.[33]

One of Polk's territorial objectives—settling a border dispute with Britain over the Oregon Territory—was resolved in 1846, establishing the US border at the 49th parallel. It gave the United States land that would become the states of Oregon, Washington, and Idaho.[34]

But as the dispute with Britain was being settled, the United States was veering toward confrontation with Mexico. Although Polk had made the acquisition of California one of his key objectives, the immediate source of conflict with Mexico concerned Texas. Texas had declared independence from Mexico a dozen years before, and on March 1, 1845, seventy-two hours before he left office, President John Tyler signed a bill officially annexing it.

In his inaugural address three days later, Polk picked up where his predecessor left off, urging the Lone Star Republic to formally join the United States—and for Mexico not to meddle in American affairs. "I regard the question of annexation as belonging exclusively to the United States and Texas," he said. Alluding to the Louisiana Purchase—of which Texas had originally been part—he added that Texas joining the union was no "conquest by a nation seeking to extend her domination by arms and violence, but . . . the peaceful acquisition of a territory once her own."[35]

But Mexico recognized neither Texas's independence nor its inclusion into the United States; it viewed American efforts to seize the Lone Star territory as nothing less than pure robbery.[36] The outraged Mexican ambassador to Washington, Juan Almonte, packed his bags and went home, but not before calling American designs on Texas "an act of aggression the most unjust which can be found recorded in the annals of modern history."[37]

Mexico beefed up its army, and in response Polk sent General Zachary Taylor and thirty-five hundred men to Texas in June.[38] On the 16th of that month, the Texas Congress accepted an American offer of annexation; six months later, on December 29, 1845, Texas was formally admitted to the union as the twenty-eighth state. With Texas officially part of the United States, Polk provoked the Mexicans still further by ordering Taylor and his men to the banks of the Rio Grande itself.[39] "Any acts of hostility" against American forces, the president warned, would immediately result in him asking Congress to declare war.[40] For its part, Mexico interpreted Polk's show of force as tantamount to an American invasion.

If the president was itching for confrontation, he would not have to wait long to get one. Months of diplomatic maneuvering—which some historians have characterized as insincere on Polk's part[41]—gradually gave way to border skirmishes between US and Mexican troops. Finally, on May 11, 1846—"a day of great anxiety with me," he wrote in his diary[42]—the president asked Congress to declare war.

It was a conflict that would cement American dominance over the North American continent—and lay the groundwork for the ascension of four men to the presidency: Zachary Taylor, Franklin Pierce, James Buchanan, and Abraham Lincoln.

In asking Congress to declare war, the president accused Mexico of attacking American troops on US soil north of the Rio Grande (though Mexico considered the United States to be the invader). Secretary of State James Buchanan argued that the case for war "already existed by the act of Mexico herself."[43] Despite opposition to war in parts of the country, notably New England, Congress quickly backed the president, with the House voting for war by a 174 to 14 margin[44] and the Senate 40 to 4.[45] James Polk finally had his war.

Americans rallied around the flag as the war began, and US troops quickly racked up a series of military victories inside Mexico. But as fighting dragged on for nearly two years, support began to ebb, presenting political difficulties for Polk. The president would learn—as later successors would—that starting wars was easier than ending them, events were often uncontrollable, and that the press often had an agenda of its own.

Perhaps most frustrating of all to Polk was that he could not take his support on Capitol Hill for granted. Much to his disgust, many a lawmaker made it clear to the president that they would back his legislative priorities only if he did something substantive for them—such as awarding a military commission to a relative, friend, or themselves. This horse-trading even extended to Polk's own Cabinet, which repulsed the president. He hated this so-called "spoils system," even though it began in the era of his hero and mentor, Andrew Jackson. "The patronage of the government will destroy the popularity of any President," Polk wrote, "however well he may administer the government."[46] The constant demands had begun to sour the once energetic president: He would famously scribble in his diary that "With me it is emphatically true that the Presidency is no bed of roses."[47]

Polk's troubles even extended to his two top military commanders—Brigadier General Taylor and Major General Winfield Scott, both members of the opposition Whig party. The president suspected his commanders had future political ambitions, and were using the war to pursue them. Polk's diaries frequently mention how "ungrateful," "narrow-minded," and "partisan" Taylor was, while Scott was "arbitrary" and "tyrannical."[48] The president was right: His generals *were* politically ambitious. He wasn't the first commander in chief to have issues with his generals—nor would he be the last.[49]

While Taylor and Scott were fighting in Mexico proper, American commanders were seizing other territory. On August 18, 1846, General Stephen Kearny declared New Mexico under US control. One day earlier naval commodore Robert Stockton, in the small town of Los Angeles, issued a similar proclamation about California, declaring that the entire province was now American territory.[50] Stockton's proclamation itself came two months after another naval officer, John Sloat, raised the Stars and Stripes over San Francisco.[51] With the United States firmly in control of both southern and northern California, Polk's ultimate prize appeared to be his at last.

But despite the fulfillment of his territorial ambitions, the president, as 1847 began, had new problems. His Democratic Party suffered a humiliating blow in the midterm election of 1846, losing a stunning fifty-nine seats and, with it, control of the House to the Whigs. The war, despite its battlefield successes, appeared to be the reason.[52] Polk saw it as a stinging rebuke to both the war and his presidency.

The vote also widened an ongoing rift between Polk and Secretary of State James Buchanan. As was the case with Generals Taylor and Scott, Polk accused Buchanan of using his position as the nation's chief diplomat to further his own presidential ambitions."[53] As his term wound down, Polk would belittle Buchanan, writing that he was "in small matters without judgment and sometimes acts like an old maid."[54] James Polk, an intensely ambitious, focused, and driven man, often seemed astonished and resentful that others harbored ambitions of their own.

But he was right. Buchanan *did* aspire to be president, and would see his own dream fulfilled in 1856. Aside from the Second World War a century later, no war helped propel more men into the presidency than the short-lived US war against Mexico. Polk's most prominent commander, Taylor, became a national hero for his battlefield exploits and would succeed Polk in the White House in 1849, though he would die in office just a year and a half later, probably of cholera.[55]

Franklin Pierce certainly benefitted. When the war began, he was a forty-one-year-old private in the New Hampshire Volunteers, recruiting men to enlist in the Army. But Pierce wanted more, and had the best of connections: He had helped deliver the Granite State and its six electoral votes to Polk during the campaign of 1844. Writing to the president, Pierce asked for a battlefield commission, and Polk was happy to help an old political ally. Within short order, Pierce, a man with virtually no military experience, was a brigadier general commanding more than two thousand men.[56] Just four years after the war ended, he was elected president himself. Pierce's unhappy and unsuccessful presidency would be succeeded by yet another political beneficiary of the war: Buchanan.

Taylor, Pierce, and Buchanan would go down in history as three of America's least-accomplished and least-respected presidents. But the same certainly could never be said of the fourth president to garner attention during the Mexican-American War: a young congressman from Illinois named Abraham Lincoln.

Elected to Congress in 1846, Lincoln would serve only one term, and a rather undistinguished one at that. By the time the Thirtieth Congress gathered in Washington—in December 1847—the bulk of the war with Mexico was over.[57] But its first month happened to coincide with a request from President Polk for additional war spending, to bring, as Polk claimed, the conflict to a close. Lincoln, who privately harbored concerns about the war, used this as an opportunity to speak out. On December 22, 1847, the freshman congressman decided to challenge the president.

Lincoln began by questioning Polk's insistence that the war was fought in defense of American territory. Polk, he argued, should provide the House with "all the facts which go to establish whether the particular spot of soil on which the blood of our *citizens* was shed, was, or was not, *our own soil.*" Lincoln clearly believed that Polk had started the war by making an unprovoked attack on Mexican territory.[58]

Two weeks later, Lincoln joined his Whig colleagues in supporting a resolution declaring that the war had been "unnecessarily and unconstitutionally begun by the President of the United States." Of Polk, who was a lawyer by training, Lincoln, himself a man of the law, said: "Mr. Polk is too good a lawyer not to know that he is wrong." He said Polk's desire for war was motivated by a thirst for "military glory—that attractive rainbow, that rises in showers of blood. . . . " He added that the president was "half-insane."[59]

Although they had just taken the House in the 1846 midterms, Whigs were pessimistic about their chances in the more consequential presidential election of 1848. They had to acknowledge privately that Polk had successfully achieved the goals he had outlined in 1844, and that his likely successor, Michigan senator Lewis Cass, would be hard to beat.[60]

But the Whigs, including Lincoln, did see one vulnerability: the president's role in starting the war. It's worth noting that Lincoln said essentially nothing about this during his run for Congress in 1846, and nothing from the point he was elected in November of that year until his attack on the president thirteen months later.

In any case, for all of Lincoln's sharp-tongued oratory, nothing came of his attacks and demands on the president. The House generally ignored him, as did the president himself. There is no record that Polk ever uttered the Illinois backbencher's name either in public or in his quite detailed diaries.[61] That an obscure newcomer to Washington like Lincoln would be treated with such disdain and indifference by a powerful wartime president came as a surprise to practically no one save Lincoln himself. What does seem to have surprised Lincoln, though, was the chilly reaction he received from some members of his own party.[62]

There were lessons learned that would serve Lincoln well in a few short years when he too found himself in the role of wartime president. But unlike Polk, the war Abraham Lincoln would face was far graver—not a war of choice fought on some distant battlefield, but one waged, quite literally in his very backyard—a war of raw survival.

In his anti-Polk tirades, Lincoln argued another point that was probably true. The president, the congressman charged, had no plan to end the war.[63] Indeed, Polk thought that the quick seizure of California would convince the Mexican government of the futility of continued resistance to American forces. He was wrong. The president, noted historian John Seigenthaler, "badly misjudged the will and pride of the Mexicans and their enmity for the United States." It would slowly dawn on Polk that no simple, diplomatic solution to the war existed.[64]

But Polk's uncertainty about how the war would end was alleviated by events on the battlefield. With California secure, Mexico City fell to American forces in September 1847.[65] There was talk of seizing the rest of Mexico as well.

But the president knew that the war was now hurting him politically. The opposition Whigs, now in control of the House, passed a resolution by an 85 to 81 margin calling the conflict "unnecessarily and unconstitutionally begun by the President of the United States."[66] Though tempted by the "All Mexico" crowd, Polk now wanted peace—with the Rio Grande serving as America's southern border.[67] Peace talks began, and on February 2, 1848, while Lincoln and his fellow Whigs were attacking the president, the Treaty of Guadalupe Hidalgo was signed. The Senate would ratify it five weeks later—over the objections of Whigs, who opposed the philosophy of Manifest Destiny—and it was signed by Polk on July 4th.

The treaty added more than five hundred thousand square miles of territory to the United States, and the Stars and Stripes now flew from Texas to
the Pacific coast. With the Oregon territory now part of the nation as well,
Polk's vision—controversial to some, despised by others—had been realized.
The United States was now a continental power, stretching from the Atlantic
to the Pacific Ocean. "The results of the war with Mexico," he told Congress,
"have given to the United States a national character abroad which our country never before enjoyed."[68]

Partisan criticism notwithstanding, James Polk would retire in 1849 as
probably the most consequential one-term president in American history.
The giant map that had greeted him upon entering his White House office
for the first time had been rendered quite outdated by his actions; it no doubt
gave him immense satisfaction to know that his focus and determination had
made it so.

CHAPTER EIGHT

Abraham Lincoln: The Gettysburg Address

The Shop

HIS REPUTATION IS AS SOLID AND ENDURING AS THE GRANITE INTO WHICH his bust is carved at Mount Rushmore, in the Black Hills of South Dakota. He entered office just as the gravest crisis America has ever faced—the Civil War—was beginning, when the nation's very survival was far from certain. Over the next four terrible years, 25 percent of Americans would be killed,

The White House as it looked during the administration of Abraham Lincoln; that's a statue of Thomas Jefferson on the North Lawn. Today, a fountain sits there. The president often spoke to well-wishers from the middle window under the portico. LIBRARY OF CONGRESS

In this painting by Francis B. Carpenter, the First Family is shown in 1861. Willie Lincoln, seated at left next to his mother, Mary Todd Lincoln, would die the next year, plunging the Lincolns into depression. Willie, eleven, died in what would become known as the Lincoln Bed, which today sits in the Lincoln Bedroom. The bed was probably never used by the president himself, though several successors have slept in it. LIBRARY OF CONGRESS

the equivalent of 7.6 million Americans perishing today. Like them, he would also make the ultimate sacrifice, falling to an assassin's bullet less than a week after the guns of the war fell silent. But this last and most prominent casualty of America's bloodiest conflict died knowing that he had seen the nation through its darkest hour. For this, Abraham Lincoln is, and will almost certainly always be, regarded as our greatest president.

His overwhelming preoccupation with the war did not preclude Lincoln from contemplating and planning for what lay beyond—assuming, of course, that the Union would prevail in the great conflict. "The struggle of today is not altogether for today," he said in his first annual message to Congress

In another Carpenter painting, Lincoln is unveiling his Emancipation Proclamation to his Cabinet. The president's Cabinet meetings, like this July 22, 1862, gathering, were held in what Lincoln called "the shop"—his office on the second floor. Today it is the Lincoln Bedroom. LIBRARY OF CONGRESS

(today known as the State of the Union), "it is for a vast future also."[1] That vast future must be secured by all-out fighting, he knew, and Abraham Lincoln waged it with every means at his disposal.

In the White House today, there is a room on the second floor that overlooks the South Lawn that is known as the "Lincoln Bedroom." It's a misnomer: Lincoln probably never slept there, for it was his office, which he called "the shop." In the four years, one month, and eleven days he served as the sixteenth president of the United States, he would spend the bulk of his time in this room, making the grave wartime decisions that meant life or death for hundreds of thousands of his fellow citizens.

It was here where he pondered what he called "the central act of my administration, and the greatest event of the 19th century"[2]—the Emancipation Proclamation, which freed—beginning on January 1, 1863—all slaves in any state (or part of a state) that was fighting the Union. It was here that he crafted his stirring, elegiac, second inaugural address. And it was here that he contemplated that "vast future," so eloquently articulated in what is widely

This Peter Waddell painting shows another view of Lincoln's office (again, the present-day Lincoln Bedroom) on the second floor of the White House. Maps on the wall helped the commander in chief follow the Civil War. From his windows, the president could see Confederate encampments in Virginia—and the unfinished Washington Monument. PETER WADDELL FOR THE WHITE HOUSE HISTORICAL ASSOCIATION

regarded as the most magnificent and consequential 272 words ever spoken by an American president: the Gettysburg Address.

That Lincoln would be a great president, or merely the latest in a string of mediocre ones, was unknown when he and his wife, Mary, moved into the White House in March 1861. The Civil War had been brewing for decades, and none of his successors had been able to stop it. The previous December, a month after he was elected—he wasn't even on the ballot in the Deep South—South Carolina announced that it was seceding from the Union. By the time he was sworn in three months later, Florida, Alabama, Georgia,

Louisiana, and Texas had joined them. After the bombardment of Fort Sumter, a federal base in South Carolina, and the new president's call for volunteers to put down the southern rebellion, four more states—Virginia, Arkansas, Tennessee, and North Carolina—left the Union as well. No president—with the possible exception of Franklin D. Roosevelt in 1933—has ever entered office amid such truly desperate conditions.

The White House as it first appeared to the Lincolns reflected their gloomy spirit. The exterior remained an imposing facade as visitors approached the entrance, but such visions of grandeur quickly vanished when they stepped inside. Wooden floors sagged. In the basement, caretakers propped up the East Room with logs, fearing the weight of visitors during receptions—and soldiers who slept there in the early stages of the war—would cause the floor to collapse. As far back as 1842, Charles Dickens thought the interior worn and drab;[3] two decades later, it remained so.

Not that attempts weren't made to spruce things up. First Lady Mary Lincoln—who asked to be called "Mrs. President" and wanted a say in how the government should be run—made the White House her own little fiefdom.[4] Allocated $20,000 by Congress to redecorate the mansion,[5] she spent it all in less than a year and kept on going. She bought two sets of Haviland china—one for official entertaining and one for her own everyday use. Custom-made carpets, drapes, wallpaper, and a fancy seven-hundred-piece set of glassware—her shopping list was as long as it was extravagant. To hide her massive overspending from congressional critics, she got public buildings commissioner Benjamin B. French to bury the bills in the budgets of various government agencies. She "loved glitter, show, pomp and power," the first lady's sister Elizabeth once noted.[6]

Her spendthrift ways sent her "always rigidly frugal" husband into a rage. "It would stick in the nostrils of the American people to have it said that the President of the United States had approved a bill over-running an appropriation of $20,000 for *flub dubs* for this damned old house, when the soldiers cannot have blankets."[7]

Like many a husband and wife, the Lincolns argued about money. He wanted to reimburse the government for cost overruns out of his own pocket, but "Mrs. President" refused to let him do it. During one fight, she was reported to have thrown stove wood at him; another time, she chased him about with a butcher's knife.[8] As if the commander in chief, who was already desperately trying to win a war, didn't have enough problems.

For reasons of security and privacy, much of the White House's ground floor was closed to public view during Lincoln's presidency, including the State Dining Room (formerly Thomas Jefferson's office) and a smaller dining room, both used by the First Family just about every day. But aides, messengers, members of Congress, and sometimes ordinary citizens visited, making their way from the north entrance, through the East Room, and up to the second floor, where the president worked, and where he and his family slept.[9]

This steady stream of visitors was often so crushing that it reduced the area where the First Family could truly be alone to just a handful of rooms at the far west end of the second floor. Lincoln could have easily closed the White House as President James K. Polk did in the 1840s; but as a congressman during those years, Lincoln thought that made the people's house aloof and unfriendly. Abraham Lincoln, the humble rail-splitter from Illinois, reasoned the American people had put him in the White House. They should be allowed to see him if they wished.[10]

And see him they did. In the early stages of his presidency, Lincoln— who admitted that when he became president he was "entirely ignorant"[11] about how to do his job—allowed these visitors to take up most of his time, from ten o'clock in the morning until late at night. Ushering them in with his standard greeting, "What can I do for you?"[12] he sat for hours listening to their often petty concerns. Many were office seekers; others sought government business. Some just wanted to shake the hand of the president of the United States. One of his secretaries, John Nicolay, said the crush of visitors was so great that "we have scarcely had time to eat sleep or even breathe." Responding to criticism, Lincoln said his callers "don't want much and don't get but little, and I must see them."[13]

Lincoln's insistence on mixing with the general public is also a reflection of his personal bravery, as he received scores of death threats in the mail. Much to the dismay of his guards, the president considered the threats "nonsense," although he kept the letters, pushing them through a little pigeonhole in his desk.[14]

Other than when he retired to his personal quarters each evening, the president was frequently exposed to danger. Anyone who could make their way to the White House basement could, in theory, get a glimpse of Lincoln as he emerged from the winding service stairs that connected the ground floor to the work/living space on the top floor. The president would often walk from the basement under Thomas Jefferson's West Wing colonnade, pass through a contingent of soldiers camped between the mansion and the War Department next door, and enter its telegraph room, where the commander in chief pored over battlefield dispatches that came in frequently over the wires.[15] Lincoln spent so much time in the telegraph room—an early iteration of the modern-day Situation Room—that he sometimes slept there as he awaited news from his generals.[16]

But the president did make efforts to be careful. Because it offered more privacy and security than the grand staircase or the business staircase, Lincoln used the service stairs most of the time. The passageway was enclosed in its own small hall and guarded by the doorkeeper, whose room was adjacent. This gave the president the ability to privately access any part of the house (except for his own office); he could also come and go from the mansion itself in secrecy.[17]

The Oval Room (today the Yellow Oval Room) was at the heart of the small portion of the second floor—just nine rooms—reserved for the personal use of the First Family. During the day, these rooms proved a welcome sanctuary from the daily invasion of aides, members of Congress, nosy reporters, businessmen, and plain tourists. Mrs. Lincoln, who often relished attention, perhaps didn't mind all that much. But Robert, Willie, and Tad, the Lincolns' sons, quickly found upon moving into the mansion that the freedom of movement they had taken for granted in Springfield was a thing of the past. For security reasons Willie and Tad, ages ten and seven, respectively, were also homeschooled in the Oval Room. (Robert, seventeen, was a Harvard freshman when his father was elected.)[18] [19]

In addition to the central heating system—installed during the Polk era—that helped keep Washington's long winters at bay, the Lincolns were the first occupants of the White House to enjoy the convenience of running water in their private quarters. James Buchanan had ordered the system, which used water from the nearby Potomac River, installed, but it wasn't ready until after the Lincolns moved in.[20]

Except for the Oval Room, every room in the family quarters had washstands with fancy porcelain sinks topped by marble. Each featured a single faucet, off when turned parallel to the wall, gushing when turned toward the sink. Servants placed linen towels at each sink daily.[21] For a man born on the frontier, in a one-room log cabin with a dirt floor and no glass windows, Abraham Lincoln's White House years were quite comfortable.

In fact, despite its generally shabby appearance, Lincoln considered the White House the nicest place he had ever lived. His satisfaction with the house, as well as his utter preoccupation with the war effort, resulted in a general disinterest in making any changes to it. He only made one alteration during his four years in office, and it was for reasons of convenience and privacy: He ordered that a partition be built across the southern side of a reception room on the second floor. This created a closed, private passage he could use to walk, unobserved and unbothered, from his office on the southeast side of the floor, to the Oval Room—used by the First Family for private relaxation. It was off-limits to all but a few aides and guests.[22]

The Lincolns' private quarters were lined with bookshelves, an addition to the mansion courtesy of Abigail Fillmore, who was given funds from Congress in 1851 for a White House library.[23] Mrs. Lincoln added to the existing collection, buying English novels for herself and poetry and plays—with an emphasis on Shakespeare—for her husband. There was never much leisure time, but whenever they could, the president and first lady would retreat here, relaxing in upholstered rocking chairs.[24]

Next to the Oval Library, on the western side, were two bedrooms. The bigger chamber, next to the Library itself, was the first lady's; the Lincolns had separate, connected bedrooms in Springfield, so they were accustomed to this arrangement. Next to it was a smaller room where the president slept, which in turn led to a small dressing room with fireplace and water closet, in the southwest corner. The suite stood over the State Dining Room one floor below. This was the true Lincoln Bedroom.

Across the hall stood the "Prince of Wales Room," where Prince Albert Edward (the future King Edward VII) stayed during an 1860 visit to President James Buchanan. The irony was rather odd: A nation that sought independence less than a century before to rid itself of an overbearing English monarch now named one of its most exclusive chambers in honor of a future king.

It was in this homage to royalty that Mary Lincoln placed, in 1861,[25] what is today the most famous piece of furniture—with the possible exception of the famous "Resolute" desk in the Oval Office—in the entire White House. Ordered from the Philadelphia firm of William Carryl, it came to be known as "the Lincoln Bed." But like the bedroom that is incorrectly named for him, there is no evidence that Lincoln ever slept in the Lincoln Bed either[26]—though at 6'4" (the tallest president along with Lyndon Johnson), Lincoln could have easily stretched out on the gargantuan frame with feet to spare. One Lincoln did sleep in the room, however: Robert, the eldest son, who visited during his breaks from Harvard.

The bed was enormous: eight feet, six inches long, framed by a towering rosewood headboard and large footboard—both featuring carved grapes, grapevines, and birds.[27] Above the giant headboard itself was a gold American shield surrounded by plush purple satin curtains fringed in gold, which flowed all the way to the floor. Sheets and blankets were topped by a purple and gold bedspread. Some today might call it gaudy, but in 1861 it was said to be spectacular, "the best in the family suite," in the words of one of Mrs. Lincoln's cousins. Next to the Prince of Wales Room was a small room with a bathtub, and next to that, two smaller bedrooms. This was a fairly new development. The smaller bedrooms had once been a bigger chamber but were later divided, probably during Franklin Pierce's administration. Between them stood a small passageway, which led to a window overlooking the North Portico of the White House. President Lincoln would occasionally appear in the window to safely address crowds below.[28]

A long hallway ran down the middle of the floor, just like the great transverse on the main floor below. At the western end was a grand staircase, which stood just outside the president's suite—right where the original architect of the White House, James Hoban, had intended it to be. Rebuilt during the mansion's reconstruction after the War of 1812, the handrail was mahogany—traditionally the wood of choice for White House interiors—and the spindles a gleaming white. The stairs were covered in Brussels carpeting, held into place by long brass rods. At the head of the stairs, Lincoln could look west through the spectacular half-moon window; the sunsets must have been lovely—though he enjoyed the same view from his dressing room next door.[29]

Regardless of where his bedroom was, Lincoln, under enormous pressure and stress, slept poorly in the White House.[30] He spent the bulk of his time down the hall, in his office. It was in this room, situated on the southeast side of the mansion's top floor, the president saw America through the Civil War.[31]

But it was also where the president engaged in more mundane activities, like opening his mail and getting his hair and beard trimmed. A restless man, Lincoln often paced about and certainly spent time gazing out the windows, which offered a sweeping view of the South Lawn, encampments of Union troops, the unfinished Washington Monument,[32] and the Potomac River. Beyond that, the president could also see, depending on how the war was progressing, Confederate flags fluttering in the distance—an ominous reminder of the threat that dominated his every waking moment.[33] Never before had a president of the United States stood in his own home and seen, from such a close distance, the very enemy determined to destroy what he had sworn to defend.

To Americans today, the principal workspace of the president of the United States—the Oval Office—is a quiet enclave that conveys great power and dignity. It is a humbling, even intimidating, space—both literally and symbolically. In contrast, Lincoln's office was seen in more modest terms—an extension of sorts of the personality of the man who occupied it. It was, in short, far less impressive than the soaring oratory and momentous decisions that emanated from it.

A sketch made in October 1864 shows his office dominated by a long black table, crafted from walnut. This was used for Cabinet meetings, which were held on Tuesday and Friday. A table lamp was fueled by a rubber hose that extended from a chandelier above. The walls were covered in dark green wallpaper. Along one wall stood a sofa, framed by two upholstered chairs; above them hung maps where the president could track the movements of Union and Confederate forces. There were two desks. One was quite big, made from mahogany and topped with a series of cubbyholes that served as the presidential filing cabinet. Relegated to one corner, it was so shabby that one of his secretaries thought it must have come "from some old furniture auction."[34] Lincoln's working desk stood between the two windows that looked south. Pulling a nearby cord would summon one of the president's two assistants, John Nicolay or Nicolay's assistant, John Hay.[35] Lincoln affectionately called them "the boys."[36] There were carpets, but most of the president's office was covered with oilcloth as well, to protect floors and carpets from poor aim into spittoons, or when they began to overflow.[37]

Aside from the president's own family, Nicolay and Hay were closer to Lincoln than anyone. Both men, still in their twenties, lived on the second floor of the mansion, just down the hall from the First Family. They wore many hats: chief of staff, press secretary, and political advisor; they also guarded the "last door which opens into the awful presence" of the president himself, as Noah Brooks, a top Washington journalist, noted. Hay and Nicolay always addressed their boss as "Mr. President," of course, though in private, they affectionately referred to him as "the Tycoon" and "the Ancient."[38]

Lincoln was an arrive-early, stay-late president. After a meager break-fast—typically black coffee, toast, and an egg[39]—he went to the office and immediately buried himself in paperwork, reading dispatches from military commanders that had been received overnight. He also reviewed the day ahead with his assistants, and discussed concerns with members of his Cabinet. Appointments typically ran from 10:00 a.m. until noon, at which point Lincoln took a lunch break. Like breakfast, the midday meal was also modest: "a biscuit, a glass of milk in the winter, some fruit or grapes in the summer."[40] Lincoln then received more visitors until 5:00 or 6:00 p.m. each night.[41] He often worked until midnight.[42]

As the Civil War was the most devastating conflict in American history, Gettysburg was its most devastating battle. Lasting from July 1st to July 3rd, 1863, it marked the high-water mark of the Confederacy. Robert E. Lee's Army of Northern Virginia had been dealt a stinging defeat and would never again seriously threaten the North. But casualties had been horrendous.

In just three days of vicious fighting, some forty-six thousand men on both sides would be killed, wounded, or missing. The toll on Lincoln, who had spent an agonizing seventy-two hours monitoring the great battle, was visible to all who saw him. One visitor wrote of the president's anxiety and weariness, his "drooping eyelids, looking almost swollen; the dark bags beneath the eyes, the deep marks about the large and expressive mouth."[43] The Battle of Gettysburg would haunt Lincoln for the brief remainder of his life.

On November 2, 1863, David Wills, a prominent banker, judge, and member of the Gettysburg Cemetery Commission, invited the president to speak at the dedication of a new national cemetery. Because Edward Everett, the former secretary of state, governor, and senator from Massachusetts, would deliver the oration, Lincoln could deliver just "a few appropriate remarks," Wills said.[44] The president immediately accepted.

Lincoln knew that his presence on the battlefield, which had already begun to take on the aura of a national shrine, called for words of unusual eloquence and power. In his mind, he outlined three parts to the address. He would begin by looking to the past and explaining what led to the battle. He would then touch upon the present situation. Finally, Lincoln decided he would look to the future, placing Gettysburg and its significance in a broader context. Around this framework he would use, as he always preferred, short simple words.[45]

As he developed his address, Lincoln sought advice. Inviting William Saunders, a landscape architect who was designing the cemetery, to the White House on November 17th—just two days before he was to speak—the president got a lesson on the topography of Gettysburg.[46]

It was a helpful complement to what he already knew from battlefield dispatches that had been sent by his commanders in July. He began to write his speech on White House stationery.

Lincoln left for Gettysburg on November 18th. As usual, he had been quite busy and told Ward Lamon, who doubled as both presidential aide and body-guard, that he had misgivings about making the trip. Although he knew the broad outlines of what he wished to say the next day, the speech was unfinished and the president fretted about it. Some witnesses claim to have seen Lincoln jotting notes on an envelope, using the top of his famous stovepipe hat as a desk. But Nicolay, who sat with the president, denies this, insisting that Lincoln relaxed and chatted with fellow passengers during the trip and wrote nothing.[47] There is no definitive account to support either narrative.[49]

But even if Nicolay was right, it doesn't mean that the president's speech was ready. That night, he asked a servant to find a few sheets of paper. He pored over the address, making edits, particularly to the ending.[49] Clutching his papers, he departed the home in which he was staying around 11:00 p.m. and strolled over to a nearby house, where Secretary of State William Seward was staying. The two men supposedly spent about an hour together, prob-ably spending a portion of it discussing the speech. Even then, the president wasn't done: He would make a few, final changes in the morning.[50]

At the cemetery, a small platform had been built for the ceremony. The president sat in the front row, in a rocking chair, with Everett on his right, Seward on his left.[51] Gathered before them: an audience of some nine thou-sand people.

After a prayer and a performance by the Marine Band, Everett spoke. His speech, which he had memorized, lasted two hours. Then another band played. Now, it was the president's turn.

It was a cold day, the wind brisk as Abraham Lincoln rose. Although he had cobbled his address together over the last few days, not really finalizing it until that very morning, what he would say had been inside him for years. During his famous debates with Stephen Douglas during the campaign for the Illinois Senate in 1858, for example, Lincoln had scoffed at the notion that one race was superior to the other. In March 1862, twenty months before his visit to Gettysburg, he told his assistant, Hay, that the central theme of the Civil War was to show "that popular government is not an absurdity," and that "if we fail it will go far to prove the incapability of the people to govern themselves."[52]

These thoughts, deeply ingrained within the president, had now been condensed and rephrased, to be uttered in a far more powerful and eternal way:

Four score and seven years ago our fathers brought forth on this continent a new nation, conceived in liberty, and dedicated to the proposition that all men are created equal.

Now we are engaged in a great civil war, testing whether that nation, or any nation so conceived and so dedicated, can long endure. We are met on a great battlefield of that war. We have come to dedicate a portion of that field, as a final resting place for those who here gave their lives that that nation might live. It is altogether fitting and proper that we should do this.

But, in a larger sense, we can not dedicate, we can not consecrate, we can not hallow this ground. The brave men, living and dead, who struggled here, have consecrated it, far above our poor power to add or detract. The world will little note, nor long remember what we say here, but it can never forget what they did here. It is for us the living, rather, to be dedicated here to the unfinished work which they who fought here have thus far so nobly advanced. It is rather for us to be here dedicated to the great task remaining before us—that from these honored dead we take increased devotion to that cause for which they gave the last full measure of devotion—that we here highly resolve that these dead shall not have died in vain—that this nation, under God, shall have a new birth of freedom—and that government of the people, by the people, for the people, shall not perish from the earth.

Whether these "few appropriate remarks" had in fact been written down as the president's train approached the war-ravaged Pennsylvania town is, to some degree, immaterial. The broad theme, even specific phrases, had been in Lincoln's head for years. He had even delivered key passages before in public.

In an Independence Day message to Congress in 1861, just three months into the Civil War, the president referred to the United States as "a democracy—a government of the people, by the same people."[53] On July 7, 1863, as word of the Union's victory at Gettysburg brought an explosion of joy to Washington, he appeared before a cheering crowd that had gathered outside the White House. It has been "eighty odd years," he told them, since the nation's founders had gathered and, for the first time, "declared as a self-evident truth that 'all men are created equal.'"[54]

That last line—that all men are created equal—was a paean to his hero, Thomas Jefferson. Indeed, if there was any one person who influenced the president as he framed what would become the Gettysburg Address, it was the man from Monticello. Of all the Founding Fathers, it was Jefferson who gave Lincoln the most inspiration and direction throughout his life. Indeed, on his way to Washington in 1861 to assume the presidency, he stopped in Philadelphia to speak at Independence Hall. "I have never had a feeling politically that did not spring from the sentiments embodied in the Declaration of Independence," he declared.[55]

Jefferson's insistence that all men are created equal so moved Abraham Lincoln, in fact, that in that Philadelphia address, he said something quite ominous, considering what would happen to him four years later: "If this country cannot be saved without giving up that principle," Lincoln declared, "I was about to say I would rather be assassinated on this spot than to surrender it."[56]

CHAPTER NINE

Ulysses S. Grant: The Secret Swearing-In

The Red Room

RUMORS OF A COUP SWIRLED ABOUT THE NATION'S CAPITAL. IT WAS MORE than idle talk: Someone had already fired at the president-elect's home—hitting the dining room—and now the entire city of Washington was on edge.

Among those fearful of unrest was the outgoing president of the United States, Ulysses S. Grant. A Civil War hero who was no stranger to violence, Grant, in his last full day in the White House, had only learned who his successor would be the day before: Rutherford B. Hayes, the Republican governor of Ohio. But the circumstances of his election were so contentious and ugly—along with the Bush-Gore debacle of 2000, the most disputed election in American history—that the fight over who won would drag on for four long months, beginning on Election Day, November 8, 1876, and not ending until March 2, 1877—a mere forty-eight hours before Inauguration Day.

Now, as Hayes prepared to take the oath of office, security across Washington had been tightened.

An honest president, Ulysses S. Grant was nevertheless surrounded by scandal, with both friends and family attempting to take advantage of their access to him. LIBRARY OF CONGRESS

FRANK LESLIE'S ILLUSTRATED NEWSPAPER

No. 915—Vol. XXXVIII.]   NEW YORK, JUNE 6, 1874.   [Price, 10 Cents, $4.00 per year.

THE WEDDING AT THE WHITE HOUSE

The Grants spent big to renovate the East Room, finishing in time for their daughter Nellie's 1874 wedding. Some critics called the renovation "steamboat Gothic." LIBRARY OF CONGRESS

But inside the White House itself, Grant was taking no chances. Staging a dinner party in Hayes's honor on the night of March 3rd, the president and president-elect stole away for a few minutes to the room next door—the Red Room—where Morrison Waite, the chief justice of the Supreme Court, was waiting. There, in a room dimly illuminated by flickering gas lamps and brimming with flowers, he administered the oath of office to Hayes. The president-elect, who declined to use a Bible, simply raised his hand and took the oath.[1] It was the first time a president had been sworn in in the White House itself. Of the forty-two men who have taken the oath as required by the Constitution, the March 3, 1877, swearing in of Rutherford B. Hayes was the most controversial transition of power in American history.

⌒

If the rise of the forty-fourth president, Barack Obama, from an obscure Illinois lawmaker to the White House in nine years is remarkable, consider Grant: In 1860 he was working at his family's leather shop in Galena, Illinois; one war and eight years later, he was president of the United States. It was a swift and remarkable rise for a man who had failed at so many things in his life that even his own father nicknamed him "Useless" as a boy.[2]

But Grant (whose real first name was "Hiram") did have one very useful skill: He could fight. He was a West Point graduate and fought under another future president—Zachary Taylor—during the Mexican-American War of 1846–1848. Twice cited for bravery, a bright future in the Army all but assured, he suddenly resigned his commission in the spring of 1854. Known to be a heavy drinker, Grant may have been forced to quit; in his autobiography he wrote that had he remained in the Army, he would not have been able to support his wife and two children "out of my pay as an army officer."[3]

But the private sector proved to be no more lucrative. He tried half a dozen careers, and nothing stuck. One bleak year he pawned his watch for $22 so he could buy his four children Christmas presents.[4] In 1860, desperate, he went to work at the family store.

The Civil War would revive Grant's career. The North needed experienced officers, and Grant was reappointed to lead a regiment of volunteers. Given a fresh opportunity to make something of himself, he flourished. Moving up the ranks, earning larger commands, and showing a battlefield zeal that struck fear into the enemy, Grant acquired the nickname "the butcher." The man once dubbed "useless" quickly won the admiration of Abraham Lincoln, who had had his fill of useless generals; in the spring of 1863, after the Battle of

Vicksburg, Mississippi—in which Grant dealt Confederate forces a devastating blow—he received a letter from the president. "I write this now as a grateful acknowledgement for the almost inestimable service you have done the country."[5] The next year, Grant was promoted to Lieutenant General of the Union Army, a rank previously held by only one man: George Washington.

Lincoln and Grant would grow personally close. On April 14, 1865—five days after Grant accepted the surrender of Robert E. Lee's Army of Northern Virginia, bringing the Civil War to a close—the president invited him and Mrs. Grant to join him and Mrs. Lincoln at Ford's Theatre that evening. But the Grants, anxious to see their children, politely declined and left town.[6]

The war—and the martyred Lincoln's admiration for him—made Grant a national hero. At first he expressed no interest in running for elected office, but a groundswell of support changed his mind; he swept into office in 1868 by a comfortable margin.

Grant was lucky he even had a White House to move into. If government bureaucrats had gotten their way, it might have been torn down—and a new home built in another part of Washington. In 1864, when the war was raging, the commissioner of federal buildings in the District of Columbia, Benjamin Brown French, declared it unfit for habitation and in need of replacement.[7]

This probably came as news to most Americans. After all, from the outside, the White House maintained its imposing grandeur. But on the inside, the building's bones were showing their age. French said that the mansion—even though it had been rebuilt after the fire in 1814—was outdated compared with current building standards. The commissioner, not a man to be trifled with, had a powerful ally: Mary Lincoln. The first lady wanted a new house too, and had been lobbying for one on the grounds of the Soldiers' Home, a cool, leafy rest area on the outskirts of Washington where she and her husband spent much of their time. President Lincoln himself first visited the grounds three days after he was inaugurated in 1861—as well as the day before his fatal visit to Ford's Theatre. Between 1862 and 1864, in fact, the Lincolns spent the bulk of their time in a cottage there, with the president commuting to the White House.[8]

Where could a new White House go? One site high atop a cliff in Rock Creek was considered, as was a two-hundred-acre estate east of the Capitol.

The latter site, called Harewood, already had roads, trees, and walking paths—all laid out by President Andrew Jackson more than three decades before. All it lacked was a "princely mansion" for the commander in chief.[9] And because of its remoteness, the Soldiers' Home so loved by the Lincolns was again considered following the president's assassination. Whatever the venue, it should be located "away from the constant turmoil of city life, at such a distance where his privacy cannot be intruded upon, and still sufficiently accessible for all practical purposes."[10] Other critical factors: "healthfulness, good water and capability of adornment."[11]

So why wasn't the White House torn down and rebuilt in another location? We can thank, in a way, Lincoln's handpicked vice president, the mediocre Andrew Johnson. Even though he was Lincoln's number two, Johnson didn't exactly see eye-to-eye with the Great Emancipator on a lot of things, namely blacks and the issue of postwar Reconstruction. "This is a country for white men," Johnson had reportedly declared, "and as long as I am president, it shall be a government for white men"[12]—a sentiment that did not exactly conform with Lincoln's belief that all men were created equal.

Johnson also tried to block postwar Reconstruction of the South, a key Lincoln priority, believing it unconstitutional. Finally, he infuriated Congress by trying to fire Secretary of War Edwin Stanton, a violation of the 1867 Tenure of Office Act, which banned presidents from sacking senior government officials without Senate permission.[13] The House impeached Johnson; in the subsequent Senate trial, the president was acquitted by a single vote.

Johnson's impeachment and trial consumed Washington. It was a circus, with lawmakers so focused on removing the president from the White House that they largely forgot about the White House itself.

—~—

When he moved into the mansion in March 1869, Grant—who had been perfectly comfortable living in a canvas Army tent during the war—let it be known that it suited him just fine. Any talk of tearing it down faded away;[14] the mansion had survived its most serious threat since the British had burned it down half a century before.

Although Grant's status as a Civil War hero propelled him into office, the war itself began to fade into the history books during his presidency. It was the beginning of what Mark Twain coined "the Gilded Age," an era of rapid economic expansion and the creation of vast wealth, much of which was controlled by a small handful of men, who came to be known collectively as robber barons.

Oil, steel, railroads, high finance, and more reflected the brains and brawn of this new era, and that their names are familiar even today—Astor, Carnegie, and Rockefeller; Morgan, Mellon, and Vanderbilt—is testament to the power these masters of industry wielded, and their sweeping legacies that have endured to this day. Rich beyond belief—in real terms wealthier than modern-day titans like Bill Gates or Warren Buffett—they enjoyed lifestyles of opulence and ostentation that were simply beyond the imagination of the average American.[15]

It was inevitable that the era's lifestyle would seep into Grant's White House. Entertaining was both gaudy and grand, with state dinners overseen by an Italian chef and featuring up to twenty-five courses, accompanied by six types of wine. There were weekly dinners as well, each costing about $700. The total cost of these dinners alone would have broken the bank for the Grants, who lived on the presidential salary of $25,000 (which doubled in 1873 as the president began his second term). But thanks to deep-pocketed friends, the president and his wife, Julia, could maintain the lifestyle to which they had become accustomed—and to which Americans had come to expect of their president.

But even though Grant was comfortable in the White House, he acknowledged that it needed work. With a $25,000 appropriation from Congress, the Grants refurnished both the family quarters on the west end of the second floor and the president's offices on the east end. One of the first things to go were the hallway carpets, which the first lady described as "much worn and so ugly I could not bear to look at them."[16]

On the western side, the large, grand staircase (also known as the "double staircase") that had been built during the Jefferson era and rebuilt after the 1814 fire was replaced with a smaller, single staircase. This allowed for a small sitting area by the "elegant half-moon window,"[17] the origin of what is today known as the West Sitting Hall—a favorite gathering place for many First Families. The open space allowed the small hallway leading to the president's bedroom, located in the southwest corner, to be removed. The bedroom would open directly into the sitting hall, as it still does today.[18]

Mrs. Grant also bought new furniture; her taste ran toward Renaissance Revival–style furniture, which featured heavy crests, rounded pediments, and angular scrolls. Described as "a sunny, sweet woman,"[19] Julia Grant spent hours decorating rooms, arranging flowers, and going out of her way to greet thousands of visitors at countless events. The historian William Seale speculates that Mrs. Grant loved the White House so much that she played a role behind the scenes in killing plans to tear it down and rebuild elsewhere. "If I could have my way," she wrote, "[I] would never have it changed."[20][21] This profound joy in her surroundings continued until the very end. "My life at the White House was like a bright and beautiful dream . . . it was quite the happiest period of my life."[22] On her last day in the mansion—March 4, 1877—she wept.[23]

As for "Ulys," as Mrs. Grant called her husband, he was at the time, at forty-six, the youngest president ever elected.[24] Unpretentious, soft-spoken, and easily embarrassed[25]—odd traits for a war hero called "the butcher"[26]— he had simple desires: whiskey, cigars, and billiards, often enjoyed together. It was a stark contrast to his lavish official entertaining he did in an official capacity. Underneath, it seems Ulysses S. Grant was just a simple soldier who craved a simple life.

Billiard tables had been in the White House before, but usually in the basement. Grant put his in a more prominent spot, between the mansion and a greenhouse just off the mansion's west end. No photos of the room are known to exist, but it has been described as a grand space, framed in "heavy exposed timber work and paneled in beaded boards," with "rows of tall windows [that] admitted light from the north and south." The presidential billiard table itself was illuminated by gaslights overhead, and "stood on a floor of brilliant encaustic tiles laid in a geometric design." Grant spent considerable time here, playing not with the rich and fancy who flocked to the mansion, but with his fellow war veterans; he also spent many hours practicing alone.[27]

Unlike James Polk and Abraham Lincoln, Ulysses S. Grant was not a workaholic president. He typically arrived at his second-floor office around ten in the morning, where he spent about two hours. Lunch, which began at noon, lasted sixty to ninety minutes. Back in his office, the president would receive visitors until three o'clock. Then taking the winding service stairs, he would descend to the White House basement and walk outside to his stables, where he would spend another two hours or so tending to his horses. Dinner was at five o'clock. All told, the president usually spent about four hours a day behind his desk. But perhaps comparisons with Polk, the ultimate micromanager, and Lincoln, who was overwhelmed with the Civil War, are unfair. Grant, a military man, knew how to delegate effectively, and many of his White House aides were former officers whom he had commanded in the Army.

His office was the same room used by his hero Lincoln, in what is today known as the Lincoln Bedroom. Next to this, heading west, was the Cabinet Room. The Cabinet met with the president on Thursday and Friday, gathering around a long magnificent table that remains today one of the most notable pieces of furniture in the White House. Made by New York's Pottier & Stymus, it was originally built for Andrew Johnson but didn't arrive until after he left office. It featured eight lockable drawers, so Cabinet members could, in theory, keep their important papers secure.

Sitting in the same room today, the table has had a starring role in several momentous events in American history, including the pact ending the Spanish-American War in 1898, the Nuclear Test Ban Treaty of 1963, the first Strategic Arms Limitation Treaty (SALT) with the Soviet Union in 1972, and a peace treaty between Israel and Egypt in 1979. For this reason, the table is referred to as the Treaty Table.[28] The room itself was renamed the Treaty Room by Jacqueline Kennedy.

After Grant's 1872 reelection, Congress appropriated a much larger sum—$100,000—for further renovations of the mansion. This time, the Grants turned their attention to the State Floor, specifically the East Room. Other than gas lighting, which was installed in 1848 during the Polk administration, the vast chamber had essentially been unchanged since its completion in the late 1820s. The Grants began by having two beams installed on the ceiling, twenty-two feet up; this created three spaces in the room. The ceilings were painted in blues and pinks, as if to resemble the sky, and gold and gray wallpaper was put up.

The room's four fireplaces received new mantles, with tall mirrors hung above each, and four large gas globe chandeliers were hung from the ceiling. The beams were supported by imposing Corinthian-style columns—leading some observers to dub the decor "pure Greek." Others, less than impressed with all the bronze and glitter, sneered that "steamboat Gothic" was more like it.[29]

Running east to west across the State Floor, the Green, Blue, and Red Rooms also acquired a modern sheen; all were completed in time for the most important social event of President and Mrs. Grant's entire eight years in office: the 1874 marriage of their daughter, Nellie, to Englishman Algernon Sartoris.

With the exception of a minor remodeling job during the administration of Chester Arthur in 1882—when Louis Tiffany installed silver paper on the ceiling and added several potted plants—Grant's improvements to the East

Room would last a quarter-century, when Theodore Roosevelt would over-haul the room yet again.

———

Grant would go down in history as a better general than president, largely for a series of scandals that plagued his administration. The president himself appears to have been a honest man, but his loyalty to those around him made him oblivious to their corruption. He allowed himself to accept gifts from some whose intentions were less than benign.

One of the worst abuses of the public trust came when two railroad magnates used their access to Grant—via an unscrupulous presidential brother-in-law—to try and corner the gold market. Learning of this scheme to manipulate the market, the president stopped it, ironically by manipulat-ing the market himself by flooding it with government-owned gold. Prices plunged, sparking "Black Friday," September 24, 1869, when the financial markets crashed. The so-called "Gold Panic" and a subsequent congressio-nal investigation into it dented the president's hard-earned reputation.[30] That reputation would absorb additional blows in the years ahead. Ulysses S. Grant was not the first president to be tarnished by scandal; nor, of course, would he be the last.

———

In 1797, George Washington announced that eight years in the presidency were enough for him, and that he would retire to Mount Vernon, his stately home overlooking the Potomac River. Three-quarters of a century later, Ulysses S. Grant, worn down by scandal and weary of presidential life, decided that two terms were enough for him as well (term limits wouldn't be legally established until after the death of four-termer Franklin Roo-sevelt) and that he would retire. "I do not want to be here another four years. I do not think I could stand it," he told the first lady. Julia Grant was crushed.[31]

And thus set in motion the nasty, contentious scramble to replace him. In circumstances that ring familiar to Americans today, Samuel Tilden, the Democratic governor of New York, won the popular vote over Rutherford Hayes, the Republican governor of Ohio, by more than three percentage points. Tilden also got more electoral votes than Hayes: 184 to 165. But Til-den was one electoral vote short of the 185 he needed to have the necessary *majority* of electoral votes—and twenty additional electoral votes from four additional states—Florida, Louisiana, South Carolina, and Oregon—were contested.

Allegations of fraud, violence, and intimidation were slung back and forth; 1876 became 1877. Four months after election day—and forty-eight hours before Inauguration Day—the nation still didn't know who the next president would be.

In the end, Congress appointed an Electoral Commission, made up of five senators, five members of the House of Representatives, and five Supreme Court justices. Seven were supposed to be Republicans, seven Democrats, and one independent. As it turned out, there were eight Republicans and seven Democrats. The commission gave the disputed electoral votes to Hayes. But Republicans gave into the Democratic demand to end postwar Reconstruction in the South. Hayes, with 185 electoral votes, would be president, while southern Democrats could reverse gains that blacks had made during Reconstruction.[32]

When the news became public, Democratic outrage over the so-called "Grand" (or "Corrupt") bargain boiled over. Grant increased White House security. But the threat of violence wasn't the only thing that worried the outgoing president. Inauguration Day, March 4th, fell on a Sunday in 1877. Because presidents traditionally were not sworn in on Sunday, the ceremony would have been, in more placid circumstances, delayed until Monday the 5th. But this would have meant that the presidency would have been constitutionally vacant for a twenty-four-hour period—from noon on Sunday the 4th until noon the next day.

Thus, in the final act of his eight-year presidency, Ulysses S. Grant threw a dinner party. Thirty-eight guests were invited to honor the incoming president and Mrs. Lucy Hayes. Perhaps some who were familiar with the Grants and their preference for entertaining in the Red Room thought it odd that guests were received not there but in the East Room down the hall. When it was time for dinner, guests were led down the great hall to the State Dining Room; in the commotion no one seemed to notice that the president and his successor slipped into the Red Room. Waite, the chief justice, had snuck in earlier, unseen. And thus, with dinner guests strolling down the hall just outside the room's thick door, Rutherford B. Hayes was sworn in as the nineteenth president of the United States—in complete secrecy.

CHAPTER TEN

Rutherford B. Hayes:
The Wired White House

The Telegraph Room

IN THE YEARS AFTER THE CIVIL WAR CAME TO A CLOSE, AMERICA'S ECON-omy grew rapidly. On May 10, 1869, a golden spike was hammered into the ground at Promontory Summit in the Utah Territory, linking the Union and Central Pacific Railroads together for the first time. People and commerce could now flow seamlessly by rail from East Coast to West, from the Atlantic to the Pacific. The symbolism of a physically united country, coming just four years after the end of a war that nearly tore it apart, was powerful and reflected a postwar optimism that radiated across the land.

This optimism was best exemplified in 1876, when the United States marked its centennial with coast-to-coast celebrations. For one hundred years America had withstood economic downturns and invasion from both foreign and domestic enemies, yet now stood bigger and stronger than ever. In just ten decades, it had grown from a hardscrabble union of thirteen colonies with a tenuous grip on the Eastern Seaboard to a vast power straddling the North American continent. The dawn of America's second century was also the dawn of an era in which its transformation from a rural, agriculture-based economy to an urban, industrial one accelerated.

It was that centennial year when Alexander Graham Bell—a Scottish scientist and engineer living in Boston—obtained a patent for an "apparatus for transmitting vocal or other sounds telegraphically." It came to be known as the telephone. The next year, Thomas Alva Edison, at his laboratory in Menlo Park, New Jersey, perfected a cylindrical device that could record and reproduce sound. He called it the phonograph.

Perhaps the most disputed presidential election in US history, the 1876 contest between Republican Rutherford Hayes (beard in poster on left) and Democrat Samuel Tilden (left in the poster on right) dragged on four months—until the eve of Inauguration Day 1877. LIBRARY OF CONGRESS

During this time of rapid technological change, the political spotlight fell on the nineteenth president of the United States, Rutherford Birchard Hayes. A dignified, forward-thinking man, Hayes embraced the future, inviting Bell, Edison, and others to the White House to demonstrate their astonishing wares. He knew this publicity would speed their integration into the US economy. The president integrated them into the White House as well: Shortly after Bell's visit, the telegraph room, which had been moved near the president's office on the second floor of the mansion by Andrew Johnson, soon had a telephone.

Rarely has the White House been a more suitable abode for a president and first lady than it was for Rutherford and Lucy Hayes. The mansion indulged their deep interest in history, art, and old houses; one of their first improvements to their new old house was to assemble a collection of presidential portraits for

The Red Room: site of the secret swearing in of Hayes on March 3, 1877. Fearing a coup by supporters of Tilden after the bitterly contested 1876 election, President Grant, on his last full day in office, staged the event during a White House dinner party. LIBRARY OF CONGRESS

visitors to enjoy.[1] The most prominent portrait can still be seen by visitors today: E. F. Andrews's magnificent painting of Martha Washington, which hangs near the Gilbert Stuart portrait of her husband in the East Room.[2] "I love this house for the associations that no other could have," noted Mrs. Hayes.[3]

Nearly a century before Jacqueline Kennedy earned great renown for her efforts to restore the mansion's original authenticity, Lucy Hayes—the first first lady to have a college degree[4]—scoured the White House basement and attic looking for original pieces to restore and display. William Crook, a White House employee who served twelve presidents for over half a century[5] wrote that "many really good things owed their preservation to this energetic young lady."[6] Mrs. Hayes's efforts were thwarted by vindictive House Democrats, who ended the practice of giving new First Families funds to decorate the mansion. Still angry over the nasty election that thrust

A true high-tech president, Hayes invited Alexander Graham Bell and Thomas Edison to the White House to display their wares. He knew the publicity would speed the integration of their inventions—the phonograph and telephone—into the US economy. Hayes loved the telephone so much that he ordered one for the White House; the number in those days was easy to remember: 1. LIBRARY OF CONGRESS

Lucy's husband into the White House, lawmakers withheld appropriations for two years.[7]

When Congress finally opened its purse strings, Mrs. Hayes returned Ulysses S. Grant's beloved billiards room to the ex-president and converted the space into a greenhouse for plants. She liked greenhouses so much she had a dozen of them built; their upkeep would consume a quarter of the White House's entire budget.[8] Sitting on the current location of the West Wing and Rose Garden, they produced oranges, lemons, pineapples, and a variety of flowers, their fragrance often wafting into the mansion.[9] Mrs. Hayes also started a "mini-zoo" on the White House grounds, replete with a mockingbird, goat, and the nation's first Siamese cat.[10] Some animals were unwanted: The White House had a problem with rats, which sometimes would "scamper over the presidential bed and be so bold as to nibble on presidential toes."[11]

Rodents aside, life in the Hayes White House was quite pleasant, known for its "friendliness, good humor, openness and unpretentiousness."[12] In this respect, Lucy Hayes was seen as a great political asset, well liked for her "large warm heart and lively sympathy for or with all around her."[13] She also began a White House tradition beloved to this day: the annual Easter Egg Roll.

But the first lady, for all her charm and vivaciousness, did one thing that rubbed hard-drinking Washington the wrong way. With the encouragement of her husband, she banned all alcohol, including wine, at the White House. Hard liquor had been prohibited in the White House before, by the Polks.

Sitting on the site of today's West Wing, conservatories (greenhouses) grew everything from flowers to tropical fruits; when the wind was just right, wonderful aromas wafted into the executive mansion itself. LIBRARY OF CONGRESS

But White House guests had come to expect at least wine.[14] For her teetotaling ways Lucy Hayes would earn perhaps the most famous moniker ever associated with a first lady: "Lemonade Lucy."

Yet the alcohol ban appears, in fact, to have originated with the president.[15] Although he enjoyed an occasional glass of wine himself,[16] he believed all alcohol made men reckless.[17] Before moving into the White House, Hayes was pressured by temperance groups to institute the ban.[18] "It seemed to me," Hayes wrote, "that the example of excluding liquors from the White House would be wise and useful, and would be approved by good people generally."[19]

So instead of wine with dinner, followed by a civilized after-dinner brandy, the president and first lady would lead their guests on a brisk after-dinner walk along the White House grounds, ending about half an hour later at the foot of the grand staircase. It was their way of signaling that the evening was over.[20]

As word spread throughout the city that the president and first lady were serious about their booze ban, a few saloons near the White House, seeing an opportunity to snag new customers, advertised their fully stocked bars. One proprietor changed the name of his watering hole to "Last Chance."[21]

In the White House of the 1870s, the telegraph, which had first been used heavily by Lincoln, was still the quickest way to communicate over great distances. In working areas on the second floor of the mansion, presidential aides, busier than ever, relied on surface-mounted speaking tubes to communicate; the tubes linked offices and also allowed officials to speak with doormen downstairs.[22]

But just as the telegraph rendered the Pony Express outdated in the 1860s, Bell's invention—the telephone—spelled the eventual demise of the telegraph. Bell would demonstrate it to Hayes in 1877,[23] and the president, suitably impressed, ordered one for the White House. On May 10, 1879, the first telephone—courtesy of the National Telephone Company—was installed in the telegraph room,[24] which Andrew Johnson had moved to the second floor near the president's office.[25] The president tried it out by making his first call to Bell himself, who was thirteen miles away.[26]

Although Bell's end of the conversation is not known, he must have been very excited, for the president reportedly asked him to "Please speak more slowly!"[27] Hayes ordered that this first White House telephone be connected to the Treasury Department next door. It was no doubt unsightly: Wires ran out the window of the telegraph room, which was on the east side of the mansion, and extended some four hundred feet to the Treasury, where Secretary John Sherman had already beaten the president to the punch with a phone of his own. Phones were so rare, in fact, that the president's phone number was, simply, "1."[28] Few calls came in, but when they did, callers were probably surprised to find the person answering was sometimes none other than the president himself.[29]

The president took to the era's other great inventor—Edison—as well. Late on the evening of April 18, 1878,[30] Hayes learned that Edison was in town demonstrating the phonograph, which could record and play back the spoken word.[31] He asked Edison to come over and show him how it worked. Edison came to the White House immediately, and left at 3:30 the next morning.[32] Rutherford B. Hayes would become the first president to have his voice recorded. Astonishingly, Hayes, who kept a diary for most of his life, didn't mention this, and the recording itself was probably destroyed.[33]

There was even "wireless technology" in the White House. It arrived in a wooden crate on February 12, 1880.[34] Workers opened the crate to find a boxy steel device with a rolling pin, around which paper could be inserted. It had dozens of small surfaces featuring the alphabet, the numbers 0 through 9, and a variety of punctuation marks. When forced down by fingers, the small surfaces, which were called keys, struck the paper with enough pressure to leave an imprint of ink. The contraption was rather large and took up not a small amount of desk space, but this seeming inconvenience was easily outdone by the device's sheer efficiency. It was the White House's first typewriter, a Fairbanks & Company Improved Number Two model, and was so quick and easy to use that it would soon produce practically all presidential correspondence—a setback for White House clerks, who earned a living with their penmanship.[35]

Prior to the Lincoln assassination, the notion that a president of the United States could be murdered was practically unthinkable. But it was a constant fear for Hayes, who received numerous death threats both during his bitter election fight with Tilden and after he moved into the White House. This all but ensured that security—both for himself and his family—would always be on Hayes's mind. After taking office, the president ordered guards posted at White House gates. The practice of holding concerts on the mansion's grounds ended.[36] A vegetable garden, used by prior First Families as a place to stroll, was deemed too exposed, as was the South Portico, where the Grants enjoyed many pleasant hours sitting in their rocking chairs.

In fact, other than to play an occasional game of croquet, the Hayes family—unlike the Lincoln, Johnson, and Grant families—rarely set foot on the White House grounds. It was the beginning of what has today become a pervasive fortress mentality at 1600 Pennsylvania Avenue.

This stress, and that of the job itself, made for a man who was relieved to be leaving the White House after just one term—a pledge Hayes had made in 1876. As time wore short, he expressed no regrets. "I am now in the last year of the Presidency and look forward to its close as a schoolboy longs for the coming vacation," he said in a letter to a friend.[37]

It was a bitter irony to Hayes, upon his return to Ohio in 1881, that for all the fears over his safety during his four years in the White House, that his successor and good friend, James Garfield, also from Ohio, would fall victim to an assassin's bullet just six months after taking office.

CHAPTER ELEVEN

William McKinley:
The Spanish-American War

The War Room

PRESIDENT WILLIAM MCKINLEY stood at the head of the table wearing a scowl. With fourteen other men, sporting similarly grim expressions, he watched as a peace treaty ending the Spanish-American War was signed.

That hot, muggy day—August 12, 1898—represented the only time in American history when a war fought by the United States came to an end with a formal treaty signing at the White House.

The conflict with Spain—the defining event of McKinley's four and a half years as president—was America's first two-front war. It was also the first time the United States had waged war thousands of miles from its shores. As the Navy steamed into Manila Bay in the Philippines to deliver a crushing defeat to the Spanish fleet, the Army was preparing to do battle against Spanish

William McKinley in his office on the second floor of the White House. He worked at the long table behind him, which was used to sign the treaty ending the Spanish-American War in 1898. The desk—today perhaps the second-best known piece of furniture in the White House after the famous Resolute desk in the Oval Office—is known as the Treaty Table. The room itself is today the Treaty Room. LIBRARY OF CONGRESS

An early iteration of today's Situation Room, McKinley managed the Spanish-American war from this war room on the second floor of the mansion, next to his office. Clerks managed twenty-five telegraph wires and fifteen telephone lines around the clock, enabling the president to communicate directly with commanders in the field. LIBRARY OF CONGRESS

forces in Cuba, with the key battle on that island famously led by Col. Theodore Roosevelt, who would become McKinley's running mate in 1900.

The war, which McKinley had desperately sought to avoid, was won swiftly and decisively. It also brought major changes to the White House, including the construction of what can be considered the first true Situation Room, from which the commander in chief could direct the conflict. That he could easily handle two distinctly separate and distant fights nearly simultaneously reflected the twenty-fifth president's managerial acumen.

But the easy US victory over Spain also, and more importantly, reflected America's emergence onto the world stage as a true global power. Many Americans saw this as the culmination of the Manifest Destiny philosophy that had first emerged half a century before during the Polk years—the last time Americans vanquished a foreign enemy.[1] Under William McKinley,

During the McKinley era, the Lincoln Bedroom was on the north side of the mansion overlooking Pennsylvania Avenue and Lafayette Square. The room—where President William Henry Harrison and Willie Lincoln died, and where Abraham Lincoln's autopsy and embalming were performed—is today the First Family's private dining room. LIBRARY OF CONGRESS

Americans bid the nineteenth century farewell stronger and more confident than ever before, oblivious to the fact that far bigger wars, of immensely greater complexity and danger, would soon confront them in the twentieth.

Prior to the Spanish-American war, William McKinley had been waging a battle at home to revive the US economy. It had yet to recover from a crippling depression between 1893 and 1895,[2] one of the worst economic downturns the nation had ever suffered.[3] Even four years later, when he was inaugurated, the unemployment rate was at least 12.4 percent.[4] By coincidence—or congressional efforts to protect American workers by raising tariffs and shifting to a gold standard—the economy began to recover in the months after he

As the nineteenth century gave way to the twentieth, telephones and electric lighting became more ubiquitous in the White House—replete with hanging cables and wires. This picture shows an office sometime between 1889 and 1906. LIBRARY OF CONGRESS

took office. McKinley, already popular, became more so; he was dubbed "the prophet of prosperity."[5] The recovery ushered in a new economic boom that was to last a decade.

McKinley was a clear beneficiary of both luck and good timing, thanks to an economic recovery and his victory in the war. He was popular with most Americans, particularly with rank-and-file Republicans. Such accolades might have gone to the heads of many a lesser politician, but they seemed to have little effect on McKinley, who "never enhanced his own power at the price of other men's reputations, nor did he take credit where it was not his due."[6]

The president's popularity was assisted by two things that marked the beginning of the modern presidency. As a congressman and then two-term governor of Ohio, he understood the importance of retail politics, of being seen by the voters. As president, he traveled widely,[7] taking advantage of railroad lines that now stretched across the country. Most Americans had never seen a president before; here was one who came to them. At the time of his death, McKinley was planning to travel abroad—the first sitting president to leave the country—which signaled America's increasingly important role in the world.[8]

McKinley also understood the importance of modern communications.[9] He had learned over the years the importance of the press and the role it played in shaping a politician's image; by the time he arrived in the White House in 1897, he was as savvy about the press as any other elected official of his time.

Reporters had been treated with hostility during the two administrations of Grover Cleveland.[10] They now found to their delight an administration that saw value in them—or at least in the audience they reached. McKinley's secretary, George Cortelyou, provided desks, chairs, and sofas for them to use in the mansion's corridors[11] and began conducting daily briefings[12] and distributing "briefing papers" containing the administration's line on the issues of the day.[13] 1600 Pennsylvania Avenue became a place where news was made. Enterprising reporters hired bicycle messengers to hang out under the North Portico, ready to rush their dispatches to the Western Union office at any moment.[14]

When McKinley traveled, Cortelyou made sure a car for reporters was attached, and that they had access to all presidential events.[15] To the president's credit, this generosity even extended to newspapers that were opposed to his policies. For the nascent White House press corps, there was only one issue: The president himself never spoke to the press.[16] Even so, news flowed from the White House during the McKinley era, fanning the public perception of a busy president—and enhancing the power of the presidency itself.

McKinley's reelection, on November 6, 1900, came five days after the one hundredth anniversary of the first president moving into the White House. In the century since John Adams first rolled up to the muddy entrance in his carriage, the White House had been home to twenty-four presidents and twenty-four First Families. It had burned to the ground, seen four major wars, four presidents die in office—two by assassination. Triumph and tragedy: The White House's first century reflected the history of America itself.

As the nation entered the twentieth century, life moved at a faster pace. Presidents who once got around on horseback enjoyed the relative comfort of trains and steamships. In Lincoln's day, it was considered a miracle that his inaugural address could be delivered to California by Pony Express in less than eight days.[17] The telegraph replaced that system, before it was eclipsed by the telephone. Cities gleamed at night as the marvel of electric light spread. As farming became more efficient and manufacturing boomed, cities burst at the seams as millions moved to urban areas in search of better lives. When John Adams moved into the White House, the largest city in the nation—New York—had a population of 60,515;[18] a century later it was 3.4 million.[19] The nation itself had grown from 5.3 million people who lived in sixteen states, to 76 million who lived in forty-five. William McKinley presided over an America that had gotten big very fast, was increasingly wealthy, and—even if most had yet to grasp this—had become a world power.

Yet for all this change, the White House was essentially the same. Some thought the president's home should keep up with the times, expand as the nation had. At a centennial luncheon hosted by McKinley on December 12, 1900, Col. Theodore A. Bingham, the commissioner of public buildings and grounds, unveiled a plan to vastly expand the White House by adding two large wings—each about three-fifths the size of the original mansion itself—to either side of it. Each would be framed by towering columns and topped by a dome.[20] Looking at a model of it today, it seems grandiose, even ugly. But Bingham pointed out that such an expansion reflected the wishes of the one president who never lived in the White House, George Washington. Washington had expected that the mansion would grow as the nation did, and—according to Bingham—would have approved of the plan.[21]

Bingham claimed to have support from McKinley,[22] but nothing in Washington, even back then, ever got done easily. The commissioner ruffled feathers in Congress, which also had a say in the matter, and the plan went nowhere. McKinley's assassination in September 1901 sealed Bingham's fate.

Despite his apparent support for expanding the White House, McKinley's life in it reflected his penchant for "Jefferson simplicity."[23] While not a workaholic like Polk or Lincoln, he nevertheless maintained a disciplined work schedule, which included writing most of his speeches and letters to Congress.[24]

Occasionally, McKinley would also indulge in a new hobby that reflected America's expanding economic and technological prowess: riding in an automobile. He didn't know how to drive a car, and never owned one, but while visiting his hometown of Canton, Ohio, in November 1899 he became the first president to ride in one.[25] It was a steam-powered vehicle called the Stanley Steamer.[26] Soon to be made obsolete by the internal combustion engine, they were nevertheless something to behold; as they lacked a roof, the president likely enjoyed them only when the weather was cooperative. When in Washington, however, the president "was rarely seen out of the White House."[27]

Whether at the White House or making one of his frequent trips around the country, McKinley was never far from his wife, Ida Saxton McKinley. The first lady was quite troubled, largely homebound, and her husband did not want to be away from her.

Her troubles dated back nearly a quarter-century. In 1873, Mrs. McKinley—by then married to the man she called "Dearest"[28] for two years—suffered a series of rapid blows: the death of her mother, followed six months later by the death of the McKinley's second child, Ida, who died in her infancy. Two years later, typhoid fever would claim the couple's first child, Katherine, at age three.[29] William and Ida McKinley would have no more children.

Mrs. McKinley, heartbroken, never recovered. She also developed epilepsy, and would suffer seizures for the rest of her life. During White House functions the first lady kept her distance from visitors, and clutched a bouquet so she wouldn't have to shake hands and reveal her tremors.[30] She always sat next to her husband, and if she was hit with a sudden seizure, the president would cover her face with a handkerchief, giving Mrs. McKinley some semblance of dignity and privacy until the episode passed.[31]

Bathed in self-pity and struggling with depression, the first lady, gaunt and frail, often lashed out at others. She became a recluse, spending much of her time in the presidential bedroom on the mansion's second floor, where she sat for hours in a rocking chair reading and knitting slippers—an estimated thirty-five hundred one friend wrote—for charity.[32]

This is not to suggest an absence of fun or frivolity in the McKinley White House. The president liked to dance, and for a man in his fifties, he tried to stay current by showing off the latest moves on the East Room floor.

He enjoyed a two-step dance called "Goo-Goo Eyes," which helped introduce a new kind of music to Americans: ragtime. For a man in such a serious position of responsibility, the sight of him cutting it up on the dance floor must have been something to behold. At an 1898 dinner for the Supreme Court, the composer and cellist Ernest Lent performed. Historians believe that his "Piano Trio in B Major" was the earliest serious chamber music performed at the White House.[33]

If ever a president was reluctant to take the nation to war, it was William McKinley. The last president to have fought in the Civil War—including seeing action in the battle of Antietam,[34][35] still the bloodiest single day in American history—the twenty-fifth president said, "War should never be entered upon until every agency of peace has failed; peace is preferable to war in almost every contingency."[36]

Unfortunately for the president—who made that vow in his 1897 inaugural address as tensions between the United States and Spain grew—other forces were at work. Tensions centered on neighboring Cuba, a Spanish colony just ninety miles from Florida. The 1890s was a time of growing American power. Jingoistic feelings radiated, and many lawmakers, pointing to the seventy-five-year-old Monroe Doctrine, which forbade European colonization of the Western Hemisphere, resented the Spanish presence. Fueling these emotions were two aggressive newspaper publishers—William Randolph Hearst and Joseph Pulitzer—who began publishing sensational stories to inflame public opinion against Spain. At one point, Hearst sent an employee (the artist Frederic Remington) to Cuba to cover an anti-Spanish insurrection. Ensconced in a swanky Havana hotel, insulated from unrest elsewhere on the tropical island, Remington cabled Hearst: "Everything is quiet. There is no trouble here. There will be no war. I wish to return." Hearst's alleged reply: "Please remain. You furnish the pictures and I'll furnish the war."[37] Hearst denied that such an exchange ever took place,[38] but there can be little doubt that both he and Pulitzer engaged in such sensationalist tactics. "Yellow journalism"[39] was born.

As 1897 gave way to 1898, hawks in Congress and powerful press barons aligned against McKinley and his desire for peace. Then, on February 15, 1898, an American battleship, the USS *Maine*, exploded in Havana harbor. It sank within minutes, killing 260 of its crew; another six would later succumb to injuries.

Within hours, and without any facts, suspicions arose that Spain was involved. The president, who had been woken in the middle of the night with the news, was cautious and ordered that "judgment be suspended until a full investigation is made."[40] At the same time, the administration stepped up its military preparations for a possible conflict.[41]

War fever quickly grew, but McKinley resisted. "I pray to God that we may be able to keep the peace," he said. "I shall never get into a war until I am sure that God and man approve. I've been through one war. I have seen the dead piled up, and I do not want to see another."[42] McKinley's calm leadership was praised in many circles, while others thought him timid.[43]

Today, it is believed that the likeliest cause of the explosion that sank the *Maine* was an onboard accident[44]—an explosion of coal gases that had built up[45]—and not a Spanish attack. But in 1898, a panel investigating the cause of the disaster told McKinley that a mine, probably from a submarine, was to blame. Their proof was that the ship's keel and bottom plates had been driven upward, indicating an external explosion.[46]

From there, the slide toward war seemed unstoppable. The president asked his new secretary of the navy, Theodore Roosevelt, for advice. The brash Roosevelt swiftly replied: "Mr. President, I would order the whole American Navy to Cuba tonight if I had my way."[47]

On April 1st, the president, still hoping for peace, made a final proposal to Spain. The Spanish government was also under pressure not to cave in, and rejected American demands.[48] On April 11th, the president asked Congress to declare war. It did so on the 25th. William McKinley, the war hero who sought to avoid war, quickly shifted into commander-in-chief mode.

⎯⬝⎯

Given the great distances and complexity of managing battles in the Pacific and Caribbean, technology played a vital role in the US war effort. The telegraph, which had been enormously helpful during the war with Mexico half a century before,[49] was still in wide use during the McKinley era. But the telephone was even more advanced, and the hands-on commander in chief wanted every tool at his disposal. He ordered that a small room on the southeast corner of the White House's second floor be turned into a war room. Clerks used to handling routine correspondence were hustled out, and a switchboard with twenty-five telegraph wires and fifteen telephone wires was installed.[50] No president had ever been so plugged in, and it enabled McKinley to stay in touch, via French and British cable lines, with his commanders in the field. "I walked the floor of the White House night after night until midnight and I am not ashamed to tell you," McKinley wrote, "that I went down on my knees and prayed Almighty God for light and guidance more than one night."[51]

McKinley ran the war at a highly granular level. "In all the movements of the army and navy the President's hand is seen," George Cortelyou wrote in his diary. Postmaster General Charles Emory Smith wrote: "He was Commander in chief not merely in name but in fact."[52]

The War Room was dominated by the communications center, which was really just an oak rolltop desk in the middle of the floor. It was manned around the clock by a clerk. One wall had a glass bookcase stuffed with history, geography, and law books; the walls themselves, wallpapered in green, were plastered with maps, covered with pins representing the location of US forces.[53]

The room was next to what had traditionally been the president's office (and today is the Lincoln Bedroom). McKinley didn't care for it, and used the room next to that, the Cabinet Room (known today as the Treaty Room), as his workspace.[54] McKinley loved the long table that Grant used for Cabinet meetings. It became his desk, with the president sitting at the southern end, his back to two tall windows. The president honored his predecessors by requesting that a series of presidential portraits by George Healy be hung on the wall—from John Quincy Adams to Grant.[55]

The swift and decisive victory over Spain came with a price: 3,289 Americans dead (the vast majority from disease) and 1,641 wounded.[56] But the United States was now a Pacific power. Hawaii became an American territory, and the United States cemented its control of the Caribbean. The presidency itself, thanks to McKinley's dominant presence, "rose to a level of power not known since George Washington occupied the office."[57]

His popularity was such that McKinley didn't take security particularly seriously. When he first moved into the White House, he ordered guard boxes on the front lawn removed. He went on early-morning walks unaccompanied, seemingly unbothered that two predecessors had been shot to death in the prior three decades. "I have never done any man a wrong, and believe no man will ever do me one," he told friends. His friends weren't convinced, and urged the president to allow one plainclothes Secret Service officer to shadow him.[58] [59]

But during the war, scores of death threats arrived in the mail, prompting a series of security upgrades. Access by visitors was tightened, Secret Service men were stationed on the first and second floors of the mansion, and on the mansion's grounds, and windows were locked.[60] Large public receptions, for decades a staple of White House social life, came to an end. There was even concern about the small dinner parties the president and first lady often gave; guests had to show their invitations and be personally vouched for by a White House employee.[61]

Even so, the president scoffed. On August 27, 1901, the *Washington Post* ran a story mentioning an alleged plot to kill him. "Mr. McKinley laughed at the report," the *Post* story said, "characterizing it as a canard, and again expressing the belief that he was enough of the people to trust the people."[62]

Ten days later McKinley toured the Pan-American Exposition in Buffalo, New York. His personal secretary, Cortelyou, was worried about the venue and twice removed it from McKinley's schedule—only to be overruled each time by the president. Cortelyou then asked Buffalo authorities to arrange for security, and three Secret Service agents (two more than usual) were assigned to guard the president.

Citizens lined up to meet him, and the president was in a good mood. McKinley had an unusual superstition: If he wore a carnation in his lapel, it would bring him good luck. He wore one that day. A twelve-year-old girl stepped forward to meet the president. McKinley, upon learning her name was Myrtle Ledger, promptly gave her his carnation.

"I must give this flower to another little flower," he said.[63]

Moments after giving up his good luck charm, McKinley greeted another visitor, a man whose right hand was wrapped in a bandage. The president, seeing this, reached for the man's left hand. The man, a Polish anarchist named Leon Czolgosz, proceeded to shoot McKinley twice with a .32 revolver concealed underneath the bandage. The president stumbled, and Czolgosz tried to shoot again when guards knocked him down.

Looking into the face of his killer, the collapsing McKinley said, "May God forgive him."[64] Asked if he felt much pain, the president put his hand into an opening on his shirt, near his heart and replied: "This wound pains greatly." He removed his hand, fingers covered in blood. His head dropped to his chest.[65]

The president was conscious as he was rushed to a hospital. On the way, he felt in his clothing and pulled out a metal object. "I believe this is a bullet," he said. After a few days, McKinley appeared to be recovering. But gangrene soon set in. The president, the Civil War hero who had seen more than his share of death, knew he was dying. "It is useless, gentlemen," he said bravely. "I think we ought to have a prayer."

On the evening of September 13th he said: "Good-bye, all, good-bye. It is God's way. His will be done."[66] At 2:15 on the morning of September 14, 1901, with Ida McKinley holding his hand, William McKinley died. He was the third president of the United States to have been assassinated in thirty-six years.

CHAPTER TWELVE

Theodore Roosevelt:
The Dawn of the American Century

The West Wing

HOURS BEFORE HIS ASSASSINATION on April 14, 1865, Abraham Lincoln signed legislation creating the United States Secret Service. It wouldn't have saved him that night, nor would it have helped James Garfield sixteen years later. That's because the original mission of the Secret Service was rather narrow: to stop currency counterfeiting. It took the assassination of a third president, William McKinley, for Congress to request, in 1901, that the Secret Service expand its portfolio to protect the president of the United States.[1] In 1902 two agents were assigned to the White House full-time.[2] They had their work cut out for them. Their protectee, Theodore Roosevelt, just forty-two when he took over for McKinley, was the youngest—and perhaps most energetic person ever to become president.

Thrust into office by the assassination of William McKinley in September 1901, Theodore Roosevelt, at forty-two, was the youngest man to ever become president. Energetic and restless, he led a confident and rapidly growing nation into what would become known as the American century. LIBRARY OF CONGRESS

Lincoln never slept in the "Lincoln Bed," but Roosevelt did; the bedroom itself was in the southwest corner of the second floor, overlooking what is today the Rose Garden. LIBRARY OF CONGRESS

If ever there was a man born for his era, it was TR. As the curtain rose on the twentieth century, the United States had quietly, and rather quickly, become a great world power. Straddling a continent, protected by the buffer of two vast oceans, rich in natural resources, industrializing rapidly and not the least bit hesitant about embracing the future, America and its bespectacled new leader could be defined in exactly the same way: forward-thinking, brash, and supremely confident.

Roosevelt quickly and with a sense of urgency made his mark on everything from business (breaking up monopolies like John D. Rockefeller's Standard Oil and E. H. Harriman's Northern Trust Railroad) and foreign policy (building the Panama Canal and brokering an end to a war between Russia and Japan—for which he won the Nobel Peace Prize) to conservation (protecting vast swaths of land and expanding America's national park system).

Home, home, on the . . . South Lawn. Archie Roosevelt on his calico Shetland pony Algonquin in front of the new West Wing. His father's square—not oval—office is on the right side of the building (near the man). LIBRARY OF CONGRESS

But when he moved in and looked around at his new home and place of work, Theodore Roosevelt was embarrassed. The Executive Mansion, as it was officially known, was run-down, decrepit, and cramped. If America was the vibrant, powerful center of the New World, TR reasoned, then its most visible symbol must reflect such grandeur.

Accordingly, Roosevelt embarked upon a massive remodeling of the mansion. He had two goals: Return it to its Federal roots, which would entail the removal of decades' worth of heavy, dark Victorian-era decor and design, and an expansion of presidential workspace. From Adams to McKinley, presidents had always worked and lived in the mansion itself. Now Roosevelt wanted some separation between work and home. Thus was born the West Wing, today the principal workspace of the president of the United States.

Before all that though—and even before the flowers from William McKinley's funeral began to wilt—Roosevelt took one step that symbolized that a new man was in charge: He officially did away with the name "Executive

The presidential office in the new West Wing. Even though this is where the president worked, some visitors felt it wasn't as prestigious as visiting the mansion itself, where Presidents Adams through McKinley worked. LIBRARY OF CONGRESS

Mansion," formally renaming the residence what millions of Americans had long called the imposing building at 1600 Pennsylvania Avenue. The name was reflected in the clean, crisp elegance of new stationery he ordered, with paper and envelopes:

THE WHITE HOUSE.[3]

Theodore Roosevelt's desire to expand the White House and separate its living quarters from its workspace was driven by two principal factors. The US government was growing, not just in size but complexity; the head of the executive branch simply needed more room. But there were personal reasons too. The new president and his wife, Edith Carow Roosevelt, had six young children ranging in age from nearly four to sixteen. The First Family also had

Once Thomas Jefferson's office, the State Dining Room took on the look and feel of a western hunting lodge under Roosevelt. Ironically, the mounted heads on the walls were not bagged by TR, a lifelong hunter, but purchased from a Manhattan interior design firm. LIBRARY OF CONGRESS

what amounted to a mini-zoo: countless dogs, birds, guinea pigs, snakes, rabbits, badgers—even a small bear named Jonathan Edwards.

Once, when Archie Roosevelt, the president and first lady's fifth child, was sick, brothers Kermit and Quentin brought his beloved pony—Algonquin—up to see him, carefully guiding the horse into the White House elevator.[4] It was a big, rambunctious family, happy, outgoing and active—the biggest First Family to live in the mansion since the presidency of John Tyler.[5] The eight rooms and two bathrooms set aside for personal use on the second floor simply weren't enough.[6] One bathroom, connected to the president's bedroom, was used by the president and Mrs. Roosevelt, leaving one for everyone else, including any visitors.[7] Clearly, something had to be done.

Presidents had come and gone over the decades, yet the interior of the White House always seemed to be described in creaky, tumbledown terms. Charles Dickens thought so in the 1840s, sagging floors had to be propped up in the Lincoln era, and a few years later there was serious discussion about tearing the mansion down entirely.

A new century had arrived, but old problems persisted. Floors still sagged. The wooden staircase leading to the second floor was clearly worn, and the new First Family was undoubtedly bothered by the "curly wallpaper and wainscots jaundiced with fifty years of tobacco spit."[8] Carpets in a hideous mustard color, peeling plaster, and exposed and wooden pipes that made "flatulent noises in wet weather" were also incompatible with the president's desire for a majestic home in which to live.[9]

Although fairly new to Washington, Roosevelt's legislative skills became apparent in 1902, when he got Congress to approve $343,945 to begin repairs of the mansion and another $131,500 for new furnishings.[10] Another $65,196 was approved for a new, separate office building for the president.[11] The Roosevelts picked a New York architectural firm, McKim, Mead & White, for the project, with day-to-day work supervised by a principal of the firm, Charles McKim.

The desire for grandeur aside, the president established several goals for the renovation of the White House. In addition to making the mansion structurally safe, he wanted the presidential workspace relocated, which would benefit both the growing executive branch and his family's personal needs. He wanted more efficient movement of large crowds at White House events. He wanted the State Dining Room—once Thomas Jefferson's office— expanded, and he wanted all the ugly appendages of technological progress (pipes, electric cords, etc.) removed or hidden away. All of this, Roosevelt insisted, was to be done in such a way that contributed to the overall image of the White House as a stately place in which to live, work, and entertain—a place that would make the American people proud. And it had to conform with the style and vision as expressed by the mansion's original architects more than a century earlier.[12] The president wanted it finished by December, in time for the holiday parties he and the first lady planned to give. McKim had five months.[13]

Where could the presidential offices go? The original plan presented to George Washington, the only president who would never live there, called for the construction of a White House five times bigger than the mansion we know today. This proved impractical, and a more modest structure—still the largest building in the United States at the time—was built. In the ensuing century, the area around the White House had been built up: The Treasury Building lay just east of the mansion, while the State, War, and Navy Building (today known as the Eisenhower Executive Office Building) stood to the west. Even if Roosevelt had wanted to dramatically expand the White House, big federal buildings on either side brought physical limits to the task.

But the famous colonnades extending in both directions from the mansion, designed by Benjamin Latrobe and Thomas Jefferson, presented Roosevelt and architect McKim with some intriguing possibilities to do something more modest, such as build in a southerly direction. Standing in the way were the massive greenhouses installed by prior administrations.

TR, the activist president and man of action that he was, was neither shy about expressing his desires nor sentimental toward parts of the mansion that he disdained. "Smash the glass houses," he bellowed,[14] and down came the conservatories that had been part of the White House since the days of James Buchanan nearly half a century before. In their place, McKim built a "temporary Executive Office" building,[15] soon to be known as the West Wing. It was square, with long windows on the ground floor and short windows on the floor above, made to resemble Federal-style architecture from the mid-nineteenth century. It included a Cabinet Room; telegraph room; rooms for secretaries, stenographers, and the press; a filing room; a reception room; and closets in the basement.[16]

A final room, of course, was the highlight: Roosevelt's office, dubbed the "President's Room." It would be in the southeast corner of the new building, overlooking the South Lawn. The room was square, with sliding doors opening into the Cabinet Room, which Roosevelt wound up using for both meetings and entertaining. McKim and his men worked so fast that the building was finished in late September. [17] It took another two weeks for paint to dry.

When Roosevelt eventually moved in, it meant the end of what had been the century-long tradition of the president of the United States living and working under the same roof. In the beginning, many visitors considered the Executive Office Building a step down in prestige from the nearby mansion, even though the president himself now worked there.[18]

Adjacent to this had been stables and a greenhouse known for the roses it produced. These were torn down and a garden—dubbed the Colonial Garden—was planted. Running parallel to the West Colonnade, it consisted of several triangular and oval-shaped areas where boxwoods, roses, and lilies flourished.[19] A decade later, another new first lady, Ellen Wilson, would rename it the Rose Garden.

As the West Wing rose, so did the East Wing. Added to the end of Jefferson's graceful colonnade, it would serve as an entry point for visitors—as it does today. A long covered entryway accommodated carriages (and soon, cars), and there was a long cloakroom for visitors to deposit their belongings before moving on to social events in the East Room and elsewhere. The construction of the East Wing accomplished Roosevelt's goal of having visitors arrive and move about the mansion's public areas more efficiently and comfortably.

As for the mansion itself, old floors, stained and scratched, were yanked up. The smell of plaster that had first greeted John Adams returned as walls were redone and painted. On the ground floor the entrance hall just off the North Portico had featured an attractive screen of iron and glass that had stood since the administration of Franklin Pierce (1853–1857). At the behest of Chester Arthur (1881–1885), Louis Tiffany made it even more spectacular with the installation of colored glass. When light struck the glass, it projected a blaze of color on the hall's cream walls.[20] Beautiful as many considered this to be, the president ordered the screen removed.[21]

Adjacent to the entrance hall, Roosevelt and McKim decided that the mansion's biggest chamber—the East Room—would no longer be an "over-ornamented salon, loaded down with crude decorations." William McKinley's potted plants were tossed, as was much of the furniture, which one influential critic sniffed was "crude in the extreme, with poorly designed frames and no taste in the color or materials of the covers."[22]

Electric lighting, which had first come to the White House in 1891 when Benjamin Harrison was president, was expanded. Three giant Bohemian glass chandeliers were wired and hung; the three chandeliers that had hung since the Grant years were sent to Capitol Hill.[23] The entire State Floor—the Green, Blue, and Red Rooms—was also wired, as was the State Dining Room at the far end of the long Cross Hall. The First Family's living quarters on the second floor and the modern new East and West Wings would be illuminated by electricity as well.[24]

It was in the State Dining Room that Roosevelt's personal taste became most apparent. Straying from the Federal style that he wanted for the rest of the mansion, he approved a country-house look, featuring heavy oak paneling and massive tapestries on the walls. The president also had animal heads mounted, including a moose over the fireplace. Ironically, these trophies weren't bagged by the president—a lifelong hunter—but purchased from a Manhattan interior design firm.[25] This veritable zoo might not have conformed with George Washington and architect James Hoban's original vision for the White House. But Thomas Jefferson had also displayed stuffed animals, so Roosevelt could have claimed that his homage to the past was accurate enough.[26]

———

The renovation was a circus. "The house is torn to pieces . . ." McKim wrote in July, "bedlam let loose does not compare with it."[27] At one point portions of the great mansion were reduced to their bones—just walls and support beams. Standing in the basement, McKim could gaze up into the Blue Room on the ground floor and, one floor above that, into Abraham Lincoln's old office, a "gawking, hollow shell, with fluttering wallpaper shreds dancing in the summer breezes."[28]

The tight schedule also threatened the president's desire that the original character and heritage of the White House be respected to the utmost. McKim knew little of the White House's history and didn't particularly care;[29] his concern was getting the job done on time. This resulted in decisions that initially seemed wise only to be seen later as folly. One of the best examples: McKim thought the problem of sagging floors could be solved by laying steel beams down and bolting them to brick walls. But it never occurred to McKim that the walls themselves weren't strong enough to hold the steel beams securely.[30] It was errors like this that contributed to the near collapse of the White House years later during the Truman administration.[31]

———

While McKim and his small army of workers toiled frantically, the First Family had wisely decamped. The president moved in June to a house a block away at 22 Jackson Place on Lafayette Square,[32] while his family went to the Roosevelt's home on Long Island. Roosevelt himself would join them in early July.

Thus Theodore Roosevelt became the third president to live somewhere other than the White House as it was rebuilt. But James Madison and James Monroe were forced to live elsewhere following the destruction of the White House in 1814—Roosevelt's departure was thoroughly voluntary. The First Family would return on November 4th, promptly throwing a dinner party for friends. When they retired that night, the second floor was theirs alone, and it felt huge. There were more bedrooms, and each had its own bathroom, shimmering with white ceramic tile and nickel fixtures.[33]

On the eastern end of the floor, the former Cabinet Room was now a presidential study; just outside was the grand staircase, which had been relocated from the west end of the hall near the presidential bedroom. Its removal left a large space that became a living room for the Roosevelts—and for First Families that followed.[34] The president was thrilled. "You will be delighted with the White House," he wrote son Kermit. "The changes have improved it more than you can imagine."[35]

The presidential bedroom itself—which was in the old Prince of Wales Room overlooking the North Lawn[36]—featured a piece of furniture that was special to Roosevelt: the famous Lincoln bed. Like millions of Americans, the twenty-sixth president revered the sixteenth. One of Roosevelt's first moves in the White House was to get rid of the brass beds in the presidential bedroom and replace them with the "Lincoln bed."[37] It's unknown whether Roosevelt knew Lincoln had likely never slept in it, but TR certainly wished for some of the Great Emancipator's luster to rub off on him. Perhaps Roosevelt did know that the room in which he slept was also used for Lincoln's autopsy and embalming in 1865.

Abraham Lincoln and Theodore Roosevelt could not have come from more different backgrounds. Lincoln, the humble, shy man, born in a log cabin with dirt floors, a man who grew up in poverty and received no formal education and encountered numerous setbacks on his way to the White House; how Roosevelt—born into wealth and privilege, educated at Harvard, a man whose rise up the ladder was swift and unimpeded—wished to emulate him! Roosevelt told friends that Lincoln was "my great hero," a man who meant "more to me than any other of our public men." Throughout his nearly eight-year presidency, Roosevelt kept a portrait of the Great Emancipator in his office for inspiration. "I look up to that picture, and I do as I believe Lincoln would have done," he said.[38][39]

"The Restoration," as it was called in 1902,[40] complete, President and Mrs. Roosevelt opened their sparkling new home to the public for the first time on New Year's Day 1903. Thousands lined up, and the president, energetic and in jaunty spirits as usual, shook every hand. Reviews were universally good. "Visitors noticed the dignified, tasteful, yet simpler and starker interiors that gave the rooms a more spacious look and reflected the nation's larger role in international affairs,"[41] while others called it intelligent and refined. The president and first lady were immensely pleased. Writing Congress to thank it for the money used on the massive project, Roosevelt wrote:

The White House, which had become disfigured by incongruence has now been restored to what it was planned to be by Washington. In making the restorations the utmost care has been exercised to come as near as possible to the early plans . . . the White House is the property of the nation, and so far as it is compatible with living there and it should be kept as it originally was, for the same reasons that we keep Mount Vernon as it originally was. The stately simplicity of the architecture is an expression of the character of the period in which it was built, and is in accord with the purposes it was designed to serve. It is a good thing to preserve such buildings as historic monuments which keep alive our sense of continuity with the nation's past.[42]

The White House under Theodore Roosevelt became a showcase, reflecting, he believed, America's prominent new position on the world stage. Great Britain was still regarded as the preeminent global power as the century began, an empire on which the sun never set. But to Roosevelt, that sun was just beginning to rise on the American empire; it was a glorious time to be an American president. He was always in a hurry, and when he was governor of New York, TR was "a young man who was eager to reform the whole world between sunrise and sunset,"[43] according to President Benjamin Harrison. That description was no less accurate when Roosevelt became president himself. He possessed an endless amount of exuberance, and made no effort to hide it. Journalist Lincoln Steffens observed, in the aftermath of the McKinley assassination:

His offices were crowded with people, mostly reformers, all day long, and the President did his work among them with little privacy and much rejoicing. He strode triumphant around among us, talking and shaking hands, dictating and signing letters and laughing. Washington, and the whole country, was in mourning, and no doubt the President felt he should hold himself down; he didn't, he tried to, but his joy showed in every word and movement.[44]

All of this was meticulously noted by the press, which, under Roosevelt, became more intertwined with the presidency than ever before. In a decision that future presidents probably wish he hadn't taken, he spotted a group of reporters standing in the rain one chilly day and invited them inside.

Scribes have shadowed presidents ever since, tracking their every move and utterance.[45]

Perhaps Roosevelt invited reporters in because he didn't want them freezing to death. But it's likely he had a more calculated reason. By the turn of the century, newspapers had become increasingly sophisticated and influential. Radio was still a generation away; any politician wanting to reach a mass audience knew that newspapers were the only way to go. William McKinley invited reporters to work on tables in the second floor hallway of the White House, but wouldn't actually speak to them. Not only did Roosevelt invite reporters in that cold damp day, he gave them an actual room—just off the new Executive Office Building's entrance—in which to work.[46] It was the first true White House Press Room.

Unlike the taciturn McKinley, Theodore Roosevelt was a chatterbox. When he had something to say (which was quite often), he would pick up the telephone and personally summon them to his office.[47] Dozens would scamper to the second floor or to the West Wing to hear what was on his mind. On topics both consequential and mundane, the president's approach was generally the same: He was informal, and often spoke to the gathered scribes "as though they were close friends."[48] Those "friends" didn't seem to know (or care, perhaps) that they were being seduced by TR, a master showman, for they "almost idolized the man"[49] and reveled in their access to him. Invariably, the end result was one that many a future president could only dream of: a press that reported things just as the president preferred.[50] His incessant ability to talk, talk, talk lay waste to one of his most famous sayings: "Speak softly and carry a big stick!"

The love fest continued when the president traveled, often on a larger scale than was possible in the crowded White House. Whenever Roosevelt hopped on a train, railroad companies would add on an entire car for reporters; sometimes there were as many as 150 of them. Sometimes wealthy friends of the president—with private cars of their own—decided they wanted to go along too. Before long the entourage was so big that instead of the presidential car and press car being attached to a regular passenger train, there were now "presidential trains" themselves.[51] George Cortelyou, the super-efficient secretary who modernized McKinley's press operation and had been kept on by Roosevelt, organized trips with the precision of a Swiss watchmaker, giving all travelers a detailed hour-by-hour itinerary. At the end of the twentieth century, it would require a small army to do the job that Cortelyou did almost single-handedly.

Beyond changing the White House, Theodore Roosevelt changed the way in which Americans saw the presidency itself. It was seen, more than ever, as a center of great and unmatched power, power wielded by just one central authority. Not since Andrew Jackson—who loved to wrap himself up in his trademark blue cape and make dramatic entrances in his own lustrous new East Room—had the citizenry seen a president with such a flair for showmanship. Indeed, "his symbolic stature was more powerful in its time than Jackson's or Lincoln's had been" in theirs.[52]

The staid, stuffy Victorian era was no more; the White House was now occupied by a man who was determined to liven things up—and to have things his way. It was all quite calculated: "To the formal setting he gave a common touch with humor and incongruous behavior, turning the simplest occasion into a theatrical production."[53] In his home, in his country, on the world stage, Theodore Roosevelt was determined to be at the center of everything, and he was.

CHAPTER THIRTEEN

Woodrow Wilson: The Secret Illness

The President's Bedroom

IN A CITY OF SECRETS, IT WAS ONE OF THE MOST CLOSELY GUARDED SECRETS of all: the perilous condition of President Woodrow Wilson. On October 2, 1919, he suffered a near-fatal stroke. It left him partially paralyzed, barely able to speak or move—and the United States without its elected leader. The presidential bedroom in the southwest corner of the White House's second floor, where Wilson was confined for virtually all of his final eighteen months in office, became the center of power. It also was the stage for one of the greatest political cover-ups in American history.

In the beginning, other than doctors sworn to secrecy by their Hippocratic oaths, few knew the president was gravely ill. Not Vice President Thomas R. Marshall, who might have assumed Wilson's constitutional responsibilities. Not the Cabinet. Not Congress. Certainly not the press nor, by extension, the American people.

Standing between all of them and the president of the United States was one person, who in many ways was acting as de facto president herself: First Lady Edith Bolling Galt Wilson. All presidential spouses wield influence in their own unique way. But in the long annals of the American presidency, the nation has never seen anything quite like it.

———

Wilson was devastated in 1914 when his wife of twenty-eight years, Ellen, died from a kidney ailment. He plunged into depression, thinking that at age fifty-seven, he was too old to meet another woman. The president also thought that being cooped up in the White House wouldn't help either. "My heart has somehow been stricken dumb," he said in a letter to his middle daughter, Jessie.[1]

Woodrow Wilson's first wife, Ellen, did away with the Roosevelts' Colonial Garden—a jumble of geometrical planted areas, and changed it to what is today's Rose Garden, seen here in 1921. She died in August 1914. LIBRARY OF CONGRESS

His romance with Edith Galt began with a bit of serendipity. Driving through Washington one day with Admiral Cary Grayson, the White House physician, they passed two women whom Grayson happened to know. Eyeing Edith, Wilson was attracted immediately. "Who is that beautiful woman?"[2] he asked.

Since the first lady's death, the president's cousin, Helen Bones, had been serving as White House hostess—and happened to be friends with Edith. In March 1915, Helen invited Edith to the White House for tea. They had been out for a walk and weren't dressed suitably, but Helen assured her guest that they wouldn't see anyone else. Yet within moments of arriving, the two women ran into President Wilson and Grayson returning from a round of golf. It turned into tea for four, and within minutes, the widower president was smitten.[3] Edith, who also hailed from Virginia and had also suffered the loss of her first spouse, was forty-two. Never again would the president's heart be "stricken dumb."

While most men of his generation gathered after dinner for brandy, cigars, and serious talk about the issues of the day, Woodrow Wilson preferred beautiful and refined women.[4] "Girls of all degrees of beauty and grace have a charm for me which almost amounts to a spell," he admitted.[5] Edith Galt was certainly all that and more. But she was conflicted, unsure if she was attracted to Wilson the man or Wilson the president. Unattached presidents were not rare, of course—Wilson was the ninth—but Edith was torn. In the end, she was pursued by both. Wilson the man invited her to dinner several times a week, while Wilson the president—in an attempt to impress her with his power and status—shared state secrets with her, a potentially foolish indiscretion.[6]

"Who is that beautiful woman?" Woodrow Wilson asked when he first laid eyes on Edith Galt. Dismissing concerns that dating so soon after his wife's death would hurt his chances for reelection in 1916, the president tried to impress his new girlfriend by sharing government secrets with her.
LIBRARY OF CONGRESS

The president's advisors, worried about what the public might think of their newly widowed leader dating again so soon, tried to keep the fast-moving relationship out of the papers. The boss was up for reelection in 1916, after all. But the press caught on. In one of the more infamous journalistic gaffes, the *Washington Post*, noting how the president and his girlfriend enjoyed being chauffeured on long drives along the Potomac River, reported that the president had been "entertaining Mrs. Galt." Thanks to a typo, however, newspaper readers learned that the president had been "entering Mrs. Galt." A joke—risqué for the times—made the rounds: "What did Mrs. Galt do when the President of the United States proposed to her?" Answer: "She fell out of bed."[7] They married on December 18, 1915. Edith Galt had only known Woodrow Wilson for nine months. Now she was first lady.[8]

❧

Theodore Roosevelt used the Prince of Wales Room on the northwest side of the second floor as the presidential bedroom; William Howard Taft, reverting to tradition, slept in the bedroom back across the hall. This was Woodrow Wilson's bedroom as well, a grand space overlooking the Colonial Garden and, beyond that, the South Lawn and Mall, where the 555-foot-tall Washington Monument towered above the city's modest skyline.

When the United States entered the First World War, Edith coded and decoded secret messages for her husband and other government officials. But the power the first lady would wield after her husband's crippling illness would be far greater. LIBRARY OF CONGRESS

The president's view soon changed, though. Ellen, his first wife, decided that she didn't care for the Roosevelts' Colonial Garden, a jumble of circular and triangular planted areas. She had it torn up, and in its place a narrow, rectangular expanse of grass was put down, surrounded on three sides by flowers, bushes, and trees. The overall look was neat and symmetrical; the first lady called it the Rose Garden.[9] Sadly, Ellen Wilson would pass away shortly after its completion. After her death, the East Garden was completed, featuring a lily pond in the center, trees, well-manicured boxwood bushes, and "borders lavishly planted in flowers."[10] The garden today is named for Jacqueline Kennedy.

"My God, the president is paralyzed," said his close friend and physician, Dr. Cary Grayson. After Wilson's near-fatal stroke, Grayson conspired with Edith Wilson and others to hide the president's true condition from Congress and the American people. LIBRARY OF CONGRESS

Edith Wilson made few changes to the White House, but one was rather significant: She had the Lincoln bed moved into the presidential bedroom on the second floor's southwest corner, deeming it more appropriate for the president than the twin beds that had been there since the Taft years.[11] The small room next door, squeezed into the southwest corner, served as a tiny living room, where the Wilsons took many meals together; it also had a fireplace in the corner and a bathroom. If the second floor, off-limits to all but a few, was the presidential retreat within the White House, these two rooms were the Wilsons' true inner sanctum.[12]

Mrs. Wilson also paid tribute to her predecessors by creating the White House China Room on the ground floor (below the East Room). She had glass cabinets built around the room and displayed china, silver, and glassware used by previous First Families.[13] It is still there today, providing a charming sense of continuity between past and present. Mrs. Wilson also ended the habit of purchasing such items from abroad, placing an order for seventeen hundred pieces with Lenox China, then based in Trenton, New Jersey.[14] The famous presidential seal that we know today came into being during the Wilson years, and the president himself asked that it—and not the Great Seal of the United States—be displayed.[15]

Next to the new China Room, Edith Wilson also had a billiard room created for her husband; she saw it as a diversion from the burdens of the presidency, particularly as the United States got dragged into the war.[16] It's hard to visualize Wilson—regarded as an aloof academic and a snob—engaging in a pastime as pedestrian as pool, but he enjoyed it. The twenty-seven-and-a-half-foot by twenty-two-and-a-half-foot space is today called the Vermeil Room, used for a variety of purposes, such as a ladies sitting room, and visitors there can see a striking group of portraits of several first ladies.[17]

The new first lady was regarded as not as intelligent as the president's first wife had been, but the president, who often worked in the evening, entrusted her with important papers to read and often discussed serious matters with her.[18] As many a husband does, the president came to rely on Edith as a close advisor. And, as many a wife does, Edith developed a good instinct for how her husband thought, approached issues, and dealt with certain problems. She would soon use these instincts to make decisions on her husband's behalf when he proved unable to do so for himself.

The president's whirlwind romance with Edith wasn't an issue during his reelection run in 1916. Americans were far more concerned about the war in Europe that had broken out in 1914, and the possibility that the United States could be dragged into it. Even when 128 Americans were killed after a German submarine sank the British passenger ship *Lusitania* in 1915, Wilson refused growing pressure to get involved. America, Wilson said, "must be a special example . . . not merely of peace because it will not fight . . . there is such a thing as a man being too proud to fight."[19] War hawks like former president Roosevelt accused him of cowardice.

Wilson campaigned on a theme of neutrality, while urging stepped-up preparedness. His slogan "He Kept Us Out of War" resonated and he won, albeit modestly, with 49.2 percent of the popular vote and 277 electoral votes. But in the winter of 1916–17, his reelection safely behind him, events forced Wilson's hand. He learned of a German plot to form an alliance with Mexico, with Germany pledging to help Mexico recover Texas, New Mexico, and Arizona—territory lost to the United States in the Mexican-American War seventy years before. German submarines also began sinking American cargo ships in large numbers. On April 3, 1917, the president asked Congress to declare war.

Like William McKinley in 1898, Wilson had tried to avoid war, but once it began, he shifted decisively into commander in chief mode. He put the nation on a war footing; more than four million men were mobilized for what was to be a devastating conflict. More than 116,000 Americans would lose their lives; another 204,000 would be wounded.[20] The war also absolutely ravaged Europe, destroying an entire generation of young men across the continent. World War I would effectively end the British Empire, and lay the foundation for far greater horrors lurking on the horizon: the rise of Lenin's Soviet Union and Hitler's Nazi Germany. All the things said at the time about the great conflict—that it was "the war to end all wars," or that America's entry into it would, as Wilson himself said, make the world "safe for democracy"—proved tragically wrong.

At war for the second time in a generation, the White House adjusted. Public tours and the Easter Egg Roll were canceled, as were the New Year's Day receptions that gave citizens a chance to shake the president's hand. Edith Wilson donned a Red Cross uniform and saw departing troops off at Washington's Union Station. Americans were asked to ration food, gasoline, and other commodities. Edith did her part, making sure lights were turned out whenever possible, and ordering that meat and wheat be kept off White House menus on certain days. She even brought a flock of sheep, twenty in all, to the White House and had their wool auctioned off to raise money for the war effort. Recognizing the growing influence of the film industry, she teamed up with early Hollywood stars like Charlie Chaplin and Mary Pickford to sell war bonds.[21]

But Edith Wilson's principal responsibility during the war, as she saw it, was to support her commander in chief husband. In this regard, she did so in a way that no other first lady before or since has done: She learned to code and decode messages for the president and other top officials, putting her at the very heart of the war effort and making her privy to the nation's most important wartime secrets.[22] It was astonishing.

America's entry into the war tipped the scales. By December 1918, it was clear that the United States and its allies (Britain, France, Italy[23]) had gained the upper hand in the fight against the Central powers (Germany, Austria-Hungary, and Turkey). Wilson sailed to Europe, the first sitting president to visit the continent. In Paris, he attended a conference aimed at establishing postwar terms with Germany, while laying the groundwork for what the president hoped would be a peaceful and just world order.

Other than a brief return at the end of February, Wilson would spend the next six months in Europe, by far the longest period of time any sitting president has spent outside the United States. It was worth it, Wilson believed, since it culminated in his signing of the Treaty of Versailles, which established the League of Nations, a collaborative international body formed to prevent future conflict. But Wilson still needed two-thirds of the Senate to support the treaty. Without their backing, the president's signature was worthless.

But conservatives, alarmed that the Versailles treaty would require the United States to cede some of its sovereign powers to the League of Nations, balked. The president took the rare step of appearing before the Senate Foreign Relations Committee to argue for ratification.[24]

Wilson's pleas fell on largely deaf ears. Both the Senate and House in 1918 were controlled by Republicans, and Wilson, frustrated, decided to go over their heads and take his case directly to the American people, with a cross-country railroad tour. But the president was not in the best of health, and Edith Wilson, worried about the toll such a trip would take on her frail husband, was strongly opposed. So was the president's personal physician, Admiral Grayson, who objected strenuously. Wilson's response: "I cannot put my personal safety, my health, in the balance against my duty—I must go," and that was it.[25]

On September 2, they departed on the grueling journey, making multiple stops a day so the president could address the crowds. It was too much. He began to suffer from asthma attacks and splitting headaches that nearly blinded him.[26] "Let's stop," an increasingly alarmed first lady cried. "No!" was her husband's stubborn response.[27] The president made it over three weeks before finally collapsing from sheer exhaustion in Colorado. He was rushed back to the White House.

Aides had worried about Wilson for months. His memory had been slipping[28] and he talked to himself; now, chief usher Ike Hoover, welcoming the president home, noticed that "he looked a little peaked and seemed to have lost some of his spirit."[29] That was September 29th.

Three days later, Hoover, in his office, received an urgent call from Mrs. Wilson. "Please get Doctor Grayson, the president is very sick." The admiral rushed to the president's private quarters. Wilson had collapsed onto the white-tiled floor of his bathroom; Mrs. Wilson had put a pillow under his head and covered him with a blanket.[30] Grayson and the first lady moved the president into his bedroom, struggling to lift his 5'11" frame and put it gently into the Lincoln bed. With the first lady watching anxiously, Grayson examined him. The president had suffered a stroke, caused by a blood clot in a brain artery. It left the left side of his body paralyzed. "An arm and one leg were useless," Mrs. Wilson said, "but, thank God, the brain was clear and untouched."[31] The lower left side of the president's face also drooped, and he had trouble expressing himself.

Emerging from the bathroom, Grayson told Hoover, who was waiting anxiously outside: "My God, the president is paralyzed."[32] When Hoover first saw the president, "he looked as if he were dead."[33]

That afternoon, Mrs. Wilson and Grayson asked other doctors to examine the president as well. They were unsparing in their consensus: President Wilson was "seriously disabled, both in a medical and constitutional sense." His "thought processes nor his conduct in office would ever be the same again."[34]

In modern times, even the tiniest of incidents involving the chief executive does not go unnoticed by the press. John F. Kennedy, once questioned about a Band-Aid on his finger, admitted that he had been cutting bread.[35] Barack Obama split his lip playing basketball in 2010 and it was a major story for a few days. But on the morning of October 2, 1919, the president of the United States suffered a crippling, and near-fatal stroke—and the crisis, from the very beginning, was enveloped in an "air of secrecy."[36] Those in the know were determined to keep it that way. The communications strategy from the outset was simple: "no details, no explanations."[37]

It was "the beginning of the deception of the American people," Hoover would write in his 1934 biography, published posthumously. Never was a conspiracy "so pointedly and so artistically formed."[38]

While no one beyond the tight circle of the first lady, Hoover, and assorted doctors and nurses knew the president's true condition, it quickly became evident—based on Wilson's sudden disappearance from the rest of the world—that something was terribly wrong. Fed misleading information by Dr. Grayson, the *Washington Post* reported the day after Wilson's collapse that the president was merely suffering from "nervous exhaustion." But the

White House was silent on the real story. Days turned into weeks, and by Christmas 1919, the president, now sporting a long white beard, began the difficult task of learning to walk again. His ability to speak also returned, though at first mumbling was the best he could manage. Throughout, the White House response remained the same: silence. It would remain this way for the next eighteen months.

The silence even extended to the president's senior advisors. Secretary of State Robert Lansing, demanding answers but getting none, suggested to the president's private secretary, Joseph Tumulty, that Vice President Thomas R. Marshall assume Wilson's duties. He began to read the relevant passage in the Constitution: "In case of the removal of the President from office, or of his death, resignation or inability to discharge the powers and duties of the said office, the same shall devolve on the Vice President." Tumulty was enraged: "While Woodrow Wilson is lying in the White House on the broad of his back I will not be a party to ousting him. He has been too kind, too loyal, and too wonderful to me to receive such treatment at my hands."[39]

Marshall himself—who had more reason than anyone beyond the First Family to know the president's true condition—was shut out. Mrs. Wilson suggested that allowing Marshall to take over would speed Wilson's recovery, but one of the president's doctors, Francis Dercum, thought it a bad idea. If the president were to resign—a first in American history—"the greatest incentive to recovery is gone."[40]

And so while a handful of people, elected by no one, discussed in utter secrecy who should run the US government, Vice President Marshall went about his business. But just in case Wilson died, the decision was made to tell him the president's true condition, via a reporter who could be trusted. Marshall thought about assuming Wilson's duties on his own, but decided against it. "I could throw this country into civil war by seizing the White House, but I won't," he told his wife.[41] But he also said if Congress or the courts ordered him to take over, he would do so.[42]

So Woodrow Wilson, despite his grave illness, remained president in name. But who was running the government? Who was running the country? Dercum advised the first lady to screen all paperwork and visitors. "Have everything come to you, weigh the importance of each matter, and see if it is possible by consultations with the respective heads of the departments to solve them *without the guidance of your husband*"[43] (italics added).

It was a selfish course of action, putting the perceived needs of one man above those of the country. The first lady herself admitted as much, saying that her top priority "was first my beloved husband whose life I was trying to save," and "after that he was President of the United States."[44]

⁓

The silence surrounding Wilson's true state sparked wild rumors. As usual, some twisted the "facts," which weren't known; others simply made things up. Those bars on the ground-level White House windows? They were there to keep the president, "who had gone insane and was in danger of killing himself," from leaving the White House. (The bars had been installed by Theodore Roosevelt so his ball-playing sons wouldn't break the windows.) Others said Wilson had gone insane, spending his days drooling and reciting nursery rhymes. Still others claimed the president had been paralyzed after contracting venereal disease in Europe.[45]

Edith Wilson could have deflated these rumors and tall tales in an instant. Two advisors to the president—son-in-law (from Wilson's first marriage) William Gibbs McAdoo and Navy Secretary Josephus Daniels—urged the first lady to be candid with the American people, arguing that the public would sympathize and rally around their twice-elected president. Edith Wilson disagreed, and the White House remained silent.

Half a century later, during Watergate, a common argument would emerge: "It's not the crime, it's the cover-up." While no crime had been committed, Edith Wilson—a devoted wife trying to help her husband—certainly participated in one of the greatest coverups in history. By hiding her husband's illness, by making decisions in his name, Edith Wilson—an acting president in all but name—placed the nation's security and well-being in jeopardy. The condition of the nation, not its chief executive, should have been of paramount concern; astonishingly, for a year and a half, it was not.

So as Woodrow Wilson rested in the big Lincoln bed on the second floor of the White House, his wife began, as she put it, her "stewardship." She claimed, "I myself, never made a single decision regarding the disposition of public affairs. The only decision that was mine was what was important and what was not,"[46] which of course were decisions in and of themselves. "I talked with him so much that I knew pretty well what he thought of things,"[47] she remarked. She also claimed that the president asked countless questions, insisting on being in the loop on everything. Clinical papers of Dr. Dercum, made public in 1991, appear to completely contradict Mrs. Wilson's account.[48]

Information vacuum or not, others caught on quickly. "We have a petticoat government, Mrs. Wilson is President," said New Mexico senator Albert Fall. The *Nashville Tennessean* called Mrs. Wilson "the nation's first presidentress." The *Boston Globe*'s phrase was more convoluted: "Acting First Man."[49]

Abroad, it was big news as well. The *London Daily Mail* called Edith Wilson "the acting president of the United States."[50] Newspapers speculated about what it all meant, whether the government was functioning smoothly—or at all. If Marshall wasn't making decisions, was the Cabinet? And how did that work? Did Cabinet decisions have to be unanimous or require a simple majority vote? As usual in this extraordinary period, there were far more questions than answers.

Had the contingent of Edith Wilson, Cary Grayson, Joseph Tumulty, and Francis Dercum looked toward the past for clues on how to manage the situation, they would have found as much confusion as clarity. When William Henry Harrison died after a month in office in 1841, the debate was not whether Vice President John Tyler would succeed him; the question was whether he would be president, or merely acting president—decisions subject to approval by Harrison's Cabinet.

And while the deaths of two presidents—Zachary Taylor in 1850 and Abraham Lincoln in 1865—had been quick, the passing of two others—James Garfield in 1881 and William McKinley in 1901—had not. Garfield, who lingered for two and a half months after being shot by an assassin, was clearly incapable of fulfilling his duties.[51] His Cabinet wanted Vice President Chester Arthur to take over as acting chief executive. But it took no action, fearing that Garfield, should he recover, might be unable to retake the office he had surrendered.[52]

William McKinley's condition wavered during the eight days he lived after being shot—yet Vice President Theodore Roosevelt, after initially rushing to the president's bedside, went on vacation in the remote Adirondack Mountains of upstate New York. He was unplugged from the machinery of government and only learned of the president's death when a park ranger tracked him down and thrust a telegram into his hands.[53]

But Woodrow Wilson's situation was like no other. He hadn't been shot; his brain functioned and he could communicate—just not enough to fully uphold his responsibilities to the nation. It was a constitutional crisis the likes of which the nation had never seen—except they didn't see it, since the drama played out behind the closed doors of the White House. The twenty-eighth president of the United States, who once dreamed of winning a third term in 1920, would live in virtual seclusion for the remainder of his second term.

Wilson would depart the White House diminished in body, but not in spirit. In the fall of 1920, he learned that he had been awarded the Nobel Peace Prize for his efforts on behalf of the League of Nations. His futile campaign for it nearly cost him his life, but at least he had some form of validation for his efforts. He would not attend the ceremony in Oslo that December, but the US ambassador to Norway read a telegram. It reads, in part:

> *Mankind has not yet been read of the unspeakable horror of war. I am convinced that our generation has, despite its wounds, made notable progress. But it is the better part of wisdom to consider our work as one begun. It will be a continuing labor. In the indefinite course of the years before us there will be abundant opportunity for others to distinguish themselves in the crusade against hate and fear and war . . . whatever has been accomplished in the past is petty compared to the glory and promise of the future.*[54]

CHAPTER FOURTEEN

Warren G. Harding: Scandals Galore

The Yellow Oval Room

HE WAS A GAMBLER IN EVERY SENSE OF THE WORD: WOMEN, REPUTATION, marriage—and ultimately, his place in the history books. He put it all on the line to satisfy his seemingly endless desire for kicks, for lust, for a quick buck. Today, it would be almost impossible for any presidential candidate to win with that kind of baggage. But Warren Gamaliel Harding did—and by a landslide. In fact, his winning percentage in the 1920 election, 60.3 percent of the popular vote, was bigger than anyone who preceded him, and has since been topped by only three others: Franklin Roosevelt in 1936, Lyndon Johnson in 1964, and Richard Nixon in 1972.

If nothing else, the huge winning margin only validated the reckless life he had led up to that point. Harding brought it with him into the White House, where some of its most august surroundings—including the Oval Office itself—became his personal playground. Though short-lived—just two and a half years—his administration has forever been defined by some of the biggest political scandals in American history.

He died suddenly in 1923, highly popular and widely mourned. This was a reflection of the fact that the scandals, the personal failings, the sleaziness, were little known by the public until long after his passing. There was the longtime mistress he frequently snuck into the West Wing, just beyond the gaze of his suspicious wife. There were payoffs, sometimes by him, usually by others, to keep the women quiet. During one of his regular Oval Room nights of poker and drinking (he hypocritically supported Prohibition in public), Harding once gambled away a case of fancy White House china. The gambling, the booze, the pursuit of flesh: All were fueled by a sense of entitlement that reflected both Harding's arrogance and feelings of inadequacy. "I am not fit for this office, and never should have been here," he once confided.[1]

As the nation entered what would become known as the Roaring Twenties, Harding seemed like just the right man to lead America. The scars of World War I—which killed or wounded 320,000 Americans in just nineteen months—were still fresh. A recession gripped the nation. And the outgoing president, Woodrow Wilson, was an invalid, crippled in the fall of 1919 by a devastating stroke that left him a shadow of his former self for the last eighteen months of his presidency—while First Lady Edith Wilson and others hid his true condition and assumed some of his responsibilities.

It was a golden opportunity for Harding, who in 1920 was nearly a decade younger than the stern, shriveled Wilson. The contrast between the two could not have been more striking. "He was tall and handsome, age 55, with silver white hair and a brilliant smile . . . he looked every inch a President,"[2] the White House historian William Seale wrote. Women were attracted to Harding like a moth to light (he was "handsome as a matinee idol," it was said),[3] and conveniently enough, the Nineteenth Amendment to the Constitution had recently given them the right to vote. Their support swept Harding into the White House.

Despite his failings, Harding may be deserving of more credit for his achievements than some historians are willing to give. Assuming the presidency during a recession, he cut taxes to jumpstart the economy. He instituted a formal and disciplined budget process for the federal government. As

The biggest landslide in history up to that time propelled Warren Harding into the presidency in 1920. Women loved Harding, a flashy, good-time president— and he loved them right back. As often as possible. His administration is today remembered as perhaps the most scandal-tainted in American history. LIBRARY OF CONGRESS

Well aware of her husband's lifelong philandering, First Lady Florence "Flossie" Harding was tipped off one day that the president was entertaining a woman in the Oval Office. Rushing to the West Wing, a Secret Service agent blocked the door. LIBRARY OF CONGRESS

automobiles became more ingrained in the lives of Americans, Harding signed the federal Highway Act of 1921, designed to expand the nation's road network. He hosted a disarmament conference that was regarded as a triumph. And the president spoke on behalf of African Americans and civil rights more forcefully and effectively than any president since Lincoln. For a time, he "was probably as popular as any past president other than Washington."[4] But after his sudden and still mysterious death in August 1923, the skeletons Harding had so cleverly concealed came tumbling out. His reputation would never recover.

Because of security concerns during World War I and Wilson's long, crippling illness, the White House had been closed to the public since 1917. The doors flung open under Harding, who ordered tours resumed. The openness played to the image that Harding wanted to project—a "regular"

American, not an Ivy League elitist like Wilson. The new president especially got a kick out of dropping in on tours to greet surprised and delighted visitors.[5]

But because the White House had been closed to the public for so long—and hadn't been refurbished since 1902—the interior seemed outdated, even chilly to visitors. Thick carpeting and dark, heavy drapes muffled voices and footsteps. Furnishings gave the appearance of yesteryear.[6] President and Mrs. Harding demanded that everything be polished and clean, and the first lady did replace old curtains and upholsteries—with the same dark, heavy patterns—but in terms of architecture or decor made no substantive changes to the mansion's public spaces.[7]

Even in the private quarters upstairs, the Hardings made few alterations. Citing the need to be frugal during a recession, they declared that the $20,000 given to incoming administrations for decor would not be spent. But the money was quietly shifted to another account and spent on entertaining. The Hardings also got rid of the famous Lincoln bed used by Wilson during his long illness, moving it out of the presidential bedroom to a nearby guest room. They replaced it with twin beds used a decade before by President and Mrs. Taft.[8]

It's a miracle Harding even made it to the White House in 1920. His Senate record was mediocre. Representing Ohio since 1915, he often skipped work (he was a no-show for 1,163 of 2,692 roll calls)[9] and generally avoided decisions on controversial issues of the day like Prohibition and women's suffrage. When the going got tough, Warren Harding was usually nowhere to be found.

It was hardly the stuff of presidential timber, yet at the 1920 Republican Convention, Harding's was one of eleven names to be placed in nomination. Convention delegates were deadlocked, and after ten rounds of balloting, Harding—considered a dark horse—emerged the victor.

Even so, the GOP's new standard-bearer impressed few. He was a "party hack," some said. Connecticut senator Frank Brandegee, a GOP kingmaker, was blunt: "There ain't any first-raters this year . . . we got a lot of second-raters and Warren Harding is the best of the second-raters."[10]

Even Harding himself didn't think he was up to the job. "The only thing I really worry about," he had fretted the year before, "is that I am going to be nominated and elected."[11] It was no tongue-in-cheek comment; Harding genuinely feared serious responsibility: "I am sure I should never have any more fun or any real enjoyment in life if I should be so politically fortunate as to win a nomination and election. I had much rather retain my place in the Senate and enjoy the association of friends and some of the joys of living."[12] Hardly the words of a leader.

Had Harding been vetted as thoroughly as presidential candidates are today, his Senate record—and absences—wouldn't have been the only red flag. While everything about modern-day candidates is known—education, work, achievements, voting records, embarrassing flubs, family, and finances—much of Harding's background, particularly his private life, escaped serious scrutiny. Someone with that kind of personal baggage simply could not be elected today.

The worst of it was his weakness for women. Married since 1891 to an older woman, Florence ("Flossie") Kling DeWolfe, the domineering daughter of a wealthy Ohio businessman, Harding engaged in a series of affairs throughout their marriage. Two stand out: his long, intense flings with Carrie Phillips and Nan Britton.

In 1905 Harding—then lieutenant governor of Ohio—plunged into a six-year fling with Phillips, a knockout brunette and wife of a close friend. The Phillipses and the Hardings often vacationed together, offering Carrie and Warren ample opportunities to see each other—often under the noses of their spouses. Incredibly, despite his desire to keep the affair secret, Harding created a vivid paper trail—eight hundred pages long—of love letters to Phillips. It never occurred to him that this indiscretion would come back to haunt him, that the higher he advanced in politics, the more vulnerable the letters would make him. Harding called Carrie "Sis" and she called him, intriguingly, "Constant." He wrote her on Christmas Eve 1910:

My Darling:
There are no words, at my command, sufficient to say the full extent of my love for you—a mad, tender, devoted, ardent, eager, passion-wild, jealous reverent, wistful, hungry, happy love—unspeakably encompassing, immeasurably absorbing, unendingly worshipping, unconsciously exalting, unwillingly exacting, involuntarily expounding, everlastingly compensating. All the love a man can know and feel and endure, and gladly, oh, so gladly give. It flames like the fire and consumes. . . . [13]

The future commander in chief's literary efforts even included crude attempts at poetry:

> I love your back, I love your breasts
> Darling to feel, where my face rests,
> I love your skin, so soft and white,
> So dear to feel and sweet to bite. . . .
> I love your poise of perfect thighs,
> When they hold me in paradise. . . .[14]

It wasn't until three years later—as he weighed a run for the US Senate—that Harding realized, too late, that his paper trail to Phillips was a problem. His solution? Write her another letter. This from January 3, 1913:

I have been thinking of all those letters you have. I think you [should] have a fire, chuck 'em! Do. You must.[15]

In 1911, the affair was discovered by their spouses. Florence Harding, enraged, felt betrayed and considered divorcing Harding, before he promised not to see Phillips again. James Phillips, humiliated, took Carrie and their two children and fled to Germany. It had no impact on Harding's career: He was elected to the Senate in 1914. After World War I broke out, Carrie returned to the United States, and the two reignited their affair. Letters written in his own hand on Senate stationery show the affair—by now more than a decade old—remained passionate. It was remarkably reckless behavior for such a powerful man. But Warren Harding, though increasingly cautious, dwelled in a world where friends and associates were to be trusted.

This naive mind-set would land him in hot water. Carrie eventually tired of her affair and had developed sympathies toward Germany (there is some evidence that she was a German agent[16]). As the United States contemplated entering the war against the Germans, she blackmailed Harding, threatening to publicly expose their affair if he voted for it. Harding successfully called her bluff.

Shortly before the 1920 convention, Republican officials approached Harding to ask the skeletons-in-the-closet question: Was there anything in his background that might prove an embarrassment during the fall campaign? Harding, figuring that he had won three statewide elections in Ohio without having to divulge any secrets, said no. He also neglected to mention that he had heart troubles and that he had checked himself into a sanitarium a few times to deal with nervous exhaustion.[17]

But after locking up the nomination, Harding was blackmailed by Phillips again, who threatened to release his love letters to the newspapers if he didn't pay her off. It was only then, with the presidency hanging in the balance, that Harding reluctantly came clean. Yes, he told Republican Party officials, there had been an affair with a woman, Carrie Phillips—and she wanted money. Angry over their hand-picked candidate's duplicity, party officials felt like they had no choice but to pay off the Phillipses.

Though details of what it took to buy their silence are disputed, it was an enormous amount of money. Some historians say $20,000, nearly seventeen times the annual salary for the average American in those days; another Harding expert, the author David Pietrusza, claims the Phillips were given as much as $50,000. In any case, James and Carrie Phillips, flush with cash, embarked upon a long tour of the Far East that conveniently lasted until well after Harding had been safely elected president of the United States.

But Harding, only revealing as much as he thought necessary, made no mention of Susie Hodder, a childhood friend of his wife, who he began seeing three years after getting married—and with whom he fathered a daughter. Nor was anything said about his long-term fling with Grace Cross, a typist in his Senate office (the night before his inauguration, she and Harding are said to have met in the Willard Hotel near the White House).[18] Harding's appetite for women didn't end when he became president; if anything it appeared to increase. There was Rosa Hoyle, who reportedly bore him a son, and Augusta Cole, who aborted a pregnancy by him. There were chorus girls named Maize Haywood and Blossom Jones, and "Miss Allicott," an employee of the *Washington Post*, all said to be procured by his good friend Ned McLean, the paper's owner and publisher. Then there was an unnamed New York woman who committed suicide when Harding refused to marry her.[19] In the words of his attorney general, Harry Daugherty, no president had more "women scrapes" than Warren Harding.

Yet despite all of these affairs, allegations, and cover-ups, the most infamous of Harding's flings involved a woman from his hometown: Nan Britton. A ravishing blonde thirty-one years his junior, Britton grew up infatuated with Harding, a friend of her father's. Harding hired her to work in his Washington office, and one night in the winter of 1919, according to Britton, the two conceived a child, Elizabeth Ann.[20]

When Harding became president, two Secret Service agents, James Sloan and Walter Ferguson, helped sneak her into the West Wing, where she and her presidential lover sometimes retreated to a large closet near the Oval Office itself. "My God, we've got a president who doesn't know beds were invented, and he was elected on a slogan of 'Back to Normalcy,'" smirked Alice Roosevelt Longworth, Teddy's daughter and a White House regular during the Harding years.[21]

On one occasion, Mrs. Harding, apparently tipped off by another agent, rushed to the Oval Office only to find the door blocked by Ferguson. "She stood and glared at me like she couldn't believe it. Finally she spun around and returned to the White House. . . . As soon as I thought it was safe, I went to the car and took the girl to a hotel."[22] Once, during a visit to New York, Harding and Britton even enjoyed each other's company alfresco, in a secluded part of Central Park. Even by the standards of later presidents, it was beyond brazen. And showing that he hadn't learned a thing, Harding also wrote Nan long love letters—sometimes forty pages in length.[23]

Some White House reporters seemed aware of Harding's appetite for women, but kept quiet. This sometimes encouraged the president to let his guard down. "It's a good thing I'm not a woman," he told them once in a rare moment of candor. "I would always be pregnant. I can't say no."[24]

His endless philandering wasn't the only way in which Harding mocked the dignity of the presidency. His public and private behavior were also different things when it came to alcohol. The eighteenth amendment to the Constitution, which banned the production, transport, and sale of alcohol, was in force during his presidency. When he was sworn in, Harding vowed to preserve, protect, and defend that Constitution. And he did. Until he wanted a drink.

Mark Sullivan, a prominent newspaper columnist during the Harding years, said that while sitting with the president on rocking chairs on the South Portico one evening, Harding "wished to offer me a drink. He, with Mrs. Harding, took me into their bedroom, saying they felt that since Prohibition was in effect, they ought not to drink in the ordinary rooms of the White House, nor offer drinks to their friends, but in their bedroom they might properly follow their personal standards."[25]

Millions of Americans flouted Prohibition, of course, but they hadn't taken a public vow to uphold it. And Harding didn't restrict his drinking to the private confines of his bedroom. Down the hall from the First Couple's bedroom on the second floor of the mansion is the present-day Yellow Oval Room. Here, in the forty-by-thirty-foot room, draped in "Harding blue,"[26] the president hosted long evenings of poker several nights a week, with drinks often mixed and served by the first lady herself from a table groaning under the weight of numerous liquors, wines, and ales. Longworth, a regular, recalls "the air heavy with tobacco smoke, trays with bottles containing every imaginable brand of whiskey, cards and poker chips ready at hand—a general atmosphere of waistcoat unbuttoned, feet on the desk, and spittoons alongside."[27]

Harding's preference was scotch, often followed by ale as the night wore on. As hand after hand of cards were dealt, the room filled with smoke, with Harding switching back and forth between pipes and cigars—even putting entire cigarettes into his mouth and chewing on them.[28] Standing watch over these presumably ribald evenings was, on a series of bookshelves, a pink doll of Mrs. Harding's that "shook and winked" and her eclectic collection of miniature elephants (the president was a Republican, after all). Friends were always giving her these statuettes, which "paraded in single-file in great numbers" throughout the room. Some were made from wood, brass, or ivory; some were cheap souvenirs, while others were quite exquisite pieces.

Walls and tables were covered with photos of the president in official and informal functions: giving speeches, playing golf, walking down the street with admirers.[29] When the men wanted to stretch their legs, they could stroll over to the tall windows on the room's south side and take in the sweeping vista of the South Lawn below, the round pool and fountain near the perimeter fence and—in the distance and slightly to the left—the Washington Monument.

The booze-filled nights in the Oval Room were hidden behind the Hardings' teetotaling public veneer; at least one defender of the president, Secret Service agent Ed Starling, maintains that the poker evenings were harmless affairs, akin to a night at a small-town Elks Club.[30] But anecdotal evidence shows that these were more than mere penny-ante games.

One night, Harding, upping the stakes on one hand, bet part of the White House china—and lost. And the winner was none other than the first wife of Gen. Douglas MacArthur. Louise MacArthur, married to the general between 1922 and 1929, said she often sat in on games in the Library with the president, Secretary of War John Weeks, and Gen. John J. Pershing. Mrs.

MacArthur, telling the story to a newspaper reporter, recalled that at one point, Harding turned to her and said: "Louise, let's just play a cold hand of poker—just the two of us—winner names the stakes."

The general's wife beat the president, and when asked to name her prize, replied "I'll take a set of White House china."

The very next day, "a barrel of china of the Benjamin Harrison administration was delivered at my door."[31]

—⁓—

Personal weaknesses weren't the only source of Harding's problems. Committed to putting the "best minds" on his Cabinet, he did in fact make several distinguished Cabinet picks, including Charles Hughes at State, Andrew Mellon at Treasury, and a future president, Herbert Hoover, at Commerce.[32] Yet with others, he displayed appallingly poor judgment, selecting old friends who saw public service as a way to line their own pockets—and line them they did.

The worst of it concerned a huge government oil reserve in Teapot Dome, Wyoming. When all was said and done, it was, in some respects, a scandal more brazen than even the Watergate outrage that brought down the Nixon administration half a century later.

On April 7, 1922, Interior Secretary Albert Fall decided, by himself, that he could secretly lease Teapot Dome and another reserve in Elk Hills, California, to an oilman named Harry Sinclair. It was a sweetheart deal with no competitive bidding, and Fall received at least $300,000 in bribes. Eight days later, word of the deal got out and a Senate investigation was launched. Meanwhile, the president was tipped off that his good friend Charles Forbes, an Army deserter who was nevertheless appointed to the Veterans Bureau (precursor to today's Veterans Administration) might have been involved in the private sale of government property stored in a bureau warehouse.

Harding remained loyal to both initially, before forcing their resignations on January 2, 1923 (at one point, told of Fall's dealings, Harding said "If Albert Fall isn't an honest man, I'm not fit to be President of the United States").[33] Fall eventually became the first member of any president's Cabinet to go to prison. Forbes, for peddling alcohol and drugs from veterans' hospitals to bootleggers and drug dealers, and for taking kickbacks from contractors building veterans' hospitals, was also thrown in prison. He is estimated to have stolen some $200 million—the equivalent of billions today.[34]

Harding's poor judgment also extended to an old Ohio friend and political confidante, Harry Daugherty, who became attorney general. Accused of embezzlement, Daugherty survived congressional attempts to remove him. Jess Smith, an aide of Daugherty's and friend of the Hardings, was swept back to Ohio after the president became suspicious. Smith was soon found dead of a gunshot wound in an apparent suicide. Another Harding friend, Charles Cramer, who had been caught up in the Veterans Bureau scandal, also appears to have killed himself. "My God, this is a hell of a job!" the president told journalist William Allen White, who asked Harding about his enemies. "I have no trouble with my enemies. I can take care of my enemies all right. But my damn friends, my Goddamn friends, White, they're the ones that keep me walking the floor nights!"[35]

CHAPTER FIFTEEN

Calvin Coolidge: The Roaring Twenties

The Sky Parlor

A LEAKY, CRUMBLING ROOF CAN BE A NIGHTMARE, AND CAN HAPPEN TO anyone—even the president of the United States. That's the position Calvin Coolidge found himself in after living in the White House for two years. During particularly heavy rainstorms, water often made its way to the mansion's second floor, where Coolidge, wife Grace, and, occasionally, son John lived. There were also cracks in the walls, which suggested an even greater problem: the stability of the White House itself.

Like any homeowner, Coolidge—known for being tight with a dollar—might have been expected to fix the problem as cheaply and quickly as possible. Instead, he decided the best solution to the leaks and crumbling infrastructure was to build an entire third floor on top of the White House. It was the most significant addition to the original mansion since the North and South Porticoes were constructed a century before. Unfortunately, the new White House floor created more problems than it solved; twenty years later it would contribute to the near collapse of the entire mansion.[1]

Coolidge's 1920s are seen today as a golden era, a decade sandwiched between a great war and a great depression. Despite three downturns in the 1920s—including two on the president's watch—the economy expanded overall, with wages growing and unemployment remaining low. Americans prospered, connected as never before by electricity, automobiles, telephones, radio, and movies. Life moved faster, though driven partly underground by Prohibition. It was an era of materialism, hedonism, and excess, depicted so wonderfully by F. Scott Fitzgerald's *The Great Gatsby*. In short, times were good, they were loud, and they were fun; the decade came to be known as the "Jazz Age," the "Roaring Twenties"—and the era of "Coolidge Prosperity."[2]

Even before the death in 1924 of his youngest son, Calvin Coolidge was quiet and prone to depression. He often slept ten or eleven hours a night—and took long naps during the day. Asked why he attended dinner parties when he seemed so uncomfortable, he said "got to eat somewhere." LIBRARY OF CONGRESS

Warren Harding, the flashy, good-time president who died suddenly in 1923, would have enjoyed the rest of this colorful, decadent decade. But John Calvin Coolidge Jr., his serious, button-downed successor, seemed rather incongruous with the nation's mood. Unassuming, taciturn, and frugal, he wore a pale, often grim expression, and was slow to smile.[3] It was a visage that was often interpreted as aloofness, but was in fact a reflection of his simple

Another floor was added to the White House during Coolidge's presidency, forcing the First Family to move out for six months in 1927. The president inspected the construction site each day. LIBRARY OF CONGRESS

New England stoicism. Appearances aside, the thirtieth president possessed leadership qualities his shady predecessor did not: honesty and integrity.

After Harding's death—he had been president just two and a half years—Coolidge didn't move into the White House right away. Florence Harding lingered in the mansion for a few weeks, and the new president, not wanting to pressure the former first lady, continued to live two blocks away at the Willard Hotel,[4] walking to his White House office each morning with his Secret Service agent, Edmund Starling. After a few weeks, Mrs. Harding finally left, and Coolidge and new first lady Grace Coolidge moved into their new home.

The First Couple moved into the bedroom in the southwest corner of the second floor—then as now, the traditional presidential bedchamber. The twin beds used by the Hardings were moved into a bedroom across the hall. The presidential bedroom was of the utmost importance to Coolidge, given how

The president and first lady with Charles Lindbergh and his mother in June 1927. Coolidge's 1920s are seen today as a golden era, a decade sandwiched between a great war and a great depression. Despite three downturns, the economy expanded overall, and Americans prospered, connected as never before by electricity, automobiles, telephones, radio, and movies. LIBRARY OF CONGRESS

much time he spent there: He typically slept up to eleven hours a night—plus a two-hour nap each afternoon.[5] This was likely the result of Coolidge's lifelong battle with depression, which during his presidency was made still worse by the 1924 death of his youngest son and namesake, Calvin Coolidge Jr., from blood poisoning. In his autobiography, penned months after leaving the White House, Coolidge wrote "When [Calvin] went, the power and the glory of the presidency went with him."[6] The boy's passing sent the president into a "state of clinical depression from which he never recovered."[7]

Depression generally wasn't discussed in those days, and Coolidge never let on how deeply his malady affected him. One coping mechanism was to poke fun at himself. Once when a White House staffer awoke the president from his nap, Coolidge grinned and asked "Is the country still here?"[8] At the theater one evening, Groucho Marx, spotting the president in the audience, cried out "Isn't it past your bedtime, Cal?" Coolidge laughed along with the audience.[9] When Coolidge passed away in 1933, writer Dorothy Parker asked, "How can they tell?"[10] Coolidge would have enjoyed the joke.

The Coolidges were met with a surprise when they moved into the White House: Despite the fact that the reconstruction job ordered by Theodore Roosevelt was barely twenty years old, the mansion was in serious need of repair. Specifically, the roof appeared to be in danger of collapsing. That was the conclusion of a study by Army engineers that had been ordered by Harding before his death.[11]

The problem, Coolidge was told, was the very work that had been done for Roosevelt in 1902: The truss that architect Charles McKim had installed to expand the State Dining Room was failing. Timbers holding up the attic above the second floor were splintering. They recommended a major overhaul, and informed the president it could be done for half a million dollars. Coolidge, no spendthrift, asked, "If it is as bad as you say, why doesn't it fall down?"[12]

The president had no intention of spending that kind of money to fix the White House.[13] But by 1925, he realized that something had to be done. Walls on the second floor, where the First Family lived, were cracking. There were cracks on the ceiling too, through which bits of debris occasionally fell. The wooden frame holding the mansion together was failing.[14]

The president wanted repairs to be made without disturbing him or his family. But since the White House's roof, attic, and second floor ceilings would have to be removed, and Maj. J. C. Mehaffey, the chief of design and construction for the government office that oversaw public buildings, suggested that perhaps Coolidge should leave.

"It is my opinion," Mehaffey wrote, "that if the replacement of the roof were started as proposed, the President would soon find the conditions intolerable and would either stop the work or decide to move out." Mehaffey then appealed to the president's frugality: To work around the First Family, "the cost of the work would be approximately 50 percent more than it would be if the White House was vacated."[15] Coolidge reluctantly agreed to move out of the White House.

Despite the urgency of the problem, it took another year for plans to be finalized. Congress approved $375,000 for the project, which included making the White House roof steeper than before, which would create more room below.[16]

For the second time in a quarter-century, the president of the United States and his family found themselves forced out of the White House. On March 2, 1927, the Coolidges moved into a mansion at 15 Dupont Circle, about a mile away. Ironically, the home had been built by McKim, Mead & White—the firm whose shoddy work for Theodore Roosevelt in 1902 was responsible for the Coolidges' departure.[17] Unhappy about being displaced, the president told representatives from N. P. Severin Company of Chicago, which won the bid for the White House job, that they had 125 days to finish.[18]

At the White House, Severin got to work, removing furnishings from the second floor and scattering them about rooms on the State Floor below and elsewhere. On March 14, the real work began.[19] Passersby soon saw the entire mansion covered with an enormous temporary wooden roof, made to protect the interior when the rotting roof was torn away. Also taken down was the timber frame installed by James Hoban after the fire of 1814; much of the wood was turned into various souvenirs and sold.

The four months the president gave Severin turned out to be unrealistic. It wasn't until September 11, 1927, that the First Couple returned, after a six-month absence.[20] They had been away slightly longer than Theodore and Edith Roosevelt during the renovation of 1902.

The biggest change to the White House was that an entire third floor had been plopped down on top of the First Family's private quarters one floor below. The new floor added fourteen major rooms to the mansion, in addition to numerous small spaces that would be used for storage. Plumbing had also been extended to the third floor for several new bathrooms.

What had been an attic above the North Portico was now three large storage areas; skylights had been cut into the roof of each.[21] A long hallway ran the length of the new floor, broken up by a large round hole, several feet in diameter. Just above this was yet another skylight. Thus sunlight streamed through the new roof and third floor down into the Coolidges' private quarters.[22]

The First Couple could also now enjoy what came to be known as the "sky parlor." The idea came from Grace Coolidge, who decided that it would be nice to have a sunroom on the new roof of the White House. The first lady stocked it with warm carpeting and wicker furniture, including day beds—where the president occasionally enjoyed an afternoon snooze. There was also a phonograph and a radio.[23] It offered glorious views of the South Lawn and beyond, past the Washington Monument on the Mall, past the Potomac, all the way to Virginia. No First Family had ever enjoyed such a perk, and to this day the solarium, as it is now called, remains a favorite refuge for First Families.[24]

In what is practically unheard of in Washington today, the White House renovation came in well under budget. Of the $375,000 allocated by Congress for the job, $53,226 was left over.[25] Mrs. Coolidge, told she could spend more money, decided that rooms on the State Floor could use some new furniture. The Green Room was her greatest contribution. Beginning with a "flamboyant" green-patterned rug, she set out to pay tribute to presidents past, beginning with a reproduction of a settee owned by George Washington,[26] a striking round mahogany table with claw feet[27] that had been purchased by Andrew Jackson, and a black marble clock believed to have been used by Abraham Lincoln.[28] But there were more current—and controversial—touches as well. Art Deco was a new design style that was all the rage in the 1920s; the first lady displayed sculpture that some visitors considered too risqué for the White House.

The Roosevelt renovation of 1902 solved some problems—at least for the short term—but created more substantive long-term ones. A quarter-century later, history had repeated itself during Coolidge's tenure. The third floor and its roof were built with a steel frame and concrete blocks. This was sturdy and kept the rain out. But it was heavy, and the added weight was placed directly on top of the existing, century-old structure with its masonry shell and load-bearing walls.[29] That wasn't all: The truss that McKim had installed in 1902 to make the State Dining Room bigger was now supported in part by the steel frame above the mansion—putting still more pressure on the mansion.[30] Decisions on the White House renovation made in 1927 proved to be foolish, short-sighted, and, twenty years later, nearly disastrous.

———

Grace Coolidge's influence was defined by more than sky parlors and green rooms. Vivacious and charming, she was enormously popular, particularly with women who admired her taste in fashion. The Coolidges entertained frequently, inviting glamorous guests like Hollywood stars and newsmakers like broadcaster/columnist Will Rogers and Charles Lindbergh, fresh off his historic solo plane trip across the Atlantic. Prohibition was still the law of the land, however, and unlike Warren and Florence Harding—who drank with their private guests—social events in the Coolidge White House were dry affairs.[31]

Given the president's famous reticence, the first lady conversed with guests more than the president did. This came as no surprise to visitors who were familiar with Coolidge's reputation, which is best illustrated by one story from his time as vice president. At one event, Coolidge was seated next to a woman who had heard of his quiet demeanor. She turned to the vice president and said she had wagered that she could get more than two words out of him that night. Coolidge's response: "You lose." Grace Coolidge turned the seemingly uncivil episode into a funny anecdote in an attempt to soften her husband's reputation.[32] The deference he was given as president gave Coolidge little incentive to change, and he did not.

For a man with such a taciturn reputation, Calvin Coolidge seemed to enjoy talking with reporters—a lot. Keeping a campaign pledge that no modern president would deign to make, he met with the White House press corps on Tuesday and Friday throughout his presidency.[33] But Coolidge dealt with the press largely on his terms. Reporters had to submit questions in writing and had to attribute answers not to the president himself, but a "White House spokesman." Those were the president's rules, but the press abhorred the practice and often mocked the president behind his back.

Coolidge himself offered this explanation of his press policy: "The words of the president have an enormous weight and ought not to be used indiscriminately. It would be exceedingly easy to set the country all by the ears and foment hatreds and jealousies, which, by destroying faith and confidence, would help nobody and harm everybody." But it did allow the president to speak candidly, which Coolidge obviously saw as a plus, and in the end, most newspaper readers knew who was doing the talking anyway.[34]

Coolidge's adroitness extended beyond the White House press. Knowing that radio and movies were rapidly immersing themselves in American culture, the president decided he needed to be on the radio and in the movies himself. On December 6, 1923, he gave his first State of the Union address to Congress; it was broadcast to more than half the country, making Coolidge, as the *New York Times* noted, "heard by more people than the voice of any man in history."[35] Silent Cal's speech ran some seven thousand words.[36] While he was not as masterful on the radio as Franklin Roosevelt proved to be a decade later, it seemed to Coolidge as if the medium had been invented just for him. It eliminated the need to go on the kind of grueling railroad trips that had nearly killed Woodrow Wilson.[37]

At the time, Americans were flocking to movie theaters that were springing up across the nation, eager to see the latest Hollywood releases, which were shown after short newsreels. Coolidge, sensing that audiences wanted to see their president and know what he was doing, went out of his way to be in them—and his face adorned the big screen as often as, if not more than, big stars like Rudolph Valentino, Buster Keaton, Greta Garbo, and Claudette Colbert. While appearing not to seek publicity he sought it; "he was never too busy to be photographed," noted Jay Hayden of the *Detroit News*.[38] The so-called "photo op"—where aides arrange to have a president photographed in a picturesque or newsworthy setting—began not in the television age but with Calvin Coolidge's newsreels.

Then, as now, there were critics. One journalist found Coolidge's constant face time "nauseating" and said it was corrupting the system. "Cultured Americans wince at the thought of their president putting on a smock frock to pose while pitching hay and milking a bossy."[39] Substitute "playing golf" for "pitching hay" and the comments might be as relevant in the twenty-first century as they were in the twentieth.

Appearances notwithstanding, Calvin Coolidge was ultimately always more comfortable saying less—or nothing at all. On the morning of August 2, 1927, he was on vacation in Rapid City, South Dakota, accompanied by his usual contingent of reporters. It was the fourth anniversary of his swearing-in after Harding's death, and Coolidge was in a rare, expansive mood. The president spoke of his time in office: America was at peace. Wages were up. Taxes had been cut. The national debt was lower. It sounded like Coolidge was making his case to run for reelection the following year. He invited reporters to return at 12:00, teasing that "I may have a further statement to make."[40]

When reporters returned for what they thought would be their second news conference of the day, the president had a little surprise waiting for them. An hour before, he had written a terse message on a piece of paper and asked that twenty copies, on small slips of paper, be made for each reporter.[41] "I am going to hand these out myself," Coolidge said. "I am going to give them to the newspapermen, without comment, from this side of the desk." He instructed an aide to block the door "and not permit anyone to leave" until each had a copy "so that they may have an even chance."[42]

Looking at the assembled press, the president asked, "Is everybody here?" He then handed each one a slip of paper. Opening it, they found a terse bombshell:

I do not choose to run for President in nineteen twenty-eight.

The journalists were stunned. They asked the president if he would comment. "No," Coolidge said.

A stampede ensued, with reporters running out of the room to telephone or telegraph their story in. The president's dozen words, with no further comment or explanation, caused some fifty thousand words to be transmitted that day from Rapid City.[43]

Silent Cal Coolidge had struck again.

CHAPTER SIXTEEN

Franklin D. Roosevelt: The Fireside Chats

The Diplomatic Reception Room

In the twelve years and one month he was president, Franklin Delano Roosevelt gave nearly one thousand news conferences—usually unscripted and freewheeling—about one and a half per week. Reporters loved the constant interaction, bombarding FDR with questions and getting bombarded in return with answers and jokes. The president, who presided over these sessions from behind his desk with his cigarette holder pointed upward at a jaunty angle, gave as good as he got. He was what the newspapermen in those days called good copy; that FDR engaged so freely and frequently with them reflected the supreme confidence he projected at all times to a nation that, in the Depression-ravaged 1930s, sorely needed it.

But in contrast to the frequent and boisterous news conferences Franklin Roosevelt gave, it was just thirty highly scripted, thoroughly buttoned-down interactions that had the greatest impact on the nation. They were a series of groundbreaking radio talks the president gave—that quickly became known as the Fireside Chats. In harnessing the power, the intimacy, and the ubiquitousness of radio, Franklin D. Roosevelt transformed his presidency and the nation itself. He was the first true mass medium president, and his methods would be carefully studied by others who followed, notably John F. Kennedy and Ronald Reagan.

———

If anyone was ever destined to become president of the United States, it was Franklin Roosevelt. By blood or by marriage, he was related to an astonishing *eleven* of his predecessors: John Adams, James Madison, John Quincy Adams, Martin Van Buren, William Henry Harrison, Zachary Taylor, Andrew Johnson, Ulysses S. Grant, Benjamin Harrison, William Howard

Afflicted by polio, Franklin Roosevelt had an indoor swimming pool built after he became president in 1933, and used it daily. Connecting the mansion with the West Wing it is the site today of the press briefing room. HARRY S. TRUMAN LIBRARY AND MUSEUM

Taft, and his distant cousin Theodore Roosevelt.[1] FDR sometimes stayed in the mansion and joined TR for what must have been some of the most colorful and engaging dinner conversations ever held in the White House.[2]

A seven-year-old Franklin also had a rather odd encounter with a twelfth president. In 1889, FDR's father, a big donor to the Democratic Party, took his son to meet Grover Cleveland. The president put his hand on Franklin's head and said, "My little man, I am going to make a strange wish for you. May you never be President of the United States."[3] The wish backfired: FDR would be elected not twice, as Cleveland was, but an unprecedented four times—serving twelve years before dying just three months into his final term. Roosevelt must have thought Cleveland's remarks amusing. "Wouldn't you be President if you could?" he asked a friend years later. "Wouldn't anybody?"[4]

His career, in fact, was eerily similar to that of his famous presidential cousin Theodore. Both sailed through Harvard. Both were New York

With one of his beloved model ships behind him, Roosevelt delivers a Fireside Chat on September 6, 1936. FDR shrewdly limited his exposure to the American people, giving just thirty such radio talks in twelve years. His media mastery would be closely emulated by future presidents, notably John F. Kennedy and Ronald Reagan. LIBRARY OF CONGRESS

state lawmakers, assistant secretaries of the Navy, and New York governors. Each even ran for vice president on tickets led by one-time governors from Ohio: TR was forty-two when he ran with William McKinley in 1900; FDR was thirty-eight when he was Governor James Cox's running mate in 1920. In 1905 Franklin married his distant cousin, Eleanor. At the wedding, she was given away by her uncle, the sitting president, who slapped Franklin on the back and said "Well, Franklin, it's nice to keep the name in the family."[5]

Franklin and Eleanor Roosevelt certainly kept the White House in the family—or the other way around—when they moved into the mansion in 1933. Eleanor, the new first lady, was so familiar with her surroundings that

The White House press corps expanded during the Roosevelt years. Here, radio technicians set up equipment prior to what is believed to be the president's Fireside Chat concerning Nazi Germany's invasion of Poland in 1939. LIBRARY OF CONGRESS

she recognized workers who were still there from the TR era. Usher Ike Hoover, upon seeing her, greeted her as "Miss Eleanor."[6]

Familiarity aside, the last thing Eleanor Roosevelt wanted was to become first lady and live in the White House; she thought it would detract from her work as a social activist. "I never wanted to be the President's wife," she said.[7] But as Eleanor Roosevelt did throughout her life, she plunged in, determined to make the best of it. In the end, she would do much more than that. She would singularly redefine the role of first lady and set a standard for all who followed—that none have been able to match. While historians consistently rank Franklin Roosevelt as one of America's greatest presidents, they consistently rank Eleanor Roosevelt *the* greatest of first ladies, citing her advocacy for women's issues, overall public service, and as a political value to the president himself.[8]

The Roosevelts brought two vanloads of furniture from their home in Hyde Park, New York, along with an extended network of family and friends. Even with the extra room created by Theodore Roosevelt's 1902 expansion and Calvin Coolidge's a quarter-century later, it was crowded. So many celebrities visited that the White House became known as "Little Hollywood."[9] But boldfaced names weren't the only ones to receive an invitation. The first lady sometimes invited strangers in uniform she met on the street to stay in the mansion, and at times "didn't know who was sleeping down the hall." Sometimes there were more guests than bedrooms.[10]

In a rare gesture, the president invited one close confidant to live in the family quarters: Louis Howe, perhaps FDR's most trusted advisor in the early

One of the few photographs of President Roosevelt in a wheelchair. For a president who instilled such confidence in the American people, FDR himself was not confident enough to have his polio-afflicted body photographed this way. The Secret Service often seized cameras and ripped out film of anyone caught trying to do so. FRANKLIN D. ROOSEVELT PRESIDENTIAL LIBRARY AND MUSEUM

After taking office in 1933, Franklin D. Roosevelt expanded the West Wing and moved the presidential office to its current location on the southeast corner, where it would be more accessible for his wheelchair. Here is the Oval Office in 1934; FDR chose to keep the desk used by his predecessor, Herbert Hoover. The famous Resolute desk wouldn't be used in the Oval, until the Kennedy years. LIBRARY OF CONGRESS

stages of his administration. Howe had enough clout to ask—and receive—permission for him and his wife to sleep in the Lincoln bed, which was moved to their small bedroom under the North Portico. When Howe died in 1936, he was accorded a rare presidential honor: an East Room funeral.[11] Harry Hopkins, a key architect of the New Deal—the name that encompassed the many domestic programs of Roosevelt's economic recovery plan—would live in the mansion during World War II. Marguerite ("Missy") LeHand, the president's longtime secretary, also lived in the White House, in a small but pleasant room on the third floor that looked out over the South Lawn.[12]

Mrs. Roosevelt, in a rare move of her own, invited a female reporter, Lorena Hickok of the Associated Press, to live in the family quarters too.

Hickok, one of the nation's most prominent journalists, was given a bedroom on the northwest corner of the second floor.[13] Historians believe that Mrs. Roosevelt and "Hick darling," as she called her close friend, were lovers. The two women would travel together extensively during their White House years, often to meet ordinary Americans and listen to their troubles. The first lady's presence reinforced the public perception that Franklin and Eleanor Roosevelt cared about the common man—which, of course, they did.

The president and first lady themselves slept apart, continuing a practice that had been established many years before (sex was an "an ordeal to be borne," Eleanor reportedly told her daughter Anna).[14] Mrs. Roosevelt took what had traditionally been the presidential bedroom on the southwest corner of the second floor and turned it into her office, installing a narrow single bed in the adjacent dressing room. The president slept farther down the hall next to the Oval Room, which he used as a study.[15]

The Great Depression devastated the United States. At its darkest point—just as Roosevelt came to power—thirteen to fifteen million Americans were out of work and the unemployment rate was a staggering 24.9 percent. The stock market had plunged 89 percent from its 1929 peak, national income fell 60 percent, and millions lost their homes. As poverty soared, bread lines and soup kitchens sprouted; many scoured garbage cans for scraps to eat.[16] A popular song reflected the grim era: "Brother, can you spare a dime?" Few could.

Wasting no time—"this nation asks for action, and action now," he said in his inaugural address—Roosevelt skipped every inaugural ball thrown in his honor and got down to work. It was the beginning of a frantic 105 days in which he pushed fifteen major pieces of legislation through Congress. It was a "presidential barrage of ideas and programs," historian Arthur Schlesinger Jr. observed, "unlike anything known to American history." The sense of urgency was palpable; save Abraham Lincoln, no president ever entered office amid such dire conditions, and to this day every new president's first "100 days" are compared with Roosevelt's.

But busy as he was—and Depression or not—Roosevelt found the time and money to focus on creature comforts at the White House. His first summer in the mansion, 1933, must have been a sweltering one, for he ordered the installation of air-conditioning units in family quarters on the second floor.[17]

He also ordered that the mansion's electrical system be rewired, to support the many appliances and gadgets that were becoming part of American life. This included the installation of hotel-size electric ranges and ovens in the White House kitchen. Made of stainless steel, always polished and gleaming, they were the heart of what might have been the most modern and convenient kitchen in America. One of the smaller kitchens was converted into a pantry, complete with warming ovens; this room in turn was linked to the State Floor above it by an electric dumbwaiter and a narrow, twisting staircase for staff.[18]

The president also had an indoor swimming pool installed. Swimming was physical therapy for Roosevelt, who contracted polio in 1921 at the age of thirty-nine. A New York newspaper launched a fund-raising drive, raising $22,656.90—big money in 1933. A typical donation would be twenty-five or fifty cents from a class of schoolchildren.[19] The location was convenient enough: smack dab between the mansion and the West Wing, adjacent to Thomas Jefferson's famous colonnade. When work began, the space had been a combination of "laundry rooms, a Bouquet Room, black servants' dining room, Servant's Rooms all of which were in unsanitary, dilapidated condition," according to architect Lorenzo Winslow. As the hole for the pool was dug, Winslow discovered, about four feet down, remnants of James Monroe's stable.[20]

Even by today's standards, Roosevelt's pool was a marvel. It featured underwater lighting and sterilized water that circulated constantly to keep it fresh and clean. It was also steam-heated for winter use.[21] The room itself was a work of art. Walls originally designed by Thomas Jefferson were wainscoted with terra-cotta blocks of various shades of blue, and topped by half-moon–shaped windows. Sunlight streamed in, making the water glisten. Winslow also heightened the ceiling with an arch. There were two dressing rooms, and French doors that opened onto the Rose Garden.

The overall effect thrilled the president. "I want you men to know that this pool will be a big help to me, and it will be about the only air I can get. It will be one of the greatest pleasures for me during my stay in the White House."[22] FDR would use the pool every day, often more than once.[23]

Franklin Roosevelt was so impressed with Winslow's architectural acumen that he gave him a far more ambitious job: a redesign and expansion of the West Wing. The president, despite his busy schedule, was always sketching out new ideas for the White House; in the winter of 1934 he showed Winslow his plans.[24] The Oval Office, first built by William Howard Taft in

1909, stood in the center of the West Wing's south wall. Rebuilt by Herbert Hoover following a Christmas Eve fire in 1929, it lacked the privacy FDR wanted. Winslow, indulging his boss, suggested that his idea be even bigger, proposing an addition to the existing executive office building itself. The president loved the idea.[25]

But presidents don't always get their way. Roosevelt and Winslow, an employee of the new National Park Service, ran into opposition from both Congress and the federal bureaucracy; FDR was furious. In stepped Eleanor Roosevelt, who mollified all parties with a mediator of sorts: A new architect named Eric Gugler. Gugler came up with a new redesign for the West Wing, but got little help from the president[26]; FDR, perhaps sulking, retreated to Hyde Park while construction began in August 1934. Fighting over the project took longer than actual construction, which was finished in about three months.[27] "All of us were very happy," Gugler later wrote, "but I never was quite sure FDR was."[28]

Unlike prior additions to the White House complex, like the North and South Porticoes added a century before, most of Gugler's rebuilding of the West Wing is today largely invisible to the outside eye. He dug a huge hole in the ground, allowing for an entire new floor of offices; he also added a second story to the West Wing, set back from the ground floor and hidden behind a parapet.[29]

But Gugler's most prominent feature was the Oval Office itself. He moved it to the southeast corner of the West Wing, and bowing to the president's love of Georgian architecture, stripped it of the wood trim that had characterized the room since 1909. Pediments over doors were added; built-in bookcases were topped with fluted seashell coves.[30] The graceful oval space itself was twice as big as the prior presidential office: nearly thirty-six feet at its longest axis, twenty-nine feet at its shortest.

The ceiling, eighteen feet tall, featured a stunning medallion of the United States seal—a bald eagle clutching an olive branch in one talon and thirteen arrows in the other (the eagle's head is turned toward the olive branch to signify the preference for peace). The ceiling medallion and a white marble mantle over a fireplace are the only items today that were in the original Oval Office in 1909.[31] Other than furnishings selected by new presidents, the office essentially looks like it did in 1934.[32]

For Roosevelt, greater privacy was just one benefit of having the Oval Office moved. It was also an aesthetic improvement—it opened onto the Rose Garden and gave him a view of the mansion—and a physical one. The president, confined to the wheelchair the public never saw, could be pushed by aides or the Secret Service along the colonnade and rolled directly into his new workspace.

—⁓—

Franklin D. Roosevelt has generally been described by those who knew him as a supremely confident man. In terms of his ebullient personality and certitude that he was leading the Depression-scarred nation in the right direction, this is certainly so. But he was never confident enough to let the American people see him as he truly was: a disabled man who was largely dependent upon others to get around. Barely a dozen years after Woodrow Wilson was incapacitated, his true condition hidden from all but his wife and a handful of trusted aides, FDR cleverly hid his crippling paralysis as well. Americans rarely, if ever, saw their president as he truly was, either.

He asked the press not to photograph him in his wheelchair, and anyone who didn't comply often faced the wrath of the Secret Service. Agents who spotted a photographer taking pictures of Roosevelt struggling to get into a car would seize the camera and rip out the film. In 1946, a year after Roosevelt died, a survey of White House photographers revealed that anyone taking unauthorized photos "had their cameras emptied, their films exposed to sunlight, or their plates smashed." This for a president who frequently defended the First Amendment, which gave those photographers the right to take those very pictures.[33]

Americans could read of his affliction—the *New York Times* and *Time* magazine each mentioned it before he was sworn in (*Time* referred to FDR's "lameness")—but actual images of the president in a wheelchair are exceedingly rare. Of the thousands upon thousands of photos taken of America's longest-serving president, the FDR Library in Hyde Park, New York, has just three in its vast archives.[34]

Roosevelt was so determined to hide his affliction that even longtime White House aides were surprised to learn the truth. Longtime usher J. B. West encountered the president frequently when he began working in the White House in 1941. Yet the first time he saw him in a wheelchair he was shocked: "Startled, I looked down at him. It was only then that I realized that Franklin D. Roosevelt was really paralyzed."[35] Another time, Madame Chiang Kai-shek, wife of China's leader, was leaving an Oval Office meeting. "Please don't get up," she said. Roosevelt: "My dear child, I couldn't stand up if I had to."[36]

Yet FDR never complained about being crippled. Anyone who expressed sympathy to his condition was often cut off with a terse "No sob sister stuff";[37] the president simply didn't want to hear about it. He didn't want to speak about it either. He mentioned it but once, on March 1, 1945—six weeks before his death—in a speech to Congress. "I hope you will pardon me," he said, "for the unusual posture of sitting down during the presentation . . . but I know you realize that it makes it a lot easier for me in not having to carry about ten pounds of steel around on the bottom of my legs."[38]

That he endured such a debilitating illness for years, without complaint, while guiding the country through both its worst economic calamity and a world war is testament to the man's toughness, patience, and perseverance— among the most important qualities that any president of the United States could hope to possess.

Even though radio had been a powerful force long before he was first elected, Franklin D. Roosevelt was the first president to be truly associated with the medium. It broadcast the only electoral defeat Roosevelt would ever suffer, in 1920, when he ran as Cox's running mate. The Democrats were swamped by Warren Harding that year, who became the first sitting president to be heard on the radio; his successor, Calvin Coolidge, was the first president to take to the airwaves to address the nation. Nevertheless, it was Franklin Roosevelt, far savvier than his predecessors, who truly took advantage of radio's vast power.

He had spent the previous decade listening to his less skilled predecessors. Harding was bombastic. Coolidge was stiff. Hoover lacked dynamism.[39] FDR honed his skills as governor of New York, even using a stopwatch to stay exactly on time. When he became president, Roosevelt was thoroughly polished and comfortable behind the microphone. "You'll never have any trouble with me, I'm an old hand at this," he remarked to NBC's Carleton Smith before his first Fireside Chat. His performances— and that's what they were—were almost universally flawless.[40]

He made it seem easy, but behind the scenes, Roosevelt prepared meticulously. He spent days working on each speech, reading them aloud, getting the rhythm and feel just right. Aides asked if he was spending too much time preparing for his radio talks, which after all, were only a few minutes long. To the contrary, the president answered. Preparing for his radio appearances was probably the most important thing he could possibly do, he explained.[41] The president knew that some newspapers, such as the staunch Republican *Chicago Tribune,* opposed him; radio gave him the means to leapfrog his detractors and take his case directly to the American people.

The thought of speaking to millions was banished from his mind; instead Roosevelt imagined himself chatting with a single person, a poor farmer from Hyde Park. It forced him to keep things simple.[42] He used small words, spoke slowly, and called his vast audience "my friends." The overall effect was a congenial and conversational manner that conveyed warmth and trust. Prior presidents *addressed* Americans; Franklin Roosevelt *spoke* to them. In the previous 140 years, most Americans had never even seen a president; "now almost all of them were hearing him, *in their own homes.*"[43] It was electrifying.

FDR's first Fireside Chat was given on March 12, 1933—just eight days after he was sworn in. "I want to talk for a few minutes with the people of the United States about banking," he began. "I want to tell you what has been done in the last few days, and why it was done, and what the next steps are going to be." Fearing their local bank was about to go under, panicky Americans had been withdrawing their meager savings; Roosevelt declared a bank "holiday"—closing them temporarily until safeguards could be put in place. "I can assure you," the president said in his calm, confident tone, "that it is safer to keep your money in a reopened bank than under the mattress."[44] The rest was history.

The response was instantaneous and overwhelming. Sixty million Americans—half the population in 1933—tuned in. The very next day, newspapers reported long lines of people waiting to put their money back into their bank.[45] Americans trusted Franklin Roosevelt, and his administration, less than two weeks old, had passed its first crucial test. In Herbert Hoover's day, the White House usually got around five thousand letters a week. Under FDR the number swelled to fifty thousand. Some seventy workers were hired to handle the mail—a Depression-era jobs program in and of itself.[46] A typical letter to the president came from a Mr. Simon Miller:

> *I want to thank you for your visit at 10 o'clock Sunday night. I can see you seated in the big armchair in my living room, pipe in mouth and talking on the crisis that confronts us all, telling me in words that I could understand what you had done and the reasons for your action.*
>
> *You are the first President to come into our homes. . . . Until last night, to me, the President of the United States was merely a legend, a picture to look at. . . . But you are real.*[47]

Perhaps the ultimate arbiter of how "it played in Peoria" came from one of the most famous Americans of the era, the movie star/newspaper columnist Will Rogers, who praised Roosevelt's first chat as a "home run." In his column the next day, Rogers said FDR's "message was not only a great comfort to the people, but it pointed a lesson to all radio announcers and public speakers what to do with a big vocabulary, leave it at home in the dictionary . . . he made everybody understand it, even the bankers."[48] After the haughty Warren Harding, the laconic Calvin Coolidge, and the humorless Herbert Hoover, Americans finally had a president who possessed that most powerful of political gifts: the common touch.

Ironically, the very problem Roosevelt focused on in most of his chats in the 1930s—the Depression—had helped to make his audience larger. When the economic collapse began in 1929, the average price of a radio sold in the United States was $139, about 2 percent of the average US salary that year ($6,132).[49] By 1933, when he was sworn in, incomes had plunged by half, but the price of radios had fallen even more,[50] thus making them more affordable. Depression or not, Americans bought radios: One-third of households owned one in 1929; four years later, three-fifths did.[51]

The sheer size of the audience, and the impact Roosevelt's initial Fireside Chats had on the nation, prompted calls for more. But the media-savvy president understood something that others failed to grasp: Less was more. Fewer appearances before the nation would convey greater drama and attract more attention when he did appear, or so he believed, and he was right. "I don't want the Boss to do very much," his press secretary Steve Early said. "We want to conserve him."[52]

The president timed his Fireside Chats to coincide with great events of the day. America was preoccupied with two life-and-death issues during his dozen years in office—the Great Depression and World War II—and with one or two exceptions, they were the only subjects Roosevelt ever spoke of. Between that first chat and the last, on June 12, 1944—six days after US and Allied troops invaded Nazi-occupied France—he would speak to the nation every four or five months, and that was it. The contrast between the two subjects—depression and war—could not have been more stark. Franklin Roosevelt began with an America on its knees, its economy in shambles. He ended with it an economic, military, and political colossus, standing astride the globe, dominant to an extent never seen before—or since.

CHAPTER SEVENTEEN

Harry Truman:
"The Moon, the Stars, and All the Planets"

The Rebuilding of the White House

EIGHT PRESIDENTS HAVE DIED IN OFFICE. FOUR WERE ASSASSINATED, FOUR died of natural causes.[1] When a sitting president passes away, Article II, Section I, Clause VI of the Constitution says his duties "shall evolve" on the person who is always just a heartbeat away from the top job—the vice president. The most recent example of this is Lyndon Johnson, who was sworn in aboard a stifling Air Force One on November 22, 1963, just two hours after the murder of John F. Kennedy. It was a stunning moment, frozen in time by a photo of LBJ taking the oath of office with a blood-stained Jacqueline Kennedy standing to his left, her face a classic portrait etched in grief.

But dramatic as LBJ's ascension to power was, perhaps no vice president has ever assumed the presidency under more trying circumstances, facing a greater immediate burden, than Harry Truman.

On April 12, 1945, Americans were jolted by news of the sudden death of President Franklin D. Roosevelt. FDR had been president for an astonishing twelve years—the only president many Americans had ever known, a man who guided them through America's greatest economic crisis and its greatest war. Now, like a bolt from the blue, he was gone.

Like everyone else, Truman was caught off guard. On Capitol Hill that afternoon, having a drink in the private hideaway of House Speaker Sam Rayburn, he was told to call the White House at once. He dialed National 1414 and identified himself ("this is the V.P.") and was asked to come to the White House as quickly and quietly as possible. "Jesus Christ and General Jackson," he said.[2]

Driven by a lone aide, and with no security, he arrived at the mansion within minutes—it was 5:25 p.m.[3]—and was escorted upstairs to the second

Forty-two months after Pearl Harbor and a week after atomic bombs were dropped on Hiroshima and Nagasaki, the moment Americans had been waiting for: President Truman, in the Oval Room, announcing the surrender of Japan on August 14, 1945. HARRY S. TRUMAN LIBRARY AND MUSEUM

floor. Expecting to meet the president, he was greeted by the first lady, Eleanor Roosevelt. She placed his hand on Truman's shoulder.

"Harry, the President is dead."

After a long pause, Truman asked, "Is there anything I can do for you?"

"Is there anything *we* can do for *you*?" she replied. "For you are the one in trouble now."[4]

This was the world that the bespectacled man from Independence, Missouri, inherited: In April 1945 the United States was fighting all-out wars in both Europe and the Pacific. Japan was crumbling, Hitler's Nazi empire had been reduced to a Berlin bunker, and the curtain was rising on something that would dominate America's foreign policy for the next half-century: the Cold War.

The Truman reconstruction meant an entire gutting of the White House. In this May 17, 1950, photo, walls are supported only by a web of temporary steel supports. The exterior walls rest on new concrete underpinnings, which allow earth-moving equipment to dig a new basement. HARRY S. TRUMAN LIBRARY AND MUSEUM

There was also this: In a dusty, quiet corner of New Mexico, scientists and engineers were nearing completion of the first atomic bomb. Within months, a decision on whether to use the terrible weapon would have to be made. Deliberately kept in the dark by FDR, Truman didn't even know about the Manhattan Project—the crash effort to build the bomb—until half an hour after he was sworn in as president. It was more than enough for any president. Truman, who had no foreign policy experience, was initially overwhelmed with his crushing new responsibilities.

The next day the new president told reporters: "I felt like the moon, the stars, and all the planets had fallen on me."[5]

—◆—

When President Truman and his wife, Bess—perhaps the most reluctant first lady in history—moved in on May 7, 1945, the White House could best be described as shabby. Walls sported dust and grime. Draperies were rotting, carpets and rugs were rutted by years of being trampled upon.[6]

A White House usher, J. B. West, was assigned to show Mrs. Truman around. He later said he was embarrassed to do so, since the mansion looked like an "abandoned hotel." It seems the Roosevelts hadn't even bothered to spend the $50,000 allocated to each new administration to spend on furnishings and decor. That even the Trumans, a rather modest couple, considered their personal quarters run-down attests to just how dilapidated the proud White House had become.[7]

But aesthetics were the least of it. Within a week after the Japanese attack on Pearl Harbor in December 1941, the Secret Service, conducting a security review of the White House, concluded that the mansion was structurally weak and vulnerable to fire.[8] Floors sagged, and the plaster walls needed patching up. There were scores of other problems that "no longer spoke of venerability, but of danger."[9]

But by the time the Trumans moved in three and a half years later, little had been done. The all-encompassing focus on the war had trumped other concerns; shoring up the White House could wait. But Mrs. Truman could not. She quickly ordered a thorough scrubbing of walls and a paint job. For her bedroom and study—the same rooms used on the southwest corner of the second floor by Eleanor Roosevelt—she selected lavender and gray paint. The president's bedroom down the hall was redone in green and blue. The Oval Room in between—once the site of Warren Harding's booze-filled card

Unthinkable today: Each morning Truman took a brisk walk on Washington's streets. Nervous Secret Service agents rigged traffic lights to turn green so he wouldn't have to stop. When the president found out, he complained that they were ruining his walks. HARRY S. TRUMAN LIBRARY AND MUSEUM

games and most recently FDR's study—was redone in beige. President Truman would use this for his study as well.[10]

The president himself made an important contribution to the family quarters. He ordered that bedroom furnishings that had been selected by Mary Lincoln, which had been in a bedroom on the northwest side of the second floor, be moved to what had been President Lincoln's office on the southwest corner. This room has since been known as the Lincoln Bedroom.[11] In turn, the room where Mrs. Lincoln's furniture had been now became a bedroom for twenty-one-year-old Margaret Truman—the First Couple's only child. It was painted "raspberry pink."[12]

"If I live to be a hundred years old, I'll never forget the day that I was first told about the atomic bomb," Truman wrote in his memoirs. "It was about 7:30 p.m. on the evening of April 12, 1945, just hours after Franklin Roosevelt had died at 3:35 p.m., and no more than half an hour after I was sworn in as president at 7:09 p.m. Henry L. Stimson, who was Roosevelt's secretary of war and then mine, took me aside and reminded me that Roosevelt had authorized the development of a sort of super bomb and that that bomb was almost ready."[13] It was "a new explosive of almost unbelievable destructive power."[14]

Truman realized he alone would soon have to make a tremendous decision, one that no other human being in history had ever been forced to contemplate: whether to actually use such a terrible weapon. On April 25, the new commander in chief held a secret meeting in the Oval Office with Stimson and Maj. Gen. Leslie Groves, the man in charge of the Manhattan Project. Groves snuck into the White House through a back door. Truman said, "Stimson handed me a memorandum that said, 'Within four months we shall in all probability have completed the most terrible weapon ever known in human history, one bomb which could destroy a whole city.'"[15] The president signed off on a recommendation to form a group called the Interim Committee, which would study the merits of using the bomb and offer advice accordingly.[16]

When Franklin Roosevelt first ordered the Manhattan Project in 1941, he did so out of fear. A letter signed by the prominent physicist Albert Einstein, who had fled Hitler's Germany in 1933, warned that the Nazis were racing to develop an atomic bomb of their own.[17] But now, with Germany's surrender on May 8, 1945, the focus shifted to Japan. Truman and the Interim Committee placed their decision within these parameters: What was the quickest way to end the war in the Pacific, while minimizing American— and Japanese—casualties, which were mounting as US forces clawed their way closer to the Japanese mainland?

The numbers were horrendous. The Japanese were self-proclaimed fanatical warriors who would fight to the death rather than surrender; in thirty-five days of vicious fighting on the tiny island of Iwo Jima in February and March, nearly seven thousand Americans were killed and twenty thousand wounded.[18] As the Interim Committee weighed its options, American casualties were piling up on another island, Okinawa, just 340 miles from Japan. Over eighty-three days, an estimated twelve thousand American servicemen were killed; another thirty-six thousand were wounded, in what was the bloodiest battle for the United States in the entire Pacific War.[19] The president, who closely monitored casualty reports each day, agonized at the growing bloodshed.

On June 18th, three days before the Battle of Okinawa ended, Truman met with his Joint Chiefs of Staff to discuss Operation Olympic—the invasion of Japan itself. Its chairman, Gen. George C. Marshall, gave the president sobering estimates of American casualties: 250,000 killed, 500,000 wounded. Truman was horrified: "The statistics that the generals gave me were as frightening as the news of the big bomb," he wrote. "I could not bear this thought, and it led to the decision to use the atomic bomb."[20]

On July 16th, deep in the New Mexico desert, a blinding flash of light "with the intensity many times that of the midday sun"[21] overwhelmed the dawn sky.[22] Observers ten miles away saw a massive fireball, felt a "blinding heat,"[23] and forty seconds later heard a thunderous roar; a massive shock wave was felt ninety miles beyond that.[24] A vast cloud, assuming the shape of a giant mushroom, quickly soared nearly eight miles into the air. "I am become death, the destroyer of worlds," J. Robert Oppenheimer, the Manhattan Project's top scientist intoned, quoting an ancient Hindu scripture.[25]

Five days later, the committee discussed exploding such a bomb over an isolated area of Japan, sparing casualties while demonstrating its fearsome power. "Reluctantly, we decided against that as well," Truman said, "feeling that that just wouldn't be enough to convince the fanatic Japanese."[26]

Dropping the bomb would end the war sooner, its members concluded, thus saving hundreds of thousands of American lives and a far greater number of Japanese lives. Even then, however, Stimson broadened the discussion beyond numbers and timetables, and talked about the bomb in terms of future generations and the impact (and threat) this ghastly new weapon would have. It was necessary, he said, to think of the atomic bomb not "as a new weapon merely but as a revolutionary change in the relations of man to the universe."[27] He quoted O. C. Brewster, an engineer on the Manhattan Project, who had written Stimson, urging him not to use the bomb: It might mean, Brewster had warned, "the doom of civilization."[28][29]

Moved as he was by Brewster's letter, Stimson was not swayed enough to agree. He recommended to the president that the only way to get Japan to surrender was to give it "a tremendous shock which would carry convincing proof of our power to destroy the Empire. Such an effective shock would save many times the number of lives, both American and Japanese, that it would cost."[30] The commander in chief accepted the recommendation.

Truman made one final attempt to get the Japanese to surrender. But a July 29th plea was rejected and the commander in chief issued the momentous order, sealing the fate of at least one of four targets that had been selected: Hiroshima, Kokora, Nagasaki, and Niigata—all cities thought to be heavy military manufacturing areas.[31] On August 6th, at 8:15 a.m. local time, Hiroshima was destroyed in the blink of an eye. Three days later, a second bomb fell on Nagasaki. The Japanese surrendered on August 15th (August 14th in the US), bringing history's most devastating conflict to an end.

Between the initial blast, burns, and exposure to radiation, the atomic bombings of Hiroshima and Nagasaki killed 210,000 people by the end of 1945 and 340,000 within five years—mostly civilians.[32] Horrific as they were, the bombs appeared to do what the Interim Committee and Truman determined they would do: save more lives than they took, and hasten the war's end. The Soviets' entry into the war in the Pacific on August 9th,[33] the day of the Nagasaki bombing, also influenced the Japanese decision to surrender, but Emperor Hirohito specifically referred to "a new and most cruel bomb" in his surrender proclamation.[34]

In the decades since Hiroshima and Nagasaki, it has been argued that the atomic bomb was so devastating, so morally wrong, that its use would surely open a Pandora's box of horrors for future generations. Truman always dismissed such hand-wringing. "I couldn't worry what history would say about my personal morality," he said in a 1965 speech. "I made the only decision I ever knew how to make. I did what I thought was right," he said.[35]

With the war finally over and the Great Depression a thing of the past, Truman turned to lesser matters—namely, the White House itself. Deciding that the West Wing was too small, too crowded, and unsuitable for the leader of the free world, he asked architect Lorenzo Winslow to design a large addition for it. The design called for a fifteen-thousand-square-foot extension extending south along West Executive Avenue. It would include an auditorium, working space for the White House press corps, and a staff cafeteria. It would also feature two semicircular protrusions from the new building, jutting out like the Oval Office.[36]

Congress approved the president's request and appropriated funds, and the project was set to begin—until Winslow said in an interview that it would be an extension to "the West Wing of the White House." This gave the public the false impression that the addition would transform the mansion itself. A public uproar ensued, and Congress—over Truman's objections—withdrew the funds.[37]

But Truman did want to change the White House proper. Inspired by a visit to the Jefferson-designed University of Virginia campus, he decided that the South Portico could use a balcony. Not only would it make the White House more attractive, he thought, it would make the private quarters of the First Family more comfortable.[38] The president quickly ran into opposition again. A balcony, however comfortable, would constitute a major change to the mansion.[39] The president pushed back, arguing that Jefferson himself had intended for such a balcony to be built. But Truman later admitted he was just presuming what Jefferson wanted: "Whether he designed it or not . . . I don't know, but his design came from those southern mansions at the time, which always had a portico."[40]

Truman appears to have been mistaken. Jefferson's papers contain no reference to a balcony, nor was any reference to one made by his architect, Benjamin Latrobe.[41] On the other hand, the South and North Porticoes that they had envisioned (and added by James Monroe and Andrew Jackson, respectively)[42] were not part of the original design for the President's House, either. Historical inaccuracy aside, the president, whose West Wing expansion had been thwarted, was determined to have his way this time. He ordered work begun in late 1947, and it was finished the next spring. Every president who has followed has certainly enjoyed the balcony, with its magnificent views and summer shade.

—⁓—

When he ascended to the presidency in 1945, Truman was more than jittery. "I won't deny that, at first, I felt plenty of fear myself at the added and overwhelming responsibilities that had come to me so quickly,"[43] he wrote.

He wasn't the only one. Others also wondered, at first, whether he was up to the job. This doubt was rooted largely in the fact that Truman, despite being in the Senate for a decade before being elevated to the vice presidency in 1944, was still a relative unknown. The last president who never went to college, he was portrayed in some quarters as a simple country boy who lacked the education, refinement, and bearing that a president should have.[44] Senior military officers who were long used to dealing with the only commander in chief many of them had ever known, Franklin Roosevelt, also had doubts. FDR's longtime chief of staff, Adm. William Leahy, initially considered Truman too soft,[45] while Marshall, the tough

US Army Chief of Staff, wondered aloud whether he could stand up to Soviet leader Josef Stalin. "We shall not know what he is really like until the pressure begins to be felt," he told colleagues after first meeting with the new president.[46]

Such perceptions were short-lived. His plain, earthy talk and common-man style came to be widely admired, and belied the fact that while Truman wasn't formally educated, he was a voracious reader, highly intelligent, and quite cultured. Lacking in flash or pretense, he was steeped in those most cherished of American values: hard work, decency, and loyalty. Coming after a president who was largely confined to a wheelchair and only able to move about with great difficulty, America embraced Truman's boundless energy; he took brisk morning walks around Washington each morning,[47] no matter the weather, and routinely worked up to eighteen hours a day.[48] A World War I Army officer, the president stood ramrod straight and wore suits "tailored to his trim build, ties (the former haberdasher owned no fewer than 489)[49] tied perfectly, handkerchiefs folded carefully, trousers creased sharply."[50] Above all, those who knew him best said he was a leader who possessed "courage, decisiveness and fundamental honesty."[51]

He was also charming and gregarious. From a social standpoint, the White House had been rather quiet since 1939. There had been the occasional dinner or reception, but the focus on the war was such that entertaining simply was not a priority. The Trumans changed this. In September 1946, the White House announced that the president and first lady would hold a series of events on Tuesday nights, beginning with a dinner for the diplomatic corps and ending with a reception for members of Congress.[52]

But the 1946–47 social season would be the only one the Trumans would hold in the White House. The president, and others, had begun to worry about the physical state of the mansion.

It had been 130 years since the White House was rebuilt following the British attack and fire of 1814. While old homes always creaked, Truman sensed something different about this one.[53] He noticed the chandeliers in the Blue Room and East Room actually swayed a bit.[54] He joked that ghosts were roaming about the mansion, but there were genuine concerns that the White House could actually collapse.[55] In January 1948, the president asked that engineers and architects inspect the mansion; they soon discovered the second floor—the private quarters of the First Family—was greatly overstressed. The president's oval study was a particular worry; it was recommended that no more than fifteen people be allowed in the room at any one time.[56] "The White House wouldn't pass the safety standards of any city in the country," Public Buildings Commissioner W. E. Reynolds later said.[57]

This led to a broader study of the entire mansion; Congress quickly appropriated $50,000. No sooner had the study began than a leg of Margaret Truman's piano broke through two floorboards, sending plaster crashing down onto the family dining room on the ground floor.[58] Architects found that a support beam below her room had broken in two—and that the ceiling above the dining room had dropped by eighteen inches.[59]

There were fears that the president's bedroom was sinking; for his safety, Truman was asked to sleep in the Lincoln bedroom.[60] The president himself noticed that his private bathtub was also sinking into the floor.[61] The Red Room was below; he joked that he might fall into an event below wearing nothing but his reading glasses. The entire White House was literally beginning to fall apart; it would have to be gutted and completely rebuilt.

The administration kept this from the public until after the election of 1948. "Can you imagine what the press would have done with this story?" Margaret Truman asked. "The White House would have been a metaphor for his collapsing administration."[62] Thus the Trumans lived quietly for months amid steel pipes propping up the second floor, while the president, a heavy underdog against New York governor Thomas Dewey, fought to keep his job.

Returning from Missouri following his stunning come-from-behind election victory, the president was met at the White House by usher J. B. West. "I'm afraid you're going to have to move out right away," he told the boss. "Doesn't that beat all!" Truman said. "Here we've worked ourselves to death trying to stay in this jailhouse and they kick us out anyway!"[63]

The White House announced it would be closed to tourists "because of its precarious physical condition."[64] The First Family moved into the historic Blair House at 1651 Pennsylvania Avenue, probably on November 21st; it was to be their home for the next three and a half years—until March 27, 1952.[65]

———

With the Trumans living across the street, the public finally learned just how bad a shape the mansion was in. The president, sworn in on January 20th, would leave Blair House each morning and make the three-minute walk across Pennsylvania Avenue and down West Executive Avenue to the West Wing, which was still open for business.

Some lawmakers floated the idea of completely razing the White House and starting over. An idea first raised during the Grant Administration surfaced again: Why not build a permanent home for the president elsewhere and turn the mansion into a museum? Truman fiercely opposed these ideas. "I'll do anything in my power to keep them from tearing down the White House," he vowed.

After much debate, Winslow's initial recommendation won out: The entire mansion would be gutted, leaving intact only the original stone walls, the third floor that had been installed during the administration of Calvin Coolidge, and the roof.[66] In short, a brand-new house would be built within the walls of the old one.[67]

Winslow supervised the day-to-day work. But the president made it clear to all that any major decisions would be made by him alone. Records show he made quite detailed decisions throughout the long rebuilding process. With the exception of George Washington, who approved the mansion's original design, no president would have a greater influence on the White House as the world knows it today than Harry Truman.

Furniture, artwork, bric-a-brac, everything in the mansion was carefully catalogued and moved, and after six months of meticulous planning, workers began tearing the White House down on December 7, 1949.[68] Where Jefferson, Lincoln, and two Roosevelts once trod, dump trucks and bulldozers now rumbled and cranes lifted steel into place. Trucks hauled away debris for three weeks, reducing what had been the grandest home in all the land to a dirt-stained shell propped up by a cobweb of support beams. The president, like an excited little boy, reveled in it all, giving tours and watching the small army of construction workers scurry about.[69]

The excavations and installation of a steel frame took a year to complete. By Christmas 1950, actual construction began.[70] One critical phase involved bringing the mansion's "inadequate and obsolete"[71] plumbing, electrical, heating, and cooling systems up to date.

After Japan's sneak attack on Pearl Harbor, an underground bomb shelter had been installed below the East Wing. Although adequate at the time, the forty-foot-by-forty-foot enclosure, which featured concrete ceilings nine feet thick,[72] was judged insufficient for the new nuclear age. The Soviets had just tested their first nuclear weapon after all, and the president needed something more sufficient.

Construction of the shelter took ninety-five days, 150 tons of gravel, one thousand tons of steel, and 3,030 cubic yards of concrete.[73] But even today key details, including architectural renderings of the shelter, continue to be withheld from the public.[74][75]

Even as the mansion was modernized, Winslow respectfully adhered to the past. His goal was for the new White House to reflect the spirit and wishes of the Federal era and the home's original creators, James Hoban and George Washington. He was determined to reuse as much of the original building as he could—original moldings, every window sash, every door knob and so forth.[76] Many things could not be reused, however, and were sold to the public as souvenirs (turning a $10,000 profit).[77] But there was waste too: As the pace of construction sped up to meet the president's deadline—Truman wanted to move in by Christmas 1951—many treasures wound up in a Virginia landfill: pine flooring, doors, door frames, and plaster moldings (after they had been cast for reproduction).[78]

As usual with a project of such scope, there were complications. The Korean War, which had begun in June 1950, caused steel shortages. Plasterers went on strike. These and other matters delayed construction and pushed up costs, forcing Truman and the commission overseeing the project to ask Congress for more money to finish the job.

The president would have more than his share of irritation before all was said and done. But given the perilous condition the mansion had been in, Truman knew he couldn't gripe too much. "My heart trembles when I think of the disasters we might have had—big receptions we used to hold, of fourteen hundred and sixteen hundred people downstairs, none of them knowing that a hundred and eighty tons might drop on their heads at any moment," he told one visitor. "All I can say is God must have been looking out for us."[79]

Even with some 250 men on the job working six days a week,[80] the president's Christmas deadline would not be met. Having all but announced that he would not run for reelection in 1952, Truman very much wanted to spend a full year in the mansion before departing. He set a new deadline of April 1st.

Late in the afternoon on March 27, 1952, President and Mrs. Truman returned from a week's vacation in Key West. As their car turned off Pennsylvania Avenue and passed through the White House's black iron gates, bystanders applauded and welcomed them home. Lights glistened in the mansion as dusk yielded to evening; the Trumans were escorted inside through the North Portico. After 1,222 days, the president of the United States was back in the White House.[81]

While the outside remained virtually untouched, the mansion's interior had changed dramatically. The number of rooms doubled from about sixty-five to 132, with much of the new space dug into two new sub-basements. One significant alteration: The grand staircase off the central foyer, which led to the private quarters in the second floor, had been widened and elevated, allowing Truman and future presidents to make their entrance in dramatic fashion.[82] The gleaming marble floor sported a long red chenille carpet, which ran the entire length of the Cross Hall, linking the State Dining Room with the East Room, which was reduced a bit in size and given a lemon-gold splendor.[83]

The Green Room was enhanced with yellow gold, rose, and blue, and featured a rug with the presidential seal first used during the Coolidge Administration.[84] The Red Room was accented with pinkish-white sofas and chairs. Between them, the elegant Blue Room, with its graceful oval shape, sported royal blue, with walls trimmed in white.[85]

At the end of the long Cross Hall stood the State Dining Room. Its dark oak paneling was gone, replaced with soft green paint. Hanging above the mantle, in which John Adams's famous benediction was carved, was an elegant painting of Abraham Lincoln by George P. A. Healy. It hangs there to this day. "With all the trouble and worry, it is worth it," Truman wrote in his diary that night. Architect Winslow and engineers told him the White House would last another five hundred years.[86]

The grand project—all $5,832,000 of it—was finally complete.[87] Before entering that evening, the Trumans presided over a small ceremony under the North Portico, where he was presented with a gold key in a leather box. The box was inscribed:

In a free society, the key to a man's house symbolizes his and his family's rights to those privacies and freedoms which are the heart and sinews of the American way of life. This key and the lock it operates are the products of the skills and ingenuity of American men and women living and working safe in their liberties. With God's help, may it ever be so![88]

CHAPTER EIGHTEEN

John F. Kennedy: The Blood Red Carpet

The Oval Office

PRIOR TO 1960, AMERICANS WERE ACCUSTOMED TO PRESIDENTS WHO WERE old (Dwight Eisenhower), not particularly glamorous (Harry Truman), or ill (Franklin Roosevelt). First ladies were also older, somewhat bland, and—with the exception of Eleanor Roosevelt—not particularly interested in doing much more than attending to their husband's needs. Then John and Jacqueline Kennedy moved into the White House and everything changed.

Not only was John Fitzgerald Kennedy, at forty-three, the youngest man ever elected president, he was twenty-seven years younger than his predecessor, Eisenhower (Ike called his successor "the boy").[1] Kennedy was fabulously wealthy, oozed charm, and was, to use one of his favorite words, full of vigor. His wife was probably the most beautiful of first ladies, glamorous, sophisticated, and a trendsetter at thirty-one. She looked and dressed like a model, and the "Jackie look" was closely followed on both sides of the Atlantic.[2] The new First Couple also had a very young family: a daughter, three-year-old Caroline, and a son, John Jr., born two weeks after his father's election. Suddenly the White House was home to the youngest First Family since the days of Theodore Roosevelt—a president few Americans remembered—and much of the nation was captivated.

The fascination has endured to the present day. With the exception of Abraham Lincoln, no president has been the subject of more books. But much of this interest concerns not so much how Kennedy lived but how he died: suddenly, in broad daylight, in the most shocking and brutal manner imaginable.

The final, awful day of the Kennedy administration—November 22, 1963—has, in many respects, overshadowed the 1,035 days that preceded it. That single day made John F. Kennedy, as his wife put it, "a legend when he

As John F. Kennedy claps, Caroline Kennedy and John F. Kennedy Jr. dance in the Oval Office. This charming October 10, 1962, photo reflects the juxtaposition of the White House as both workplace of the president of the United States and a home where people live. JOHN F. KENNEDY PRESIDENTIAL LIBRARY AND MUSEUM

would have preferred to be a man."[3] But the way she comported herself in those dark hours would make her a legend as well.

That television helped propel John F. Kennedy into the White House cannot be doubted. In his first crucial debate with Vice President Richard Nixon, Kennedy lost—at least those listening on radio thought so. But to the far bigger audience (sixty-six million) watching on TV—the first-ever debate between presidential nominees of the two major political parties—Kennedy was the clear victor. The dashing young senator, sporting a suntan, came off as attractive, calm, and charismatic, while Nixon, who was ill and looked it, sweated profusely and looked decidedly nervous. Simply put, Kennedy looked presidential, and any advantage the better known, more experienced VP had

Discovering that many furnishings in the White House had come from a New York discount store, Jacqueline Kennedy vowed to restore the mansion's "authenticity." She asked citizens in possession of any authentic furnishings to donate them to the White House—and they did. Shown here: a silver pitcher presented to her on December 5, 1961. JOHN F. KENNEDY PRESIDENTIAL LIBRARY AND MUSEUM

was swept away. Although there were two additional debates, it was that first clash in Chicago on September 26, 1960, that changed the tenor of the race—and the presidency itself.

The debates confirmed the ascendancy of television. JFK and television both came into their own at the same time—and were made for each other. "He was its first great political superstar; as he made television bigger, it made him bigger,"[4] and newspaper and radio reporters in the White House press corps quickly learned that the pecking order had changed.

One of the first things Kennedy did in the White House was to ask how many Fireside Chats Franklin Roosevelt had given. Learning that there were just thirty in a dozen years validated JFK's view that he should keep his appearances on TV—as FDR did with radio—to a minimum, thus maximizing their drama and impact. Knowing he could go on TV whenever he wanted, he often declined to do so. He was not eager, he told an aide, to become too familiar or a bore to the American people.[5] It was a lesson in restraint that modern presidents have, to their detriment, failed to grasp.

Jacqueline Bouvier Auchincloss was eleven when she first saw the White House in 1941, deep into the Roosevelt years, when her mother took Jackie and her sister to tour the nation's capital. Strolling through the rooms on the

Among the treasures returned to the White House during Mrs. Kennedy's restoration of the mansion were three chairs that James Monroe had ordered from a French designer. She placed them where Monroe did—in the Blue Room on the ground floor (called the "Elliptical Saloon") in Monroe's day. JOHN F. KENNEDY PRESIDENTIAL LIBRARY AND MUSEUM

ground floor, young Jacqueline was not impressed. Years later she recalled feeling "strangely let down. It seemed rather bleak; there was nothing in the way of a booklet to take away, nothing to teach one more about that great house and the presidents who had lived there."[6] Little did she know that two decades later, she would call the great mansion home, the third-youngest first lady to grace its halls.

Kennedy's frustration with the information he received during the Bay of Pigs crisis led him to create the Situation Room in May 1961. It allowed him to receive the same raw data that the CIA and Defense and State Departments got—and in real time. The bowling alley that stood on the site was moved to the Executive Office Building next door. JOHN F. KENNEDY PRESIDENTIAL LIBRARY AND MUSEUM

After her husband's election, she toured the mansion again, this time with Mamie Eisenhower. By now, this elegant habitué of finishing schools, Park Avenue, and Paris was even harder to impress. She concluded rather quickly that the White House was as she had remembered it: dowdy and unsophisticated. Its interiors, she thought, were far from suitable for a building that represented the American people and their nation's rich cultural heritage.

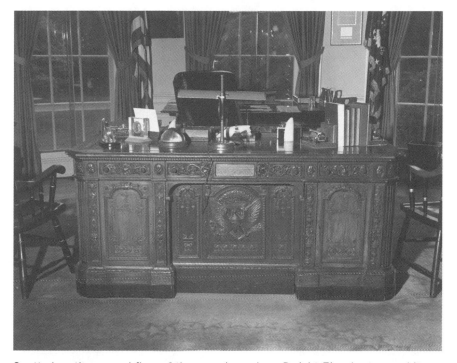

Spotted on the ground floor of the mansion, where Dwight Eisenhower used it for TV broadcasts, Mrs. Kennedy moved the Resolute desk to the Oval Office for the first time. It is today the most famous piece of furniture in the White House. Given to Rutherford B. Hayes by Queen Victoria in 1879, it has been the desk of choice for Presidents Jimmy Carter, Ronald Reagan, Bill Clinton, George W. Bush, and Barack Obama. JOHN F. KENNEDY PRESIDENTIAL LIBRARY AND MUSEUM

"Oh, God. It's the worst place in the world," she told a friend. "So cold and dreary. A dungeon. . . . I've never seen anything like it. I can't bear the thought of moving in. I hate it, I hate it, hate it."[7] Her remarks revealed more about Mrs. Kennedy's taste than the mansion itself, which, less than a decade after the Truman renovation, was in fine shape.

Specifically, Mrs. Kennedy had discovered that many of the furnishings and decor of the Truman and Eisenhower eras were reproductions of period pieces. They had been selected for financial reasons, which was unacceptable to a woman for whom the word "budget" was anathema. "It looks like it's been furnished by discount stores," she complained. "It looks like a house where nothing has ever taken place. There is no trace of the past."[8]

Jacqueline Kennedy did not get around to redecorating the Oval Office until November 1963. In the most tragic of ironies, the carpet she selected—a deep blood red—was installed on November 22—as the Kennedys were making their way to Dallas. This picture was taken the day after the president's assassination—hours after his coffin was placed in the East Room. JOHN F. KENNEDY PRESIDENTIAL LIBRARY AND MUSEUM

The White House, Jacqueline Kennedy felt, should not just *appear* grand—it must be authentically so. She vowed not to redecorate it but to restore it.[9] She was right about the discount store quip: Most of the White House's furnishings she encountered in 1961 had come from a New York department store.[10]

Armed with the $50,000 given by Congress to new First Families, Mrs. Kennedy began with the living quarters on the second floor. Rooms were brightened up. Art borrowed from museums was hung. She sent for furnishings from their Georgetown home. She ended the tradition of First Families taking all their meals in a dining room on the ground floor, creating one on the second floor where they actually lived—in the same room where Abraham Lincoln's autopsy and embalming were performed. A small adjacent room on the northwest corner was converted into a kitchen. Aside from the convenience of having a kitchen within their living quarters, it gave the young mother of two additional privacy for her family.[11]

The Oval Room on the second floor, used by Franklin Roosevelt and Harry Truman as a private study, was converted into a drawing room for the president to entertain visitors.[12] In this respect it resembled the Oval Room of the 1920s, when Warren Harding held his high-stakes card games while First Lady Flossie Harding mixed drinks. Furniture from eighteenth-century France was donated for the room, which became the first lady's favorite.[13]

As for her desire to restore "authenticity" to the White House, Mrs. Kennedy left the Lincoln Bedroom—where the sixteenth president had his office—alone. It was, she felt, "the one room in the house with a link to the past."[14] For the rest of the mansion, she formed a Fine Arts Committee to advise her on the acquisition of genuine furnishings from America's past. She asked for citizens in possession of any authentic furnishings to donate them to the White House—and they did. Treasures associated with George Washington, James Madison, and Lincoln soon arrived,[15] as did three original chairs that had stood in James Monroe's Oval Room in 1818, when the President's House first reopened following the British attack and fire of 1814.

The White House also received paintings, sculptures, and historic prints. The committee worked to find donors to pay for these treasures, and by the end of 1961, thousands of people had offered. "I hope you can realize what this means to us. . . ." Mrs. Kennedy wrote to donors: "I do hope you will come this fall to the White House—then together we will see what a difference your things have made."[16]

She found some treasures right under her nose. Scouring storage areas in the mansion and in a nearby government warehouse, Mrs. Kennedy uncovered a gilded table that had been purchased in France by one of Monroe's shoppers. To her delight she also found china that had been used during the Lincoln, Grant, Hayes, and Harrison administrations. There weren't enough pieces to use for state dinners, but she used them when entertaining small groups.

One find stood out from all the rest. In the ground floor Broadcast Room—used by Dwight Eisenhower for the first presidential broadcast from the White House in 1953—Mrs. Kennedy found a desk that had been given to President Rutherford B. Hayes by England's Queen Victoria in 1880. Built from oak timbers of a decommissioned British ship, the H.M.S. *Resolute,* its intricately carved moldings and flora swags were striking. Such a desk, Mrs. Kennedy thought, deserved a more prominent home than the White House basement. Her husband agreed, and it was moved into the Oval Office for the first time.[17]

The desk soon garnered even greater fame when a doe-eyed John F. Kennedy Jr. was photographed peering out from behind his "secret door" at the desk's base, while his smiling father studied papers. Little "John-John" called the desk "my house."[18] The picture of boy and father, perhaps more than any other, reflects the dual nature of the White House itself: as both workplace of the president of the United States and a home where people live. Of Kennedy's nine successors, five have chosen to use the Resolute desk in the Oval Office. Because of its prominent place in the White House's most important room, it has become, unquestionably, its most famous piece of furniture.[19]

To safeguard and publicize these and numerous other antiquities, Mrs. Kennedy, with the support of her husband, created the White House Historical Association in 1961 and had the mansion itself declared a museum. Her top-to-bottom restoration, all $2 million of it,[20] then became the subject of a February 14, 1962, TV show. Mrs. Kennedy guided CBS reporter Charles Collingwood through the State Floor, room by room, explaining in her now famous whispery voice what she had done. A staggering eighty million Americans watched—nearly half the nation's population. It was, CBS executives gushed, "the greatest sight-seeing trip in history."[21] Never before had a first lady been so ubiquitous—and this for a woman who once said Bess Truman was her favorite first lady because of the way she avoided the spotlight.[22]

The importance of connecting Americans with their past certainly resonated with the president himself, who told Collingwood that his wife's efforts "bring us much more intimately in contact with all the men who lived here. After all, history is people, and particularly in great moments of our history, presidents. So when we have, as we do today, Grant's table or Lincoln's bed, or Monroe's gold set, all these make these men much more alive."[23] The president said that "anything which dramatizes the great story of the United States—as I think the White House does—is worthy of the closest attention and respect by Americans who live here and who visit here and who are part of our citizenry."[24]

But Jacqueline Kennedy wasn't finished. Remembering her disappointment from her 1941 tour that there was no guidebook for visitors, she created one. The first edition of *The White House: An Historic Guide* was published in July 1962. It cost $1, with proceeds supporting the preservation of the mansion for future generations. Millions of copies have since been sold. There was one room, incidentally, that initially escaped Mrs. Kennedy's touch: the Oval Office itself. The magnificent Resolute desk aside, it too needed to be redecorated. She would turn her attention to that in the fall of 1963.

Jacqueline Kennedy wasn't the only member of the First Family who physically changed the White House. The president made one contribution as well, and it was a big one—though to this day, only a select few ever get to see it.

In February 1961, the president, in office just a month, approved a plan—originally hatched during the Eisenhower administration—to overthrow Cuba's Fidel Castro and his nascent communist government. Launched in April, Operation Zapata quickly collapsed, a spectacular failure for the young commander in chief. It came to be known to history by a different name: the Bay of Pigs.

The president was bombarded with criticism from all corners. Publicly, Kennedy took the blame for his humiliating setback; "Victory has a thousand fathers," he noted, "but defeat is an orphan." But privately, the president was furious at the Central Intelligence Agency—particularly its longtime director, Allen Dulles, who had baited the young new president, asking, "Are you going to be less anti-Communist than Eisenhower?"[25] Kennedy now threatened to "splinter [CIA] in a thousand pieces and scatter it to the winds."[26]

But the president had a second reaction. The bungled Cuban adventure made him more skeptical and less trusting of the military advice he was getting. He also decided it would be useful to be able to deal directly, whenever possible, with potential adversaries in a crisis—and ideally, to keep them from developing in the first place. To those ends, Kennedy ordered, in May 1961, the creation of a room that would monitor global hotspots around the clock and—bypassing much of the government's vast network of national security organizations—report directly to him. To make room for it, a bowling alley built for Harry Truman was quickly removed, replaced with state-of-the art communications equipment. Located on a floor below the ground level of the West Wing, it quickly became known as the Situation Room. JFK ordered every branch of the military to feed its most sensitive information to the room, which was manned by a single CIA analyst, working a twenty-hour shift, who took catnaps on a cot in a corner.[27]

In its first iteration, the Situation Room—which is actually a series of rooms—wasn't much. One conference room featured a modest table and room for about eight chairs. Wood-paneling on the walls extended up to low ceilings. The ceiling itself featured lights that looked like small megaphones, a popular style in the early 1960s. To the modern eye, John F. Kennedy's "Sit Room" looked more like a recreation room in suburban America than a 24/7 presidential nerve center.

The Situation Room changed the presidency in a fundamental way. During the Bay of Pigs, vital information that might have altered Kennedy's management of the operation never reached him.[28] Obviously dissatisfied, the president decided that he wanted the same raw data that key organizations like the CIA and Defense and State Departments had—and he wanted it in real time. This meant that the White House would be flooded with everything from embassy cables to messages sent from US military bases around the world. This suited JFK—a voracious and fast reader—just fine. Critics said the setup would enable White House staffers to second-guess members of the president's Cabinet, but Kennedy thought this was fine too, if it would help prevent future disasters like what had transpired in Cuba.[29]

It very well may have. In October 1962—just seventeen months after the Bay of Pigs debacle—what would be the gravest chapter of the entire Cold War erupted: the Cuban Missile Crisis. It was a tense standoff between the United States and the Soviet Union that nearly led to nuclear war.

The two-week showdown has been studied and written about extensively over the years. The Soviets had secretly placed nuclear missiles in Cuba that were capable of striking the United States within minutes. From the outset, Kennedy determined the missiles would have to be removed. The challenge was to remove them without letting events spiral out of control. As a last resort, the president was ready to invade Cuba itself.

Throughout the tense fortnight—as the threat of nuclear war hung over the world like the sword of Damocles—the Situation Room worked as the president had intended. Kennedy got the information he needed and he got it faster, allowing him and the so-called EXCOMM—the Executive Committee of the National Security Council—to work through the crisis more efficiently. The president himself often went downstairs to the command center itself (it was so cramped he called it a "pigpen")[30] to read newswire reports.[31] There were meetings held there as well, usually chaired by the president's national security advisor, McGeorge Bundy.[32] In addition to embassy cables and military reports, the Situation Room was also plugged into the CIA's Foreign Broadcast Information Service (FBIS), which allowed it to monitor news broadcasts from around the world.

At the height of the crisis, when an American attack on Cuba appeared imminent, this was how the White House learned that Soviet leader Nikita Khrushchev had agreed to remove his missiles. The Kremlin leader, seeking a way out of the crisis himself and fearing that information sent via normal diplomatic channels was too slow, made the announcement on Radio Moscow.[33] A relieved President Kennedy saw the bulletin on the FBIS wire almost immediately. The speed with which the president got the news helped avert war. Never had the White House had a room so inconspicuous, and yet so critically important to the nation's security.

Aside from the Resolute desk, the Oval Office itself was the one room in the White House complex that had escaped Jacqueline Kennedy's touch. In the autumn of 1963, she told her husband that she wanted to redecorate. Receiving his permission, she set about planning. The president was eager to see the final result.

A freshening up was long overdue. A blue-gray carpet featuring the presidential seal and gray drapes both dated back to the Truman administration; both would have to go, Mrs. Kennedy decided. She selected white drapes, but the most striking choice of decor she made was the rug: deep plush and dark red, the color of blood. All she needed was for the president to be away for a day and a half so workers could swoop in and make the necessary changes.[34] A trip to Texas from November 21st to 23rd provided such an opportunity.

Mrs. Kennedy had decided to join her husband in Texas, her first campaign trip with him since the 1960 election. On November 22nd, as the president and Mrs. Kennedy made their way from Fort Worth to Dallas, where they would motorcade through the city in an open car, the president's furniture, including the Resolute desk and his rocking chair, was moved so the new carpet could be smoothed out. Shortly after 1:30 Eastern Standard Time came the thunderbolt from Dallas: The president had been shot.

Within an hour the worst was confirmed: He was gone. It was the fourth time in less than a century that a chief executive had been gunned down.

Unlike the murders of Abraham Lincoln, James Garfield, and William McKinley, however, the death of John F. Kennedy played out in real time; the shock and speed of events outdid the ability to comprehend. "It is one of the ugliest days in American history," NBC's David Brinkley told a stunned nation. "There is seldom any time to think anymore, and today there was none . . . what happened has been just too much, too ugly and too fast."[35]

It was certainly too much too fast for anyone in the West Wing that tragic afternoon; no one even seemed to know, until seeing the carpet, that the Oval Office was even being redecorated. Advisor Bundy: "Oh my God, they're putting scarlet carpets in the President's office! We must stop it." Daniel Patrick Moynihan, an assistant labor secretary, thought "It looked as though they knew a new President was coming in."[36] Photographs were taken for posterity, and the late president's belongings were removed. Mrs. Kennedy would see the blood-red carpet and her husband's office for a few moments the next day.[37]

Prior to November 22, 1963, seven presidents had died in office. Now, on the hushed flight from Dallas, Jacqueline Kennedy, just hours a widow, was interested in but one. "Find out how Lincoln was buried," she instructed.[38] Working throughout the night from a May 6, 1865, issue of *Harper's Weekly* and other materials from the Library of Congress,[39] staffers draped portions of the mansion and East Room in black.

At the heart of their efforts was a rectangular-shaped platform, consisting of rough pine boards that had been nailed together and covered with black cloth. Measuring seven feet long, two and a half feet wide, and sitting atop an even larger base,[40] it was rushed to the White House and placed in the center of the East Room. It was a replica of the Lincoln catafalque, previously used to honor unknown heroes from World War II and Korea at Arlington National Cemetery. The actual Lincoln catafalque would be set up in the Capitol Rotunda, and it was upon this humble, venerated platform that the casket of John F. Kennedy would later be placed as well—four score and eighteen years after the Great Emancipator himself had been struck down.

As those around her, the nation, indeed the world, reeled from the shock of the assassination, the public saw a strong and composed Jacqueline Kennedy. Under the harsh glare of a global television audience, she projected a dignity and bearing that made a grieving nation proud.

But she also possessed an exquisite sense of history. And whether intended or not, by invoking the memory of Abraham Lincoln, she conveyed something else that tragic weekend, something more important than even the death of her husband: the continuity of the presidency itself and the notion that it was larger than any one person.

In the fourteen days she would remain in the White House following her husband's assassination—she would visit just once more over the remainder of her life—Jacqueline Kennedy made one final addition to the home she had once detested but then grew to love. In the Lincoln Bedroom, on the southeast part of the second floor, she had a plaque inscribed:

> *In this room lived John Fitzgerald Kennedy, with his wife Jacqueline, during the two years, ten months, and two days he was president of the United States.*[41]

CHAPTER NINETEEN

Richard Nixon: The Enemy Within

The Briefing Room

HAD HIS TIME IN OFFICE ENDED IN THE SPRING OF 1972, RICHARD MIL-
hous Nixon would likely have been remembered as a very good, if not
great president. At the very height of his power in February of that year, he
made what is arguably the most important journey ever taken by a president, traveling to China. It was a trip that stunned the world. A lifelong,
hard-line anti-communist, Nixon shook hands with Mao Tse-tung and
opened the door to China's entry into the modern world, a development
of monumental consequence.

Three months later Nixon became the first sitting president to visit
Moscow, where he signed a treaty with the Soviet Union—America's only
geopolitical rival—to limit each superpower's stockpile of strategic nuclear
weapons. And the most vexing, intractable problem of all—the war in Vietnam, a decade-long conflict that squandered fifty-eight thousand American
lives and tore the country apart—was mercifully winding down. Nixon saw
the world as it was, with all its complexities and dangers, and dealt with it
in a realistic, practical manner. *Realpolitik*, his approach to foreign affairs was
called.

On the domestic front, Nixon did things that by today's standards would
brand him a liberal, not the conservative Republican that he was. There were
big increases in government entitlements—Social Security, Medicare, and
Medicaid—on his watch. He cut taxes for the poor and raised them for the
rich. He strengthened workplace safety laws. He was instrumental in form-
ing the Environmental Protection Agency, tasked with making air and water
cleaner. The president "probably [imposed] more new regulation on the economy during the Nixon administration," wrote Herb Stein, his chief economic
advisor, "than in any other presidency since the [Roosevelt] New Deal."[1] He

Richard M. Nixon in the Oval Office. The president typically used the Oval Office for official or ceremonial functions, preferring to work most of the time in an office in the Executive Office Building next to the White House. This photo was taken on June 23, 1972—six days after the Watergate break-in. RICHARD NIXON PRESIDENTIAL LIBRARY AND MUSEUM

even helped establish one of the bête noires of conservatives today: National Public Radio.

In short, his achievements were demonstrable, his place in history secure. On June 13, 1972, his Gallup approval, at a solid 59 percent, was on the rise. Facing listless Democratic opposition, the president appeared headed toward a smooth reelection that fall.[2]

But none of this was enough for Nixon to overcome his inner demons. Seeking the presidency in 1960, he lost to John F. Kennedy by one of the narrowest margins in history—just 113,000 votes—amid allegations of electoral fraud. Though there was no definitive proof, Nixon was convinced "we won but they stole it from us."[3] Two years later he suffered an embarrassing defeat while seeking the California governorship. Even though he finally captured the presidency in 1968, Nixon simply could not let go of prior setbacks and perceived humiliations. Come 1972 he was determined to leave nothing to chance.

"The press is the enemy," Nixon said. Yet he gave the White House press corps a big new briefing room to call their own, installing it over the indoor swimming pool Franklin Roosevelt had built nearly four decades before. Here, the president meets the press on April 17, 1970. NATIONAL ARCHIVES

On June 17th, as the president basked in the afterglow of his triumphs in Peking (today Beijing), Moscow, and at home, five men linked to his re-election campaign were caught breaking into Democratic National Committee headquarters in a Washington, DC, office building called the Watergate. What happened in the next twenty-six months is well known: The investigation into the middle-of-the-night burglary—led by two young reporters at the *Washington Post*—eventually led to the White House itself. As he tried to cover it up, firing top aides and stonewalling Congress and the courts, his political support crumbled and he resigned in disgrace to avoid impeachment. His fall was as swift as it was stunning; never before has a president been so utterly brilliant—and yet so deeply flawed—as Richard Nixon.

What drove him to both extremes? In the end, it was the very same thing: a lifelong inferiority complex, with a generous helping of paranoia thrown in. Richard Nixon wasn't rich, glamorous, or charming like his rival John F. Kennedy. But as a politician selling himself to the voters—one of the few things that ever really mattered to him—Nixon had something that Kennedy money and connections could never buy: a good story.

Election night 1972: At the peak of his power, Nixon and his family enjoy dinner in the private dining room on the second floor of the mansion. The wallpaper depicting scenes from the American Revolution was selected a decade earlier by Jacqueline Kennedy. RICHARD NIXON PRESIDENTIAL LIBRARY AND MUSEUM

Unlike JFK, the pedigreed son of a ruthless businessman-turned-ambassador, Nixon was the impoverished kid who, by dint of sheer hard work and iron will, climbed the ladder on his own. It was a classic up-by-the-bootstraps tale that Americans could respond to. And respond they did: He was a congressman at thirty-three, senator at thirty-seven, and vice president of the United States at thirty-nine.

The humble background was very much a strength, yet to Nixon it always seemed a weakness. The nagging insecurity dogged him, even when he made it to the top. After moving into the White House in 1969, the president wandered into the Lincoln Bedroom one day and saw the plaque that Jacqueline Kennedy had installed honoring her murdered husband. Nixon callously ordered it removed,[4] a petty gesture. It personified the mind-set that would be his eventual undoing.

~

At the time just one of five men to have served as vice president for two four-year terms, Richard Nixon knew the White House well when he and

A happy respite for the president and Pat Nixon: the June 12, 1971, wedding of their daughter Tricia. The first lady quietly did as much, if not more, to restore and improve the White House than even Jacqueline Kennedy, yet has received scant public credit for it. RICHARD NIXON PRESIDENTIAL LIBRARY AND MUSEUM

first lady Patricia "Pat" Nixon moved into the mansion. While Nixon had been in the public eye since his election to Congress a quarter-century earlier, Mrs. Nixon, to many Americans, was far less known.

She was a reluctant political wife—she tried to dissuade her husband from accepting the vice presidential nomination in 1952—but acceded to his ambitions. She wasn't an extrovert like Eleanor Roosevelt, who found a way to broadcast her opinions on every issue under the sun. Nor did she evoke the glamour and cachet of Jacqueline Kennedy (who, in fairness, was twenty-five years younger). But while low key and quiet—she was the only first lady in modern times who didn't write a memoir—graceful Pat, always smiling—was effective in her own way, and very much a political asset for her husband. Traveling the world during their vice presidential years, she was a goodwill ambassador, charming and earnest at every stop. *Time* magazine described her as "one of the US's most remarkable women . . . . a public figure in her own right."[5]

In fact, and unbeknownst to most Americans to this day, Pat Nixon actually did as much for the White House as Jacqueline Kennedy had—in some respects more. In the eight years since Mrs. Kennedy refurbished the mansion, the crush of visitors—more than a million tourists and tens of thousands of invited guests each year—had taken a toll. Mrs. Nixon and her handpicked curator, Clement Conger, got to work sprucing things up. There was much to do.

"Two-thirds of the furniture was department store reproductions," Conger noted. "The curtains were in threads, the wallpaper worn right through to the plaster. No one ordered any extra materials—the chairs were simply retired to the warehouse when the fabrics wore out. In my opinion it was a disgrace second only to the burning of the White House in 1814."[6] Considering the dilapidated state of the mansion in Lincoln's day or Truman's—when an actual collapse was feared—this was so much hyperbole, but wear and tear at the White House was a never-ending issue.

Mrs. Nixon not only added to Mrs. Kennedy's more well-known restoration efforts, she exceeded them, adding more than six hundred paintings and furnishings to the White House—more than any prior administration.[7] She oversaw the redecoration of the First Family's private quarters on the second floor, and public rooms on the State Floor. On the ground floor she oversaw renovations of the Map Room and China Room. While presidential portraits have long hung on White House walls, visitors today can also see a collection of first ladys' portraits as well—thanks to Pat Nixon.

If the White House can be called the "people's house," something that belongs to all Americans, Mrs. Nixon truly made it so. She had ramps installed for the handicapped and physically disabled. She instructed tour guides to speak slowly so deaf visitors could lip-read; blind visitors were allowed to touch things.[8] She often greeted delighted tour groups herself, shaking hands and posing for photos.[9]

On one tour a little boy said he doubted the White House was where the president really lived because he hadn't seen a washing machine; Mrs. Nixon personally took him to the private family quarters on the second floor and showed it to him.[10] Unlike her husband, who was awkward around people, terrible at small talk, and craved solitude—astonishing for a politician—Pat Nixon was warm and empathetic. Had circumstances been different, she might have been a rather effective politician herself.

Anyone walking by the White House after dark can see two additional contributions made by Pat Nixon. Working quietly with the National Park Service for months, she had hundreds of lights installed around the mansion so it would be illuminated at night. Julie Nixon Eisenhower, the Nixon's younger daughter, recalls how her parents were returning to the mansion one evening in August 1970:

> . . . as their helicopter neared the mansion, suddenly hundreds of carefully concealed lights on the White House grounds were switched on. The softly

*glowing mansion was a breathtaking sight from the air. Mother had not
told my father that the project was completed, wanting him to be surprised. He was elated. Excited, he ordered the pilot to circle once, twice, a
third time. Mother beamed with pleasure.*[11]

Passersby can also see the American flag atop the White House—prior
to the Nixons, the Stars and Stripes only flew over the mansion during the
day. The first lady made sure that this ultimate symbol of the nation was
flown around the clock.[12]

For all of these efforts, Pat Nixon never sought attention; there were no
TV specials devoted to her work, no fawning by the media. After her death
in 1993, at the age of eighty-one, the *Washington Post* said that Mrs. Nixon,
with the help of Conger, "restore[d] the White House to its golden age" and
left "as one of her legacies a more historically accurate, and perhaps a more
American, White House."[13]

As for the president himself, Nixon plunged in to the job he had craved for so
long. Ironically, for a man who fought so hard to make it to the Oval Office,
Nixon did not want to work *in* the Oval Office itself. Its history and grandeur
made it appropriate for ceremonial events and greeting visitors, he thought,
but was too prone to interruption by "the constant activity in and around the
West Wing."[14]

To get his real work done, the president preferred the Old Executive
Office Building next door, a two or three minute walk from the mansion.
Harry Truman called the OEOB (named today in honor of Dwight Eisenhower) "the greatest monstrosity in America,"[15] but the solitude and insularity it offered appealed to Nixon. He turned Room 180 into his presidential
office.

While decidedly not oval in shape, and offering little in the way of views,
Room 180 offered a grandeur of its own. Towering, beamed ceilings, crown
molding, and wainscoting made it aesthetically pleasing. One of the few photos of the president in the room shows him settled into an easy chair, feet
sprawled over an ottoman. Aides say he often relaxed here, reading or writing
on a yellow-lined pad.[16]

To the right was his desk, once used by Theodore Roosevelt. A large map
of the world hung on one wall, a reflection of his intense, almost singular
focus on foreign affairs (domestic policy, he once scoffed, was like "building

outhouses in Peoria").[17] The photo shows the president talking to his national security advisor—and eventual secretary of state—Henry Kissinger, while Vicky, the family's French poodle, naps on the rug. The room would later acquire notoriety when its tape recording system captured conversations related to the Watergate scandal.

By "constant activity in and around the West Wing," Nixon was certainly alluding to the press. For decades, reporters covering the White House had worked in the same room given to them by Theodore Roosevelt, offering them an eagle eye on comings and goings in the West Wing. Their work-space, just off the lobby entrance, was a cross between a train station waiting room and a doctor's office. There were leather club chairs (each with its own tall ashtray), cubbyholes for papers, and banks of telephone booths to call in stories. Coats and hats were often tossed in a heap on a large round table in the middle of the room. Photographs taken over the years show reporters running through the room, ties flapping, to file their stories. It was no doubt colorful, smoky, and, at times, raucous, as friends and rivals competed with one another for the day's scoops.

Understanding the value of the press, every president from TR through Lyndon Johnson tolerated their presence. Some actually enjoyed having reporters around. Those who could walk fast could join Harry Truman on his morning walk around Washington; a select few were even invited to join him at the poker table. John F. Kennedy, who briefly toyed with the idea of becoming a journalist as a young man,[18] loved to trade gossip with them, but also wisely saw reporters as valuable sources of information. Johnson even allowed the three networks to build a TV studio just sixty feet from the Oval Office in the Fish Room (once Theodore Roosevelt's actual office and later where Franklin Roosevelt kept his tropical fish).[19]

But Richard Nixon hated the press and felt victimized by it. He thought big newspapers and TV networks were run by Eastern elites, men elected by no one and answerable to no one. Worst of all, in reporting items that displeased the president, they were irresponsible and unpatriotic. He sent Vice President Spiro Agnew out to attack them with highly memorable allitera-tion: The media were "nattering nabobs of negativism" and "hopeless, hysterical hypochondriacs of history." And the Nixon White House went after the press with more than words. It wiretapped reporters' phones and even ordered the Internal Revenue Service to harass some of them.[20]

Nixon hated reporters so much that several of them made a famous "Enemies List" compiled by White House staffers in 1971. The president thought journalists, particularly from organizations he considered leftist—like CBS, the *New York Times,* and the *Washington Post*—were out to get him. "Never forget," he told national security advisors Henry Kissinger and Alexander Haig in a taped conversation on December 14, 1972, "the press is the enemy, the press is the enemy . . . write that on a blackboard 100 times."[21]

And when Nixon said enemies, he meant it. There is evidence that the president, or at least close associates, considered having one of those enemies—investigative journalist Jack Anderson—killed. Nixon feared Anderson, who had uncovered numerous administration secrets and published them in his syndicated newspaper column, "Washington Merry-Go-Round."

So for a president who truly detested the media—"why don't we all get a member of the press and beat them up," he said half an hour after his 1968 election—and wanted little to do with them, it seems beyond inconceivable that he would give the White House press corps a much bigger and nicer workspace in the White House. But that's exactly what Nixon did; in 1970, he ordered that the indoor pool connecting the mansion with the West Wing itself be covered over and given to the press.

Give up a wonderful, indoor heated pool? With three rubdown rooms, a sauna, dog kennels, even a room for florists to arrange the White House's flowers?[22] Nixon—whose idea of exercise was jogging in place for a few minutes in the morning[23]—did, and replaced it with the first modern, wired press room for the burgeoning White House press corps: two floors, with broadcast booths, writing desks, and a briefing room.

The president wasn't much of a swimmer to begin with, and while turning over such valuable real estate to the fourth estate might have appeared generous, some White House reporters suspected that the president's motivation was less than altruistic. They read it as an effort by Nixon and his advisors to exert more control, and push the press farther away from the West Wing.[24] Perhaps, but it did cement the press's presence in the White House itself; it also gave the president, his press secretary, and other officials a dedicated space in which to interact with reporters.

And thus the swimming pool that soothed Franklin Roosevelt's paralyzed legs, that gave John F. Kennedy such enjoyment, was no more. Richard Nixon had no need for such indulgence, which he considered irresponsible because it took him away from "the burdens of the Presidency." This attitude applied to seemingly every facet of Nixon's life, even eating; he typically wolfed down breakfast and lunch in five minutes, and thought dining with others unproductive. When aides suggested that he invite guests to the White House for cocktails, he scoffed. "Whoever is President," he thought, "should dispense with socializing in the interest of doing his job better."[25]

The comment says much about Nixon's complicated psyche. The president, a highly intelligent man, a voracious reader, and lifelong student of politics and the presidency, knew both intuitively and from watching his predecessors that socializing was part of the job. Every president he had known since coming to Washington—Truman, Kennedy, Johnson, and Dwight Eisenhower, under whom he served for eight years as vice president—socialized with a variety of people both in and out of government.

Socializing offered two things that are essential elements of the modern presidency: a respite, however small, from the crushing burdens of the job, and an opportunity to persuade. The hospitality they offered—drinks, dinners, golf, a cigar on the Truman Balcony—was ostensibly a waste of time to Richard Nixon. But the unsociable, most tightly wound of presidents was simply incapable of it, and knew it. His lifelong insularity was his cocoon, and central to his eventual downfall.

CHAPTER TWENTY

Ronald Reagan: Lights, Camera, Action

The Family Theater

ONLY FIVE MEN IN THE WORLD TODAY ACTUALLY KNOW WHAT IT IS LIKE TO be president of the United States. The awesome responsibilities of war and peace, the constant scrutiny, the never-ending criticism—often vicious, often hateful—not just from Americans, but from every corner of the globe. It never ends.

An occasional respite from this ultimate pressure-cooker job is essential. Some presidents fish. Others play golf or ride horses. Still others ski, swim, play cards, or bury their nose in books. But one diversion seems to link all presidents—at least those in the past century—and that is that most American of art forms: the movies. For a century now, Americans have flocked to the theater to see the latest fare from Hollywood; but here, presidents have an advantage that only the well heeled can match: an expansive, private movie theater to call their own. The Family Theater, as it is known, is on the ground floor of the East Wing, a quick elevator descent from the family residence two floors up.

At first glance, the cool, dark room doesn't look much different than a theater in any neighborhood multiplex. There are forty-two seats,[1] with rows gently sloping down towards the screen. But upon closer inspection, it becomes obvious that this is no ordinary movie theater. Everything from the soft, plush carpeting to the gold-bordered wallpaper is deep red in color. The seats are cushier. And the front row consists of four additional seats— armchairs, in fact, soft, deeply upholstered, with ottomans for everyone. Standing sixty-five and three-quarter inches tall, there's also a vintage-looking red popcorn machine supplied by the Chicago firm C. Cretors & Co.[2] And, in a subtle reminder of where you are, there's a secure telephone on a small table, should reality intrude during a screening.

Ronald and Nancy Reagan enjoying a movie in the Family Theater on the ground floor. The theater, built by Franklin Roosevelt in 1942, has been a favorite of every First Family ever since. Of all the movies they starred in, the Reagans acted in just one together: 1957's *Hellcats of the Navy*. RONALD REAGAN PRESIDENTIAL LIBRARY

If the introduction of comforts and conveniences in the White House over the years—running water, electricity, the telephone, etc.—helps tell the story of the White House, a look at the movies presidents have chosen to watch is similarly revealing—telling us much not only about our chief executives but the times in which they lived, and the particular challenges they faced. And, of course, no president is linked to the movies more than the one who starred in dozens of them: the fortieth chief executive, Ronald Wilson Reagan.

The arrival of Ronald and Nancy Reagan in 1981 signaled an end to a difficult period in American history. Gone was Jimmy Carter, an honest but largely ineffective president, a puritanical scold who had outworn his welcome. Prior to Carter there was Gerald Ford, a decent man but caretaker chief executive, the only man to serve as both vice president and president without being elected to either office. Before him was Richard Nixon, who resigned the presidency ahead of what would almost certainly have been an even greater

The Reagans brought Hollywood and Washington together like never before. Here, President and Mrs. Reagan appear on the South Lawn with pop star Michael Jackson at an event for the National Campaign against Drunk Driving. May 14, 1984. RONALD REAGAN PRESIDENTIAL LIBRARY

indignity: forcible removal for his involvement in the Watergate affair. It's not much of a stretch to add Lyndon Johnson to the list: a man who did so much for the country, yet wound up tearing it apart over an unnecessary war that cost the nation dearly in blood and treasure. Come 1981, the United States was plagued by everything from rising crime and inflation to crippling shortages of energy; abroad, there had been once-unthinkable humiliations, like Iran's seizure of fifty-two Americans—mostly diplomats—which turned into a 444-day hostage crisis. In short, there were fears that both America's standing in the world and the American dream itself were in peril.

The solution, voters decided, was a sixty-nine-year-old man—the oldest person ever elected to the presidency (the oldest prior to Reagan, William Henry Harrison, died a month after being sworn in)—a man who spoke with the optimism and self-assuredness of someone one-third his age. "Those who say that we're in a time when there are not heroes, they just don't know where to look," Reagan said in his inaugural address. "And after all, why shouldn't we believe that? We are Americans."

It was a masterful performance, exactly the sort of uplifting, confident tone he had always been known for. "Life is just one grand, sweet song, so start the music," he wrote in his high school yearbook.[3] Those inclined to dislike him derided him as just an actor, and a B-list one at that, delivering his lines. They were wrong.

Reagan, of course, had been an actor—but also a two-term governor of California, the only chief executive of the nation's biggest and most complex state to become president. In fact, his eight years in Sacramento represented more executive experience than any of the fifteen prior presidents who had also been governors.[4] It can be argued therefore that Ronald Reagan, who at a far earlier age happened to share the silver screen with a chimp named Bonzo, arrived in the White House as seasoned an executive—if not more so—than many of his predecessors.

But it is also true that both careers—politician and actor—blended together for Reagan as president. He admitted as much, telling his attorney general, Ed Meese, "I don't know I could do this job if I were not an actor."[5] In fact, that he had been one—as opposed to, say, a career politician like Nixon or Johnson, a soldier like Dwight Eisenhower, or nuclear engineer like Carter—was very much a strength in his view.

In 1989, after he left the White House, he told former speechwriter Landon Parvin:

Some of my critics over the years have said that I became president because I was an actor who knew how to give a good speech. I suppose that's not too far wrong. Because an actor knows two important things—to be honest in what he's doing and to be in touch with the audience. That's not bad advice for a politician either. My actor's instinct simply told me to speak the truth as I saw it and felt it.[6]

Whether one agreed with Reagan politically or not, from the standpoint of sheer ability to inspire and persuade—absolutely essential qualities for any president—it is hard to argue that he was ineffective.

While Reagan is associated with the silver screen, it was really radio where he first honed the communication skills that would take him to the White House. In December 1932, at the very depth of the Great Depression, he got a part-time job as an announcer at WOC, a station in Davenport, Iowa.[7] Although skilled in his own right behind the microphone, Reagan, like millions of Americans, found inspiration by listening to the first true political master of that medium: Franklin Roosevelt. Reagan, then twenty-two, was dazzled by FDR, reportedly memorized his entire first inaugural address,[8] and recited portions of it to friends, using a broomstick as a microphone.[9]

Reagan, a Democrat until age fifty (he campaigned for Harry Truman in 1948), considered Roosevelt a hero. "His strong, gentle, confident voice resonated across the nation with an eloquence that brought comfort and resilience to a nation caught up in a storm and reassured us that we could lick any problem. I will never forget him for that,"[10] he wrote in his diary. As a politician—and Republican—he would carefully emulate Roosevelt's speaking style, emphasizing small words and concepts that could be easily understood by all.

After his eight years as governor ended in 1974, he took to the airwaves again, broadcasting nationally syndicated commentaries. In 1982, as president, he began taping weekly radio addresses, a practice followed by his successors. Movies brought Ronald Reagan fame and fortune but were bookended by another lifelong love: talking on the radio.

Reagan's wife of three decades, Nancy, was once a leading lady in her own right, of course. As young actors, some of their roles provided hints of bigger things to come: In high school, she performed in a play called *First Lady*; two of his films were *Going Places* and *Code of the Secret Service*. Some friends even claimed that a third movie, *Murder in the Air* (1940), in which Reagan's character, Brass Bancroft, kept saboteurs away from a secret weapon that could shoot down enemy rockets,[11] influenced his later presidential embrace of the Strategic Defense Initiative (SDI), which aimed to destroy Soviet nuclear missiles fired at the United States.[12]

The Reagan White House was the most glamorous since the Kennedy era. Longtime friends and fellow actors/entertainers like Frank Sinatra, Elizabeth Taylor, and Jimmy Stewart visited on a regular basis, and the mansion, if not Washington as a whole, soon became known as Hollywood-on-the-Potomac. After the austerity of the Carter years—like James Polk and Rutherford Hayes, Jimmy and Rosalynn Carter refused to serve hard liquor[13]—it was a welcome change to some. However, the overt display of ostentatiousness struck many as tone deaf and

Nancy Reagan in her beloved Red Room. The most glamorous First Lady since Jacqueline Kennedy, she was dubbed "Fancy Nancy" by critics who attacked her spendthrift ways, such as spending $209,508 on new china for the White House. Lost on the public was the fact that the money was privately donated, and not taxpayer funds. RONALD REAGAN PRESIDENTIAL LIBRARY

insensitive, particularly during the first two years of the Reagan presidency, when the country was gripped by a severe recession.

Like other first ladies, Nancy Reagan devoted a chunk of her time to refurbishing the mansion. Refusing $50,000 given by Congress, she tapped her wealthy friends for an estimated $1 million in contributions[14] to redo the family quarters in the second floor and parts of the State Floor below. While her efforts would not match those of Pat Nixon or Jacqueline Kennedy, she did oversee the conservation of more than 150 White House objects, including marble walls, wood doors, and floors in public rooms. Among the treasures:

As a young man growing up in the Midwest, Reagan was deeply influenced by Franklin D. Roosevelt's Fireside Chats. As president, he began taping weekly radio addresses, carefully emulating FDR's speaking style, with an emphasis on small words and concepts that could be easily understood by all. Here, the president speaks from Camp David on October 16, 1982. RONALD REAGAN PRESIDENTIAL LIBRARY

Two of the twenty-four chairs made for James Monroe's East Room in 1818 were acquired, as was a rare glass decanter made for James Madison in 1816. Various pieces of furniture that had been on loan in the Red and Green Rooms and the Library were converted to permanent acquisitions.[15]

But Mrs. Reagan's public image was dented by accusations that she lived and dressed extravagantly and, during a time of government spending cuts, ordered a new set of china at a cost of $209,508.[16] In fairness to the first lady, the funds were donated by a private foundation,[17] but this fact was lost on the public. Nevertheless, as she acknowledged in her autobiography: "The timing was unfortunate. The new White House china was announced on the same day that the Department of Agriculture mistakenly declared ketchup to be a vegetable for school lunches. As you can imagine, the columnists and cartoonists had a field day with that one."[18]

Mrs. Reagan pointed out that Eleanor Roosevelt was criticized when she, too, ordered a new set of china in 1933 (Mrs. Roosevelt even felt compelled to hold a news conference to defend herself). "People want the White House to look great," Mrs. Reagan continued, "but they don't want it to cost anything."[19] She would turn her "Fancy Nancy" reputation around with a smashing self-deprecating appearance at the 1982 Gridiron Club dinner (an annual gathering of Washington's journalistic elite), when she suddenly appeared on stage in a hideous outfit and sang a reworked version of "Second Hand Rose."

While the Reagans never lacked for rich and famous friends, they were never more content when they were alone together. A typical evening consisted of "Ronnie" and "Mommie" (as they called each other) watching TV while eating dinner on trays in a small study next to their bedroom on the second floor. Like most presidents in the television age, their viewing habits included the nightly network news broadcasts.[20]

But it was movies that the president and first lady seemed to enjoy the most. Beginning with the 1980 Jack Lemmon film *Tribute*, which they watched eleven days after the president was sworn in, to one of Reagan's own films—1954's *Cattle Queen of Montana*—which they saw six days before leaving the White House, they watched 362 films together in eight years. The bulk of these were screened on weekends at Camp David,[21] including the only movie they starred in together: *Hellcats of the Navy*, a 1957 movie about "the daring exploits of a submarine commander" and his onshore love interest.

The Reagans' tastes were eclectic; the list of films they watched included everything from musicals and comedies to science fiction and thrillers. Alfred Hitchcock movies seemed to be a particular favorite—one of the few films they watched twice was *North by Northwest*, the 1959 classic in which Cary Grant is mistaken for a government agent. They also watched two of Reagan's best-known movies. One was *King's Row* (1942), which Reagan considered his best film. Costar Bob Cummings was so impressed with Reagan's presence both on and off screen that he made a rather prescient prediction: "One day Ron, I'm going to vote for you for president."[22] It isn't known whether Cummings, who died in 1990, actually did.

The other popular Reagan film was *Knute Rockne All American* (1940), in which Reagan played a Notre Dame football player—George Gipp—who was stricken with a fatal illness. Coach Rockne, in an inspirational speech to the team, tells them "Let's win one for the Gipper." Reagan often rolled out the line during his presidency to fire up his supporters.

The president also knew that as a cultural touchstone, movies and the emotional, and sometimes patriotic, fervor they often stirred up were useful in pushing his policies—particularly if the movie had a well-known line. "Go ahead—make my day," Reagan quipped in a March 13, 1985, speech in which he threatened to veto legislation raising taxes. It was a short, simple, and easily understood line, one guaranteed enormous play on TV. He borrowed it from the popular 1983 Clint Eastwood movie *Sudden Impact* (which the president apparently had not actually seen).

Like many of his fellow citizens, the president occasionally found himself watching a movie when he should have been doing something else. On the eve of an economic summit with world leaders in Williamsburg, Virginia, in 1983, Reagan's chief of staff, James Baker, gave him a thick briefing book to read. The next day Baker was shocked to learn that the president hadn't even touched it. Baker asked why. "Well, Jim," the president said, "*The Sound of Music* was on last night."[23] At Camp David a few weeks later, when he should have been reading documents prepared for him on the MX missile, he watched *War Games*, in which a teenaged computer whiz (Matthew Broderick) accesses a Pentagon computer system and nearly touches off World War III. At a White House meeting on the MX two days later, he asked a group of congressmen if any of them had seen it, and launched into a review of the film. "Don't tell the ending," one of the lawmakers told him.[24]

Even Reagan's first meeting with Soviet leader Mikhail Gorbachev in 1985 may have been influenced in part by the 1951 science-fiction classic *The Day the Earth Stood Still*, in which a flying saucer lands near the White House. If Earth were ever invaded from outer space, the president told Gorbachev, surely the United States and Soviet Union could put aside their rivalry and work together to combat the aliens. Gorbachev changed the subject.[25] The press—and privately White House staffers—sometimes questioned whether Reagan was blurring films and facts, but aides eventually adopted the president's standard of judging stories "by their impact rather than their accuracy."[26]

But Reagan's observation was true: Politics and movies do share a great deal in common. Both require an understanding of public desire, both involve strangers projecting their lives onto yours, and both require narratives to hold the audience's interest and sympathy.

Presidents and movies date to the beginning of the film industry itself. On March 21, 1915, the first movie was screened in the White House for Woodrow Wilson; unfortunately, it was D. W. Griffith's *The Birth of a Nation*, a celebratory look at the Ku Klux Klan. The film, which sparked protests and riots across the nation,[27] was a surprising choice for Wilson, the intellectual former president of Princeton University. His secretary, Joseph Tumulty, claimed, "the President was entirely unaware of the nature of the play before it was presented and at no time has expressed his approbation of it."[28]

There was no White House theater in Wilson's time. He watched movies on the second floor of the White House, in the long Central Hall, and later in the East Room. Wilson, who had suffered a paralyzing stroke in October 1919 that nearly killed him, watched a film every day during his final year in office; chief White House usher Ike Hoover "scoured the universe" to ensure that the ailing president saw a different one each day.[29]

The theater that exists today was built in 1942, when Franklin Roosevelt had it converted from a cloakroom called the "Hat Box." Roosevelt, whose Fireside Chats on the radio reflected his media savvy, was equally shrewd about the power of movies. He knew that both reached millions while transcending racial, gender, and class divides.[30] He cultivated Hollywood, subtly enlisting producers and stars. As with his campaigns, it worked: FDR was depicted more times on the silver screen—in both fiction and nonfiction—than any other president, and in keeping with his wishes, he was never shown in a wheelchair or with a handicap. Roosevelt was as much a movie fan as anyone else. During the Depression he was known to enjoy *I'm No Angel*, a 1933 comedy starring Mae West and Cary Grant—along with Disney's *Snow White and the Seven Dwarfs*[31] and Mickey Mouse cartoons.[32] During World War II, he watched newsreels of American troops in Europe and the Pacific.

Presidents from the heartland opted for Westerns. Missouri's favorite son, Harry Truman, loved *My Darling Clementine* starring Henry Fonda. But Truman's preferred pastime was an evening of poker with the boys, and he used the theater infrequently. Dwight Eisenhower was the first president to use the theater extensively, and the man from Abilene watched just about anything with a cowboy in it. The White House projectionist in the 1950s, Paul Fischer, kept a handwritten log of everything Ike watched—more than two hundred movies over eight years—and said one of the president's all-time favorites was *High Noon*. Perhaps Eisenhower, the World War II general known for his righteousness and modesty, identified with the film's small-town marshal (Gary Cooper) who faces down a gang of killers all by himself. The theme resonated with many presidents, including Reagan, Bill Clinton, and George W. Bush, each of whom said that *High Noon* was a particular favorite (Clinton said he watched it some twenty times).[33]

John F. Kennedy watched forty-eight movies in the White House, preferring thrillers and manly movies like *Spartacus*, *From Here to Eternity*, and *Bridge on the River Kwai*. Yet during the tense Cuban Missile Crisis—when the United States and Soviet Union came close to nuclear war—he unwound one night by watching Audrey Hepburn's *Roman Holiday*.[34] Not surprisingly, JFK was also a James Bond fan, and enjoyed the first 007 thriller, *Dr. No*.[35] Kennedy, a notorious womanizer, no doubt identified with how 007 always bedded a beautiful woman or two while saving the world from disaster. But *Dr. No* was the only Bond film he would see. The second 007 movie, *From Russia with Love*, was shown in the White House theater on November 21, 1963. Staffers predicted that the president—who would be assasinated the next day—would enjoy it.[36]

Two of Lyndon Johnson's favorite movies were the John Wayne classic *The Searchers* and *Guess Who's Coming to Dinner*,[37] in which a white girl introduces her black boyfriend to her parents. The latter undoubtedly appealed to LBJ's quest for civil rights during his administration. In general though, LBJ wasn't a movie buff—unless *he* was the star. In 1966 he commissioned the US Information Agency to produce a movie about himself, which was to be shown overseas. The ten-minute short, *A President's Country*, was a yawner—except in the White House theater, where Johnson was known to watch it over and over.[38]

Richard Nixon truly enjoyed movies, especially if they featured larger-than-life characters. He was a huge fan of *Patton*, the biopic about the bombastic World War II general George S. Patton, and watched it at least five times. Some critics have suggested that it influenced his decision, in the spring of 1970, to order the US invasion of Cambodia during the Vietnam War. During a 1977 interview with the British journalist David Frost, Nixon denied being influenced by the film.[39]

The White House theater saw little use during Gerald Ford's short presidency. "I'm not a moviegoer," he wrote, "never have been." In handwritten notes for his memoirs, he said he sometimes watched comedies and musicals "because they are relaxing," but didn't name any particular favorites. Ford did enjoy "historical documentaries because they are educational and therefore interesting." But other movies, he continued, "don't interest me. I don't dislike them, but if I have a choice I prefer other entertainment."[40]

George H. W. Bush also enjoyed thrillers; *The Hunt for Red October*, based on the Tom Clancy spy thriller, was one of his favorites,[41] but in general the forty-first president pursued outdoor recreation like fishing and golf. But his successor, Bill Clinton, was captivated by the movies. "You could go to the movies for a dime when I was a little boy," he told Roger Ebert, "and so I saw every movie that came my way when I was a child and I spent a lot of time in the movies. They fired my imagination, they inspired me, you know."[42] As president, he continued to be a regular moviegoer. "I try to see everything," and the theater, he insisted, was the greatest of presidential perks—even better than Air Force One or Camp David.[43]

His tastes were so varied—everything from *Schindler's List* to the *Naked Gun* movies[44]—that it's hard to characterize him. One of his favorites (besides *High Noon*) was *The Harmonists*, an obscure 1999 film about a popular vocal group in Nazi Germany that was forced to disband because it had Jewish singers. "God, it was a moving thing,"[45] Clinton recalled. He watched the film amid ongoing peace talks between Israel and the Palestinian Authority: a timely reminder, perhaps, about the importance of Israeli security.

George W. Bush's movie habits can generally be divided into two periods: those he watched before the terror attacks of September 11, 2001, and those he watched after. In terms of the former period, he enjoyed the satirical *Austin Powers* series; in the latter he opted for more serious fare: *We Were Soldiers*, about Vietnam, and *Black Hawk Down*, about US troops in Somalia in 1993. In 2006, he screened *United 93*, a film about one of the planes hijacked on September 11th.[46]

Barack Obama said in a 2008 interview that *The Godfather* and *Lawrence of Arabia* were among his favorites. "I'm a movie guy," he said. Also mentioned by Obama: *Casablanca*, which literally translates into, of course, White House.[47]

But the all-time presidential moviegoer appears to be a president who was only in the White House for one term: Jimmy Carter. He saw an estimated 480 movies during his four years in office—about ten per month. Like Clinton, his tastes varied, from the first film he watched as president—and one that helped put him there—*All the President's Men* about Watergate, to *Midnight Cowboy*, which originally had been X-rated. Like many Americans, he used movies as an escape. On September 21, 1977, he screened *The Longest Yard*, "so that we could forget about the day's events." His budget director, Bert Lance, had just resigned amid allegations of financial wrongdoing.[48]

The close relationship that Franklin Roosevelt established between Hollywood and the White House still exists today. Studios continue to supply any movie that a member of the First Family wants to watch, whenever they want. Although even the most humble citizen can now watch anything "on demand" as well, presidents still have an edge: Thanks to the Motion Picture Association of America (Hollywood's lobbying arm in Washington), studios go out of their way to send movies to the White House before they're released to the public. Now *that's* power. And an invitation to watch a movie with the president of the United States remains one of the rarest and most coveted in Washington today.

CHAPTER TWENTY-ONE

Barack Obama: The bin Laden Raid

The Situation Room

THE VIEW FROM THE PRIVATE DINING ROOM ON THE SECOND FLOOR OF THE White House is grand. Looking across Pennsylvania Avenue, beyond the canopy of trees and fountains of Lafayette Park—named for the Frenchman Marquis de Lafayette, who fought in the Revolutionary War—one can gaze up Sixteenth Street Northwest. To the right, in the one o'clock position, stands St. John's Episcopal Church, its modest yellow sanctuary punctuated by a white spire and topped by a small golden dome. Every president since James Madison in 1815 has attended services there at least once, earning St. John's the moniker "Church of the Presidents." One wartime president— Abraham Lincoln—slipped away to St. John's so often that he became the only commander in chief to have a pew named in his honor. It is there today: far right, last row, marked by a modest brass plaque.

But the view—through windows made of bullet-resistant glass several inches thick—also offers a sobering reminder of a more recent and tragic chapter in American history. Once open to vehicular traffic, the stretch of Pennsylvania Avenue has been closed since 1995, after a truck loaded with explosives parked in front of a federal office building in Oklahoma City and blew up, killing 168 people. It was the worst terrorist attack on American soil prior to September 11, 2001.

The room itself has enough history to fill a book. The first president to die in office—William Henry Harrison—passed here.[1] Named for the Prince of Wales, who visited President James Buchanan in 1860, it was redecorated the following year by First Lady Mary Lincoln, who ordered "1 Rosewood Bedstead, 2 Arm Chairs, 4 Wall Chairs with 1 Wash Stand, 1 Bureau and 1 Sofa" for it from a Philadelphia designer for $800, along with "1 Rich Rosewood Centre Table" for an additional $350. She made it a showcase.

The long sweep of history. In the Blue Room, site of Dolley Madison's sought-after salons (parties), Grover Cleveland's wedding, and placement each fall of the official White House Christmas tree, President Obama sits on James Monroe's Bellange sofa under a portrait of John Tyler. WHITE HOUSE PHOTO

Death would soon return to Mrs. Lincoln's magnificent room. On February 20, 1862, Willie, the president and first lady's third son, died in the bed, probably of typhoid fever. He was just eleven, and his passing sent his father—already prone to depression[2]—into despair. "My poor boy, he was too good for this earth. God has called him home," Lincoln said, as he gazed lovingly into the face of his dead son. "I know that he is much better off in heaven, but then we loved him so. It is hard, hard to have him die!"[3] Returning to his office, the president told his secretary, John Nicolay, "My boy is gone—he is actually gone!" and burst into tears.[4]

To console himself, Lincoln turned to Shakespeare, burying himself in *Macbeth* and *King Lear*. But it was a passage from one of the bard's lesser-known works—*King John*—that resonated most with the grief-stricken president. He read aloud to an aide the sorrow of Constance for her son:[5]

> And father cardinal, I have heard you say
> That we shall see and know our friends in heaven:
> If that be true, I shall see my boy again.

Three years later Lincoln would meet his own end, of course, and it was in this room where his beloved son died that the president's autopsy and embalming were performed. When they were finished, his widow asked for a lock of his hair.[6]

Long after Lincoln's clay had cooled, the chamber continued to play a significant role in the history of the White House. In 1897, it became the master bedroom for William and Ida McKinley, the bedroom for Theodore Roosevelt's oldest daughter, Alice, and William Howard Taft's daughter, Helen. In 1929, the Lincoln bed—which had been moved around over the years—was returned to the room by Herbert Hoover, and the room became known as the Lincoln Bedroom. Harry and Bess Truman moved the bed again—this time for good—to a room on the southeast side of the second floor, and *that* room, which had been Lincoln's office, became the Lincoln Bedroom. Finally, in 1961, the room where one president had died and another was autopsied and embalmed was converted into a dining room by Jacqueline Kennedy. Ever since, First Families have gathered here, away from the harsh glare of the spotlight, for a few minutes of peace and quiet—and perhaps a simple cup of coffee.

And so it was here—or in a smaller dining room off the Oval Office itself—that four men found themselves gathered around the room's

A snowy evening as President Obama and Chief of Staff Denis McDonough walk along the famous West Colonnade connecting the West Wing and the mansion. On their left is the press briefing room; on the right is the Rose Garden. The walkways on both the west and east sides of the mansion first appeared In Thomas Jefferson's day, but were later removed to make way (on the west side) for a vast series of conservatories (greenhouses). They were rebuilt during Theodore Roosevelt's renovation in 1902. WHITE HOUSE PHOTO

oval-shaped table playing spades on the afternoon of May 1, 2011. Game after game they played—about fifteen in all[7]—lost in thought and deep in worry. At that very moment, as they put their cards down on the gleaming mahogany table, history was being made again—this time seven thousand miles and nine time zones to the east. President Barack Obama had done all he could. There was nothing left to do but wait. In the Situation Room, in the basement of the West Wing, the tension had been so great that the commander in chief had to clear his head, and thus the mindless card game upstairs.[8] An aide at the time, Reggie Love, recalls the president saying, "I'm not going to be down there, I can't watch this entire thing."[9][10]

The "thing" was one of the most daring military operations in US history: "Neptune Spear," the raid on a compound in Abbottabad, Pakistan, to get America's enemy number one—Osama bin Laden.

The first sign that something might have been going on that lazy Sunday afternoon came in a pool report that went out to members of the White House press corps at 2:08 p.m.

"Just nine holes of golf," it said, noting that President Obama had returned to the White House at 2:04, after being on the course at Joint Base Andrews, just outside the city, for three hours. There had been intermittent showers, but not enough to keep the president from his favorite form of relaxation. Unusual? Yes. Reason for concern? Nothing discernible.

The president, still in his golf clothes, went downstairs to the Situation Room. What transpired over the next few dramatic hours became one of the most important and best-known events in the history of the command center. A picture taken by White House photographer Pete Souza of the president and senior officers of the government crowded into a small room watching the raid on a monitor may likely be the most iconic image of the Obama presidency—and perhaps of the Situation Room itself.

As those officials watched and worried, it probably did not occur to them that the Situation Room had been formed nearly fifty years before to the very day—commencing operations on or about May 13, 1961.[11]

A command center was quickly built. It may have seemed like a new idea, but it really wasn't. A telegraph office in what is today the Eisenhower Executive Office Building—adjacent to the White House—served as a command post for Lincoln during the Civil War. In 1898, McKinley set up a watch center in the mansion itself, on the second floor—just down the hall from his bedroom—so he could monitor the war with Spain (it was later abandoned).

The closest version to the present-day Situation Room came during World War II, when Franklin Roosevelt used the Map Room—on the ground floor of the White House—as his personal command center. Telegrams and dispatches from the Army and Navy came in around the clock. The room was also used to send encrypted messages to FDR when he was away, and to wartime allies like British prime minister Winston Churchill and Soviet premier Josef Stalin. Because FDR got around in his wheelchair, furniture was clustered in the center of the room; this enabled the commander in chief to roll up directly to huge maps of Europe and the Pacific that hung on the walls.[12]

The command center was disbanded after the war, and for the next sixteen years—a period that included the Korean War—Presidents Harry

John Adams first arrived at the White House on November 1, 1800, in a carriage that was described as a "chariot" pulled by four horses. Presidents today travel in a modern-day chariot: a high-powered helicopter that can whisk them away in moments. Here, from a rarely seen vantage point, the president holds hands with daughter Sasha as they return to the White House on January 4, 2010. WHITE HOUSE PHOTO

Truman and Dwight Eisenhower had no equivalent. Three months into his short-lived term, John F. Kennedy decided one was needed.

The "Sit Room"—which also became known to insiders as "the woodshed"—got heavy use during the Vietnam War; Lyndon Johnson spent so much time in the complex that he had his Oval Office chair installed there.[13] In addition to Vietnam, numerous crises—notably the Six-Day War in the Middle East and the Soviet invasion of Czechoslovakia—kept staffers busy. Then as now, North Korea was a particular worry: In 1968 it seized the US Navy spy ship *Pueblo*; the next year it shot down a US reconnaissance plane over the Sea of Japan, killing all thirty-one Americans on board.

Despite his intense focus on foreign affairs, Richard Nixon rarely visited the Situation Room. His national security advisor (and future secretary of state), Henry Kissinger, thought Johnson spent too much time there, getting lost in the minutia of crisis management; "Situation Room syndrome,"[14] Nixon called it. Nixon's advisors—often led by Kissinger himself—typically met without the president. Even during the Yom Kippur War in 1973, when a surprise attack on Israel nearly led to the Jewish state's use of nuclear weapons,[15] Nixon remained in the Oval Office, while advisors discussed the crisis downstairs. Kissinger's deputy, Alexander Haig, would periodically go upstairs to update the president.[16]

After Nixon converted the indoor swimming pool into a briefing room for the press in 1970, an outdoor pool was built just south of the Oval Office. But to reach it, members of the First Family (starting with President Gerald Ford, who swam on a regular basis) had to walk outside. To give them more privacy, a door was built through the door of the Sit Room's communications vault. Ford usually swam after hours, and staffers sometimes had only a few moment's notice that the president was about to walk through. One worker recalls "shoving all the magazines, half-eaten sandwiches and trash into desk drawers, putting their shoes on and running combs through their hair." The door was moved during the Reagan era.[17]

Throughout the 1970s, 1980s, and 1990s, the Situation Room played an integral role in supporting Presidents Jimmy Carter, Ronald Reagan, George H. W. Bush, and Bill Clinton. Carter relied on it daily during the Iranian hostage crisis, when sixty-six Americans were seized in November 1979; fifty-two would be held until January 20, 1981, when Reagan succeeded him. Reagan's near assassination two months later sent the Sit Room into crisis mode; and Reagan used it himself during a variety of crises, such as the 1983 bombing of a US Marine barracks in Beirut, Lebanon, and the 1986 explosion of the space shuttle *Challenger*. During the principal events of George H. W. Bush's presidency—the fall of the Berlin Wall and collapse of Communism, and the first Gulf War—Bush relied on it heavily, as did Bill Clinton during the first World Trade Center attack in 1993 and war in Kosovo five years later.

On September 11, 2001, after decades of monitoring wars, crises, and catastrophes around the world, Situation Room staffers found themselves monitoring one in their own backyard. After hijacked airplanes were flown into each tower of New York's World Trade Center, air traffic controllers tracked a third plane—headed for Washington.

A supervisor at Reagan National Airport called the Secret Service command center at the White House at 9:33 a.m. and urged an immediate evacuation: "What I'm telling you, buddy, if you've got people, you'd better get them out of there. And I mean right goddamned now!"[18]

President George W. Bush was in Florida, but Vice President Dick Cheney, in the White House, was hustled through a tunnel to a bomb shelter deep below the East Wing. Other top officials, including National Security Advisor Condoleezza Rice, quickly followed.

But as the plane approached, staffers in the Situation Room refused to leave. The dozen or so men and women stayed at their desks, keeping information flowing to the president, Cheney, and other key officials. The senior duty officer, Rob Hargis, took a call from a National Security Council official urging them to get out immediately. Hargis turned to his colleagues and announced: "We have been ordered to evacuate. If you want to go, go now."

No one moved.

"We're staying," Hargis told the official.[19]

Putting their own lives at risk, every single person stayed on duty that morning. As a precaution, their names were sent to the CIA's operations center. The Sit Room staffers called it "the dead list."[20]

That plane smashed into the Pentagon, two miles away, sending thick black smoke into the air—easily visible from the White House on that crystal blue morning. A fourth and final hijacked plane was also headed for Washington—either the White House or Capitol, it was feared—but was brought down in Pennsylvania as brave passengers fought back against the terrorists. The attack on the United States killed 2,977 people—the second bloodiest individual day in American history after the Civil War battle of Antietam.[21]

The events that morning—forever seared into the consciousness of Americans as Pearl Harbor and the Kennedy assassination were for earlier generations—set in motion a manhunt that would culminate nine years, seven months, and twenty days later, on the dark, dingy third floor of the compound in Abbottabad. In the Situation Room, the electrifying message came through loud and clear: "For God and country—Geronimo, Geronimo, Geronimo." After a pause, he added, "Geronimo E.K.I.A."—"enemy killed in action."

"We got him,"[22] Obama said.

Kennedy might not recognize the Situation Room today—it is far bigger, for one, following a major renovation in 2006-07 that greatly expanded its size and capabilities, and there are now three principal conference rooms instead of one. Sources say a multi-year construction project that ended in 2012 may have been a further expansion of Situation Room facilities—tons of concrete and steel beams were seen going into a sprawling hole several stories below ground—though the official line was that the massive project was merely an upgrade of the White House's water, sewer, heating, and air-conditioning facilities. Whatever it was, it appeared to be the biggest White House construction project undertaken since the Truman era.

From its original design—selected by the only president who would never live there, George Washington—to John Adams to Barack Obama, the White House has grown and changed along with the nation it represents. Adams could not have imagined the telegraph, so helpful for Abraham Lincoln during the Civil War. Lincoln, in turn, would have marveled at Rutherford B. Hayes's telephone. In 1903, Theodore Roosevelt cheered along with everyone else when Orville and Wilbur Wright took to the skies of Kitty Hawk; just sixty-six years later, Richard Nixon, in what the White House called an "interplanetary conversation," spoke with Neil Armstrong and Edwin "Buzz" Aldrin on the surface of the moon. TR couldn't have imagined that, nor could he envision his distant cousin's future use of radio or Kennedy's use of television. As for Barack Obama, his innovative use of Facebook, Twitter, and YouTube has changed the way presidents communicate with Americans just as much as FDR and JFK changed it in their day. And the president's installation of solar panels on the White House roof—thirty years after Reagan tore down Carter's—is just as much a technological leap forward for the White House as the gas lighting that came to the mansion during the Polk years. Who can say what tomorrow will bring?

The great mansion at 1600 Pennsylvania Avenue—the People's House, as Thomas Jefferson thought of it—remains in many respects as it did on November 1, 1800, when Adams's carriage pulled up to the south entrance. There was no South or North Portico. The floor plans are somewhat different. No dripping laundry hangs in the East Room. Yet much remains the same, and Mr. Adams would be able to find his way around today's White House with relative ease.

The benediction he wrote to Abigail in his first full day in the mansion—inscribed today over the fireplace in the State Dining Room—rings as true today as it did that chilly fall day:

I pray to heaven to bestow the best of Blessings on this House and all that shall hereafter inhabit it . . . May none but honest and wise men ever rule under this roof.

ACKNOWLEDGMENTS

When I was eighteen, I took out a piece of paper and made a list of things I wanted to do in my life. Things like skydiving, traveling around the world, and watching every movie that won a "Best Picture" Academy Award. Check, check, and check. Now another item gets crossed off: writing a book. It was a privilege to write it.

Over the course of my research, I received help from a number of wonderful historians and archivists. Among them were William Bushong, chief historian of the White House Historical Association, who filled in a few holes in my manuscript. C. James Taylor, Editor in Chief of the Adams Papers at the Massachusetts Historical Society, patiently answered my questions about John Adams, and Dr. John C. Pinheiro of Michigan's Aquinas College did so concerning James K. Polk. Dr. John F. Marszalek, Executive Director of the Ulysses S. Grant Presidential Library at Mississippi State University, invited me down for a visit, and I intend to take him up on it. Dr. Eugene Trani of Virginia Commonwealth University knows all there is to know about Warren Harding, and when it comes to Harry Truman, Tammy Williams of the Truman Presidential Library and Museum in Independence, Missouri, was terrific. Abigail Malangone of the John F. Kennedy Presidential Library and Museum and Steve Branch and Michael Pinckney of the Ronald Reagan Presidential Library also deserve my thanks, as do three archivists at the Richard Nixon Presidential Library and Museum: Olivia Anastasiadis, Gregory Cumming, and Jon Fletcher. Jeannie Chen of the National Archives in College Park, Maryland, also deserves my thanks, as do Keith Wallman and Lauren Brancato at Lyons Press, who helped keep the train running on time. I'm very appreciative to everyone for their generous and cheerful assistance.

But three people in particular deserve more gratitude than I am capable of expressing here. This book simply would not have happened without my agent, Eric Nelson, who helped turn my ideas into a workable project and went out and found a buyer for it. He has been helpful and supportive every step of the way, and to him I owe my heartfelt and humble thanks. My editor, Jon Sternfeld, who brought his own love of history to the table, was wonderful in making the copy flow smoothly, suggesting better words and phrases, and shaping the overall contours of each chapter. He is truly gifted, and I am deeply appreciative. And saving the best for last, I am particularly grateful to Kathryn, my wife, for her love, support, and patience throughout. She truly is my better half—thank you for helping me to reach higher and to persevere to the end of what has been a sometimes bumpy road.

NOTES

Chapter One
John Adams: A Benediction for the Future

1 John Ferling, *Adams vs. Jefferson* (Oxford: Oxford University Press, 2004), 1.
2 David McCullough, *John Adams* (New York: Simon & Schuster, 2001), 548.
3 Ferling, 123.
4 William Seale, *The President's House* (Washington, DC: White House Historical Association, 1986), 36.
5 Ibid.
6 White House Historical Association, "Building the White House," www.whha.org/whha_classroom.
7 Hoban's inspiration for the White House can be traced to two buildings: a villa in Dublin called Leinster House and Castle Coole, a neoclassical mansion in Northern Ireland.
8 William Seale, *The White House* (Washington, DC: White House Historical Association, 1992), 6.
9 White House Museum.org; www.whitehousemuseum.org/special/renovation-1792 .html.
10 McCullough, 542.
11 Ibid., 541.
12 Ibid., 542.
13 Seale, *The White House*, 33.
14 Anna Marie Thornton, diary entries for November 1, 1800, as cited in *The President's House* by William Seale (Washington, DC: White House Historical Association, 1986), 81.
15 The White House was originally referred to as the "President's Palace." But this reference to monarchy proved to be unpopular. It was also known as the "White House" and the "Executive Mansion." The official name "White House" was officially adopted by President Theodore Roosevelt on October 12, 1901—nearly 109 years to the day after the building's cornerstone was laid.
16 Seale, *The White House*, 35.
17 Ibid.
18 Gilbert Gude, "Presidents and the Potomac," in *White House History, Collection I* (Washington, DC: White House Historical Association, 2004), 87.
19 Ibid.
20 Seale, *The White House*, 34.
21 Ibid., 24.
22 Ibid., 15.

23   Ibid.

24   Seale, *The President's House*, 80.

25   Ibid.

26   Ibid. 77

27   Betty Monkman, *The White House* (Washington, DC: White House Historical Association, 2000), 30.

28   Seale, *The President's House*, 80.

29   The original Lansdowne painting today hangs in the Smithsonian's National Portrait Gallery; a replica painted by Stuart hangs on the East Room wall (www .khanacademy.org/humanities/art-americas/british-colonies/early-republic/a/ gilbert-stuarts-lansdowne-portrait).

30   www.whitehousemuseum.org/special/renovation-1792.htm.

31   Seale, *The President's House*, 85.

32   The cold, drafty conditions required that fires be kept burning at all times; the president paid for firewood out of his own pocket.

33   www.whitehousehistory.org/whha_classroom/documents/WHHA_primary- document-1800.pdf.

34   McCullough, 503.

35   Ibid., 564.

36   White House Historical Association, www.whitehousehistory.org/history/white- house-facts-trivia/tour-state-dining-room.html.

Chapter Two
Thomas Jefferson: The Lewis & Clark Expedition

1   William J. Bennett, *America: The Last Best Hope* (Nashville: Nelson Current, 2006), 178.

2   Seale, *The President's House*, 89.

3   Ibid, 90.

4   In what could have been a conflict of interest, entries for the design of the White House first came to the Secretary of State's office, before being forwarded to President Washington for review. At one point Washington, less than impressed, wrote Jefferson, "if none more elegant than these should appear . . . the exhibition will be a dull one indeed." It isn't known if Washington was referring to entry "A.Z.," Jefferson's own anonymous entry.

5   Seale, *The White House*, 5.

6   Seale, *The President's House*, 89.

7   Dumas Malone, *Jefferson the President* (Boston: Little Brown and Company, 1970), 38.

8   Seale, *The President's House*, 83.

9   Ibid.

10   Ibid., 91.

11   Seale, *The White House*, 41.

12   Ibid., 88.

13   Seale, *The President's House*, 100–01.

14 David C. Whitney, *The American Presidents* (New York: Reader's Digest Association, Inc., 2012), 41.

15 Seale, *The White House*, 46.

16 Seale, *The President's House*, 92.

17 Donald Jackson, *Letters of the Lewis and Clark Expedition, with Related Documents: 1783–1854*, 2nd ed. (Urbana: University of Illinois Press, 1978), Vol. I, 2.

18 Ibid., 1.

19 www.monticello.org/site/research-and-collections/nicholas-lewis.

20 Jackson, 3.

21 That Jefferson cited Lewis's knowledge of America's western frontier "& it's situation" suggests that the president-elect was already thinking of the possibility of somehow taking possession of the Louisiana Territory, even before he was sworn in.

22 Jackson, 2.

23 Ibid.

24 Ibid., 3.

25 Seale, *The President's House*, 94.

26 Ibid.

27 Ibid., 95.

28 Ibid.

29 Ibid.

30 Dumas Malone, *Jefferson the President: First Term, 1801–1805* (Boston: Little, Brown and Company, 1970), 44.

31 Jon Meacham, *Thomas Jefferson The Art of Power* (New York: Random House, 2012), 353–54.

32 Ibid., 357.

33 Ibid.

34 Ibid.

35 Stephen E. Ambrose, *Undaunted Courage* (New York: Simon & Schuster, 1996), 74.

36 John Logan Allen, *Passage Through the Garden: Lewis and Clark and the Image of the American Northwest* (Urbana: University of Illinois Press, 1975), 178.

37 Ambrose, 76.

38 Jackson, 16–17.

39 Ambrose, 56.

40 Meacham, 384.

41 Ibid.

42 Ibid., 387.

43 National Archives, Louisiana Purchase Treaty, April 30, 1803, Record Group 11, General Records of the US Government.

44 Meacham, 387.

45 Ibid.

46 Ibid.

47 Ibid.

48 Meacham, 388.

Chapter Three
James and Dolley Madison: The Burning of the White House

1   Maud Wilder Goodwin, *Dolly Madison* (New York: Charles Scribner's Sons, 1898), 174.

2   Ralph Ketcham, *James Madison* (Charlottesville: University of Virginia Press, 1990), 577.

3   Goodwin, 173.

4   Architect of the Capitol, www.aoc.gov/blog/"-most-magnificent-ruin"-burning -capitol-during-war-1812.

5   Seale, *The President's House*, 119.

6   Ibid., 48.

7   Ibid., 120.

8   Ibid., 120–21.

9   Ibid., 122.

10 Seale, *The White House*, 81–82.

11 Ibid., 82.

12 Seale, *The President's House*, 123.

13 Ibid.

14 Ibid.

15 Ibid., 123–25.

16 Ibid., 126.

17 Seale, *The White House*, 53.

18 White House Historical Association, The Red Room, http://learning.whitehouse-history.org/history/white-house-facts-trivia/tour-red-room.html.

19 Ketcham, 477.

20 Seale, *The President's House,* 123.

21 John B. Roberts II, *Rating the First Ladies* (New York: Kensington Publishing Corp., 2003) 28.

22 Ibid.

23 Ketcham, 476.

24 Seale, *The President's House,* 130.

25 www.whitehousehistory.org/history/white-house-timelines/music-performances-1790s-1840s.html.

26 Seale, 128.

27 Jeff Broadwater, *James Madison: A Son of Virginia and a Founder of the Nation* (Chapel Hill: University of North Carolina Press, 2012), 118.

28 Ketcham, 527–28.

29 Ibid., 528–29.

30 A. J. Langguth, *Union 1812* (New York: Simon & Schuster, 2006), 234.

31 *Washingtonian* magazine, "Washington Burning: The 200th Anniversary of the War of 1812," www.washingtonian.com/articles/people/washington-burning-the-200th-anniversary-of-the-war-of-1812.

32 Steve Vogel, *Through the Perilous Fight* (New York: Random House, 2013), 3.

33 Cockburn, whose tactics were regarded by his fellow British officers as barbaric, had been promising for months to burn down the President's House. He would, he boasted, bow before Dolley Madison and then set fire to her home (Langguth, 294–95).

34 Langguth, 296.

35 Steve Vogel, *Through the Perilous Fight* (New York: Random House, 2013), 51.

36 Monroe would soon change his mind. Realizing that Washington could indeed be a British target, he pressured the president to form the Tenth Military Division, entrusted with the city's defense, which Madison did on July 2. He also urged the president to fire War Secretary Armstrong.

37 Goodwin, 168.

38 Ibid.

39 Langguth, 298.

40 Vogel, 97.

41 Goodwin, 171.

42 Vogel, 122.

43 Goodwin, 171.

44 Ibid.

45 Ibid., 174.

46 Ibid., 173.

47 Ibid., 176.

48 Vogel, 153.

49 Ibid.

50 Ibid.

51 Goodwin, 173.

52 Julia Moberg, *Presidential Pets* (Watertown, MA: Charlesbridge Publishing, 2012), 10.

53 Goodwin, 176.

54 Ibid., 177.

55 Les Standiford, *Washington Burning* (New York: Three Rivers Press, 2008), 272.

56 Ibid., 273

57 Vogel, 153–55.

58 Even after it was taken down from the wall of the Oval Drawing Room, the painting was nearly destroyed. Sioussat might have rolled up the canvas—cracking the paint—before Barker and De Peyster told him to just lay it flat on the floor (Standiford, 273).

59 Standiford, 278.

60 Seale, *The President's House*, 134.

61 Vogel, 157.

62 Ibid., 158.

63 Ibid.

64 Ibid., 158–59.

65 Ibid., 154.

66 Seale, *The President's House*, 135.

67 Langguth, 308.
68 Standiford, 278.
69 Seale, *The President's House,* 136.
70 Ibid.
71 Standiford, 278.
72 Seale, *The President's House,* 136.
73 Ketcham, 579.
74 Vogel, 182.
75 Ibid., 201.
76 Ibid., 202.
77 Standiford, 284.
78 Ibid., 285
79 The soldiers who attacked Congress did so because lawmakers, they claimed, had not paid them for their service during the Revolutionary War. The resulting "Philadelphia Mutiny" caused Congress to leave the city and create a new, more secure nation's capital.
80 White House Historical Association, www.whitehousehistory.org/history/white-house-facts-trivia/tour-overview.html.
81 White House Historical Association, "America Under Fire," www.whitehouse history.org/presentations/madisons-war-burning-washington-city/part-04-after math.html.
82 Ibid.
83 Seale, *The President's House,* 139.

Chapter Four
James Monroe: The Monroe Doctrine

1   Monkman, 53.
2   Monroe was James Madison's secretary of state during the War of 1812. But after the attack on Washington, Madison sacked Secretary of War John Armstrong and replaced him with Monroe.
3   Seale, *The President's House,* 145.
4   Henry Ammon, *James Monroe: The Quest for National Identity* (Charlottesville: University Press of Virginia, 1990), 13–14.
5   Ibid., 27–28
6   Biography of James Monroe, University of Virginia's Miller Center, http://miller center.org/president/monroe/essays/biography/2.
7   Bennett, 177
8   *The American Experience,* PBS, www.pbs.org/wgbh/amex/telephone/timeline/timeline_text.html.
9   Ammon, 366.
10 Seale, *The President's House,* 146
11 Ibid., 139.
12 Seale, *The White House,* 61
13 Seale, *The President's House,* 140.

14 Ibid., 147.
15 Gilson Willets, *Inside History of the White House* (New York: The Christian Herald, 1908), 47.
16 But one of Hoban's time-saving shortcuts would present future problems. Instead of using brick in parts of the mansion's interior, he used timber. Not being as strong or durable as stone, this would cause the mansion to weaken dangerously. More than 125 years later, the near collapse of the White House during the administration of Harry Truman would be blamed in part on Hoban's inauspicious choice of raw materials.
17 Seale, *The President's House*, 142.
18 Ibid., 148.
19 Willets, 47.
20 Even though the President's House itself had been rebuilt in just three years, the North and South Porticoes would take another seven and thirteen years, respectively, to complete. The main culprit for the slowdown seems to be the economic depression that gripped the nation beginning in 1819 (*White House History*, 222).
21 Ibid.
22 Secretary of State John Quincy Adams asked the president if it would not be wiser to first have a reception for the diplomatic corps. Monroe balked at first: Why should foreigners be given preferential treatment over the citizenry? But he consulted his Cabinet anyway, the result of which was that diplomats were invited thirty minutes earlier (Seale, *The President's House*, 149).
23 Seale, *The President's House*, 149
24 Ibid., 154.
25 Ibid.
26 Monkman, 61.
27 Ibid., 60.
28 Seale, *The President's House*, 155.
29 Ibid., 156.
30 Seale, *The White House*, 67.
31 Seale, *The President's House*, 158.
32 Paul F. Boller Jr., *Presidential Wives*, 2nd ed. (Oxford: Oxford University Press, 1998), 49.
33 Ibid.
34 Boller, 50–51.
35 Seale, *The President's House*, 158.
36 www.whitehouse.gov/about/presidents/jamesmonroe.
37 Bennett, 215.
38 Ammon, 462.
39 Miller Center, University of Virginia, "Biography of James Monroe," http://millercenter.org/president/monroe/essays/biography/4.
40 Wayne Fields, *Union of Words* (New York: The Free Press, 1996), 181.
41 Eric Foner and John A. Garraty, eds., *The Reader's Companion to American History* (Boston: Houghton Mifflin Company, 1991), 743.

42 History of Fort Ross, California, www.fortross.org/russian-american-company .htm#The%20Russian%20Advance%20to%20California.

43 The Monroe Doctrine, www.history.com/topics/monroe-doctrine.

44 Ibid.

45 Ammon, 476.

46 Ibid., 477.

47 Bennett, 215.

48 Ammon, 479.

49 Ibid., 478.

50 Bennett, 215.

51 Fields, 185.

52 Ammon, 478–79.

53 Ibid., 487.

54 Bennett, 216.

Chapter Five
Andrew Jackson: The Nullification Crisis

1   Princeton University, Tariff of 1828, www.princeton.edu/~achaney/tmve/wiki100k/ docs/Tariff_of_1828.html.

2   Jon Meacham, *American Lion: Andrew Jackson in the White House* (New York: Random House, 2009), 58.

3   http://worldhistoryproject.org/1830/4/13/jackson-interrupts-robert-haynes-toast -to-openly-challenge-john-c-calhoun.

4   Bennett, 236.

5   Corman O'Brien, *Secret Lives of the U.S. Presidents* (Philadelphia: Quirk Books, 2009), 42.

6   H. W. Brands, *Andrew Jackson* (New York: Doubleday, 2005), 137–38.

7   Meacham, *American Lion*, 30

8   Ibid., 4–5.

9   Seale, *The President's House*, 175.

10 Brands, 405.

11 Rachel had previously been married to another man, Lewis Robards. It was an unhappy marriage, and they separated in 1790. She married Jackson in 1791, thinking that Robards had finalized their divorce. He hadn't. The divorce would not be completed until 1794. This led to charges during the presidential campaign of 1828 that Rachel was, among other things, a bigamist and an adultress. H. W. Brands, *Andrew Jackson* (New York: Doubleday, 2005), 62–65.

12 Seale, *The President's House*, 176.

13 Ibid.

14 Gadsby's Hotel (later renamed as the National) also played host to James K. Polk, James Buchanan, and Abraham Lincoln; Lincoln's assassin, John Wilkes Booth, stayed in room 228 while plotting the president's murder.

15 Seale, *The President's House*, 176.

16 Monkman, 81–82.

17   Seale, *The President's House*, 172.
18   Monkman, 82–83.
19   Ibid., 83.
20   Seale, *The President's House*, 189.
21   Kenneth W. Leish and the Editors of the Newsweek Book Division, *The White House* (New York: Newsweek Book Division, 1972), 39.
22   Seale, *The President's House*, 189.
23   Seale, www.whha.org/presentations/waddell-artist-visits-white-house-past/andrew-jackson-president-essay.html.
24   Richard Norton Smith, "America's House: The Bully Pulpit on Pennsylvania Avenue," in Frank Freidel and William Pencak, eds., *The White House* (Boston: Northeastern University Press, 1994), 35.
25   Seale, *The President's House*, 183.
26   Ibid.
27   Willets, 102–3.
28   Wendell Garrett, ed., *Our Changing White House* (Boston: Northeastern University Press, 1995), 43.
29   Monkman, 82.
30   WhiteHouseHistory.org, Dimensions and Statistics, www.whitehousehistory.org/history/white-house-facts-trivia/facts-white-house-dimensions.html.
31   Seale, *The White House*, 88–90.
32   Ibid.
33   Ibid.
34   Ibid.
35   Ibid.
36   Princeton University, Tariff of 1828.
37   Meacham, 137.
38   Ibid., 173.
39   Bennett, 237.
40   Ibid.
41   Ibid.
42   On his deathbed in 1845, Jackson said that he only had two regrets in his life: One of them was not hanging John C. Calhoun (Bennett, 240).
43   Ibid., 240.
44   Meacham, *American Lion*, 247.
45   Ibid.

Chapter Six
John Tyler: Ten Funerals and a Wedding

1   Seale, *The President's House*, 234.
2   Ibid., 235.
3   Ibid.
4   Ibid.
5   Ibid., 236.

6 Gerhard Peters and John T. Woolley, "William Henry Harrison: Report of the Physicians," April 4, 1841, *The American Presidency Project*, www.presidency.ucsb.edu/ws/?pid=67342.

7 Paul F. Boller Jr., *Presidential Anecdotes* (Oxford: Oxford University Press, 1981), 96.

8 Ibid.

9 George Washington and Alexander Hamilton started the first national bank in 1791 to hold the government's money. After its charter expired, a second national bank was founded in 1816. But Andrew Jackson, accusing the bank of holding too much power and having little congressional oversight, shut it down in 1833 (www.history.com/topics/george-washington; www.history.com/topics/alexander-hamilton).

10 Washington *Madisonian*, August 19, 1841, as recounted in Seale, *The President's House*, 239.

11 Boller, *Presidential Anecdotes*, 96.

12 The chandeliers were not an original feature in the White House. In 1818, after moving into the White House after it was rebuilt following the 1814 fire, President James Monroe ordered two of them.

13 Boller, *Presidential Wives*, 78.

14 Priscilla Tyler, fragment of a letter to Mary Grace Raoul, Washington, May 1841, Coleman Papers (as noted in *President's House*, 242).

15 In addition to Letitia Tyler, Caroline Harrison, the wife of Benjamin Harrison, died in 1892, and Woodrow Wilson's first wife, Ellen, passed in 1914.

16 Andrew Jackson's wife, Rachel, died when he was president-elect.

17 Seale, *The President's House*, 245–46.

Chapter Seven
James K. Polk: Five Presidents, One War

1 Seale, *The President's House*, 249.

2 James McPherson, *Battle Cry of Freedom* (Oxford: Oxford University Press, 1988), 47.

3 Today Polk is merely the ninth-youngest president.

4 Monkman, 101.

5 Ibid., 102–3.

6 Seale, *The White House*, 102.

7 Ibid.

8 Seale, *The President's House*, 267.

9 Ibid., 268–69.

10 Ibid.

11 Ibid., 216.

12 Ibid., 268.

13 Ibid.

14 www.pbs.org/wnet/amerpres/presidents/pres11/main_pres11.html.

15 John Whitcomb and Claire Whitcomb, *Real Life at the White House* (New York: Routledge, 2000), 98.

16 Ibid., 99.

17 In 1836 Blair purchased a home near the Executive Mansion that today is known as Blair House, often offered to visiting heads of state. Presidents sometimes stay there as well.

18 John Siegenthaler, *James K. Polk* (New York: Times Books, 2003), 103.

19 Seale, *The President's House*, 273.

20 Ibid.

21 Robert W. Merry, *A Country of Vast Designs* (New York: Simon & Schuster, 2009), 269.

22 Ibid.

23 Ibid.

24 Seale, *The President's House*, 262.

25 At more formal White House events, Sarah Polk did serve alcohol. The wife of one congressman wrote in her diary that a four-hour dinner included multiple wines for the many courses, along with champagne, a Sauternes, and ruby port after dinner. There were so many glasses (six) that they "formed a rainbow around each plate."

26 John B. Roberts II, *Rating the First Ladies: The Women Who Influenced the Presidency* (New York: Citadel Press, 2003), 67.

27 Visitors frustrated with "Sahara Sarah's" ban on hard liquor frequently left White House receptions early and went to the nearby home of Dolley Madison, who was more than happy to accommodate them.

28 Seale, *The President's House,* 261.

29 Ibid., 262.

30 Ibid., 251.

31 Ibid.

32 Sarah Polk's morals were such that she also refused to attend the theater or racetrack.

33 Merry, 270.

34 Mark Byrnes, *James K. Polk* (Santa Barbara: ABC-CLIO, 2001), 129.

35 Inaugural Address of James K. Polk, The American Presidency Project, University of California Santa Barbara, www.presidency.ucsb.edu/ws/index.php?pid=25814.

36 John Seigenthaler, *James K. Polk* (New York: Times Books, 2003), 135.

37 Walter R. Borneman, *Polk, The Man Who Transformed the Presidency and America* (New York: Random House, 2008), 145.

38 Seale, *The President's House*, 252.

39 Ibid.

40 Ibid., 245.

41 Borneman, 198.

42 Seale, *The President's House,* 253.

43 Ibid.

44 Borneman, 205.

45 US Senate History, www.senate.gov/artandhistory/history/minute/Senate_Votes_for_War_against_Mexico.htm.

46 Seigenthaler, 132–33.

47 Byrnes, 157.
48 Seigenthaler, 133.
49 Ibid., 133–34.
50 Merry, 293–94.
51 Seigenthaler, 141.
52 Merry, 315–16.
53 Byrnes, 22.
54 Ibid.
55 Jack K. Bauer, *Zachary Taylor: Soldier, Planter, Statesman of the Old Southwest* (Shreveport: Louisiana State University Press, 1985), 314–16.
56 University of Virginia, Miller Center: Biography of Franklin Pierce, http://miller-center.org/president/pierce/essays/biography/2.
57 David Herbert Donald, *Lincoln* (New York: Touchstone, 1995), 115.
58 Ibid., 123.
59 Ibid., 123–24.
60 Ibid., 122.
61 Ibid., 124.
62 Ibid., 125.
63 Seigenthaler, 145.
64 Ibid., 143.
65 The lyrics to the US Marine Corps hymn include the line "the Halls of Montezuma," a reference to the Battle of Chapultepec, in the heart of the Mexican capital.
66 Merry, 411.
67 Seigenthaler, 147.
68 Merry, 453.

Chapter Eight
Abraham Lincoln: The Gettysburg Address

1 University of California at Santa Barbara, American Presidency Project, www.presidency.ucsb.edu/ws/?pid=29502.
2 Allen Guelzo, *Lincoln's Emancipation Proclamation: The End of Slavery in America* (New York: Simon & Schuster, 2004), 186.
3 Seale, *The White House*, 110–11.
4 Mary Lincoln decided at a young age that she would marry a president, and married her husband because she thought he would rise far in life. "He is to be President of the United States one day," she said early in their marriage. "If I had not thought so I never would have married him, for you can see he is not pretty. But look at him. Doesn't he look as if he would make a magnificent President?" (Roberts, *Rating the First Ladies*, 107).
5 Seale, *The President's House*, 390.
6 Roberts, 109.
7 Seale, *The President's House*, 390.
8 Roberts, 107.
9 Seale, *The President's House*, 376–77.

10   Ibid., 366.

11   Donald, 285.

12   www.mrlincolnswhitehouse.org/inside.asp?ID=226&subjectID=3.

13   Donald, 285.

14   "Death Threats and Cabinet Quarrels Plagued Civil War President," *St. Petersburg Times,* July 27, 1947.

15   Seale, *The President's House,* 374.

16   Tom Wheeler, "The First Wired President," *New York Times,* May 24, 2012, http://opinionator.blogs.nytimes.com/2012/05/24/the-first-wired-president/?_php=true&_type=blogs&_php=true&_type=blogs&_r=1.

17   Thomas F. Pendel, *Thirty-Six Years in the White House* (Washington, DC: Neale Publishing Company, 1902), 179.

18   David McRae, *The Americans At Home* (New York: E. Dutton & Co., Inc. 1952), 102–10.

19   Tad was quite the rascal. He aggravated visitors by pulling on their beards and threatening to set his pet goat loose on them, and when his father stood at a White House window reviewing the troops, Tad sometimes appeared in the window above—waving a Confederate flag.

20   Seale, *The President's House,* 379.

21   Letter from Nicolay to Therena Bates, Washington, February 2, 1962, and to Hay, Washington, February 9, 1864, Nicolay Papers, Library of Congress; John Hay, *Addresses,* 335–36 (in Seale, *The President's House,* 379, footnote 6).

22   Seale, *The President's House,* 377.

23   Ibid., 292.

24   Ibid., 380.

25   Seale, *The White House,* 125.

26   Ibid., 198.

27   Seale, *The President's House,* 386.

28   Seale, *The White House,* 92.

29   Seale, *The President's House,* 379.

30   Joshua Zeitz, *Lincoln's Boys: John Hay, John Nicolay, and the War for Lincoln's Image* (New York: Penguin Group, 2014), 95.

31   Guelzo, 186.

32   The Washington Monument made no progress at all during Lincoln's presidency; construction had been halted in 1854 due to a lack of funds, political squabbling, and then the war itself. It wouldn't resume until 1877, a dozen years after Lincoln's death.

33   Seale, *The President's House,* 372.

34   Donald, 310.

35   Donald, 310.

36   Zeitz, 94.

37   Donald, 310.

38   Ibid.

39 www.smithsonianmag.com/history/history-how-we-came-to-revere-abraham -lincoln-180949447/?all.
40 http://lincolncottage.org/lincolns-appetite-and-the-soldiers-home.
41 Donald, 392.
42 Zeitz, 94.
43 Donald, 446.
44 Geoffrey Perret, *Lincoln's War* (New York: Random House, 2004), 306.
45 Donald, 460–61.
46 Perret, 306.
47 Doris Kearns Goodwin, *Team of Rivals* (New York: Simon and Schuster, 2005), 583.
48 Garry Wills, "The Words That Remade America," *The Atlantic,* November 23, 2011, www.theatlantic.com/magazine/archive/2012/02/ the-words-that-remade-america/308801/?single_page=true.
49 Goodwin, *Team of Rivals,* 584.
50 Ibid.
51 Perret, 309.
52 Goodwin, *Team of Rivals,* 585–86.
53 Miller Center, July Message to Congress, http://millercenter.org/president/ speeches/speech-3508.
54 Goodwin, *Team of Rivals,* 534.
55 Ibid., 310
56 Ibid.

Chapter Nine
Ulysses S. Grant: The Secret Swearing-In

1 Willets, 93.
2 Cormac O'Brien, *Secret Lives of the US Presidents* (Philadelphia: Quirk Books, 2009), 104.
3 Ulysses S. Grant, *Personal Memoirs of U.S. Grant* (New York: Barnes & Noble, 2003), 121.
4 Miller Center, University of Virginia, Ulysses S. Grant, http://millercenter.org/ president/grant/essays/biography/2.
5 Geoffrey Perret, *Ulysses S. Grant Soldier & President* (New York: Random House, 1997), 265.
6 Grant, 669.
7 Seale, *The President's House,* 451.
8 LincolnCottage.org.
9 Seale, *The White House,* 118.
10 Michler Report (Washington, DC: US Government, January 29, 1867), as mentioned in Seale's *The White House,* 118.
11 Seale, *The President's House,* 451.
12 www.pbs.org/wnet/historyofus/web07/segment2_p.html.
13 "The Impeachment of Andrew Johnson," *American Experience,* PBS.

14 Seale, *The White House*, 122.

15 "The 13 Richest Americans of All Time," *Business Insider*, April 17, 2011.

16 Monkman, 143.

17 www.whitehousemuseum.org.

18 Ibid.

19 Boller, *Presidential Wives*, 134.

20 Ibid.

21 Mrs. Grant was instrumental in one significant change, the closing of the White House grounds "more or less permanently" because of concerns for the privacy of her children (*White House History*, 80).

22 Willets, 138.

23 Seale, *The White House*, 122.

24 Only two presidents have been elected at a younger age than Grant: John F. Kennedy was forty-three and Bill Clinton was forty-six, about five months younger. Theodore Roosevelt became president at forty-two upon the death of William McKinley.

25 William S. McFeely, *Grant* (New York: W. W. Norton & Co., 1982), 450.

26 Michael Korda, *Ulysses S. Grant* (New York: Atlas Books, 2004), 2–3.

27 Seale, *The White House*, 122.

28 Monkman, 147.

29 Seale, *The White House*, 124–25.

30 Seale, *The President's House*, 483.

31 Ibid., 486.

32 "The Rise and Fall of Jim Crow," *The American Experience*, PBS.

Chapter Ten
Rutherford B. Hayes: The Wired White House

1 Monkman, 156.

2 Seale, *The White House*, 129.

3 Ibid.

4 Monkman, 155.

5 "Col. W. H. Crook Dead," *New York Times*, March 14, 1915, http://query.nytimes.com/mem/archive-free/pdf?res=9506E0DF103DE333A25757C1A9659C946496D6CF.

6 Monkman, 156.

7 Ibid.

8 Miller Center, American President Project, http://millercenter.org/president/hayes/essays/firstlady.

9 Seale, *The White House*, 132.

10 Research provided by Becky Hill of the Rutherford B. Hayes Presidential Center.

11 Ari Hoogenboom, *Rutherford B. Hayes: Warrior and President* (Lawrence: University of Kansas Press, 1995), 348.

12 Ibid.

13 Hans Trefousse, *Rutherford B. Hayes* (New York: Times Books, 2002), 114.

14 Seale, *The President's House*, 491.

15 Boller, *Presidential Wives* 148.

16 Seale, *The President's House,* 492.

17 Hoogenboom, 384.

18 Seale, *The President's House,* 492.

19 Richard Norton Smith, "America's House: The Bully Pulpit on Pennsylvania Avenue," in *The White House*, Frank Freidel and William Pencak, eds. (Boston: Northeastern University Press, 1994), 36.

20 Seale, *The White House*, 126.

21 Perhaps it wasn't quite the last chance. It was rumored that White House stewards, upon request, would secretly spike the punch of guests attending events there (Roberts, 142).

22 Seale, *The President's House,* 494.

23 Ibid.

24 Ibid.

25 The Andrew Johnson White House, White House Historical Association, www .whha.org/photographs/white-house-administrations/andrew-johnson-white-house.html.

26 *The American Experience*, PBS, www.pbs.org/wgbh/amex/telephone/peopleevents/ mabell.html.

27 "All About the Telephone Long Before 'Press 1,'" *New York Times*, February 3, 1997, www.nytimes.com/1997/02/03/arts/all-about-the-telephone-long-before-press-1 .html.

28 White House History—Technology at the White House, www.whitehousehistory .org/history/white-house-timelines/technology-1850s-1890s.html.

29 Robert H. Ferrell, "The Expanding White House," from *The White House,* Freidel and Pencak, eds. (Boston: Northeastern University Press, 1994), 101.

30 "Exhibit Delves into Edison's Late-Night Visit with Hayes," *Toledo Blade*, March 14, 2002, www.toledoblade.com/frontpage/2002/03/14/Exhibit-delves-into-Edison-s-late-night-visit-with-Hayes.html.

31 Of all his inventions, the phonograph was Edison's favorite. "I've made some machines; but this is my baby, and I expect it to grow up to be a big feller and support me in my old age," he said. (Timeline: Thomas Edison National Historical Park [US National Park Service], www.nps.gov/edis/forkids/timeline-of-edison-and-his-inventions.htm).

32 Hoogenboom, 346.

33 "Exhibit Delves into Edison's Late-Night Visit with Hayes," *Toledo Blade*, March 14, 2002.

34 Seale, *The President's House,* 494.

35 Ibid.

36 Seale, *The President's House,* 504.

37 Trefousse, 119.

Chapter Eleven
William McKinley: The Spanish-American War

1   Some prominent Americans opposed this American expansionism. A group, the "American Anti-Imperialist League," sprung up; members included former president Grover Cleveland, industrialist Andrew Carnegie, and author Mark Twain. (Library of Congress: *Teacher's Guide to the Spanish-American War*, www.loc.gov/teachers/classroommaterials/primarysourcesets/spanish-american-war/pdf/teacher_guide.pdf).

2   Charles R. Morris, *The Tycoons* (New York: Owl Books, 2005), 246.

3   Kevin Phillips, *William McKinley* (New York: Times Books, 2003), 67.

4   Christina Romer, "Spurious Volatility in Historical Unemployment Data," *Journal of Political Economy* 94 (1): (1986), 1–37. doi: 10.1086/261361.

5   Phillips, 67.

6   Howard Wayne Morgan, *William McKinley and His America* (Kent, OH: The Kent State University Press, 2003), 29–30.

7   Phillips, 30.

8   Ibid.

9   Ibid.

10 Eugene L. Roberts Jr. and Douglas B. Ward, "The Press, Protestors and Presidents," in *The White House*, Frank Freidel and William Pencak eds. (Boston: Northeastern University Press, 1993), p.129.

11 Morgan, 245.

12 Ibid.

13 Seale, *The President's House*, 691.

14 Ibid., 625

15 Morgan, 245.

16 Ibid.

17 US Highway Administration, "Transportation in America's Postal System," www.fhwa.dot.gov/infrastructure/back0304.cfm.

18 census.gov, data for 1800, www.census.gov/history/www/through_the_decades/fast_facts/1800_fast_facts.html.

19 census.gov, data for 1900, www.census.gov/history/www/through_the_decades/fast_facts/1900_fast_facts.html.

20 Seale, *The White House*, 160.

21 Ibid.

22 Ibid., 165.

23 Willets, 118.

24 Phillips, 139.

25 Miller Center, McKinley, Key Events (Charlottesville: University of Virginia), http://millercenter.org/president/mckinley/key-events.

26 history.com, "William McKinley, First US President to Ride in a Car, Is Born," www.history.com/this-day-in-history/william-mckinley-first-us-president-to-ride-in-a-car-is-born.

27 Willets, 118.

28 Boller, *Presidential Wives*, 184.
29 Roberts, 170–71.
30 Ibid.
31 Roberts, 169.
32 Seale, *The President's House*, 619.
33 Elise Kirk, Musical Highlights from the White House, 81–83, as reprinted in WhiteHousehistory.org, www.whitehousehistory.org/history/white-house-timelines/music-performances-1850s-1890s.html.
34 National Park Service, Antietam National Battlefield, Monument to William McKinley, www.nps.gov/anti/historyculture/mnt-mckinley.htm.
35 McKinley's commanding officer was himself a future president: Col. Rutherford Hayes, who called McKinley "one of the bravest and finest young officers in the army" (Roberts, 170).
36 http://millercenter.org/president/mckinley.
37 Evan Thomas, *The War Lovers* (New York: Little, Brown and Company, 2010), 161.
38 Ibid.
39 PBS.org, "Crucible of Empire," www.pbs.org/crucible/bio_hearst.html.
40 Lewis Gould, *The Spanish-American War and President McKinley* (Lawrence, Kansas: University Press of Kansas, 1980) 35.
41 Gould, 37.
42 University of Houston, *The Spanish American War,* Digital History, www.digitalhistory.uh.edu/disp_textbook.cfm?smtID=2&psid=3160.
43 Gould, 40.
44 Thomas, 12.
45 Phillips, 94.
46 Although certain it was a mine, the board's final report to the president on March 25th said it "has been unable to obtain evidence fixing the responsibility ... upon any person or persons" (Seale, *The President's House*, 626).
47 Seale, *The President's House*, 626.
48 Gould, 45.
49 The US-Mexican War, Communications, PBS, www.pbs.org/kera/usmexicanwar/war/communications.html.
50 Leish, 78.
51 Ibid.
52 Gould, 55.
53 Seale, *The President's House,* 633.
54 Ibid.
55 Ibid.
56 The Spanish-American War Centennial Website, www.spanamwar.com/casualties.htm.
57 *White House History* (Washington, DC: White House Historical Association, 2004), 117.

58 "Why Do We Even Have a Secret Service?", *Washington Post,* October 2, 2014, www.washingtonpost.com/blogs/the-fix/wp/2014/10/02/why-do-we-even-have-a-secret-service/.

59 The Secret Service wasn't responsible for protecting public officials in McKinley's time, but sometimes did so on an informal and part-time basis.

60 Seale, *The President's House,* 630.

61 Ibid.

62 "Why Do We Even Have a Secret Service?", *Washington Post,* October 2, 2014.

63 "Flower Girl Recalls One Day of Tragedy," *Evening Independent,* February 27, 1971, http://news.google.com/newspapers?nid=950&dat=19710227&id=AWhQA AAAIBAJ&sjid=j1cDAAAAIBAJ&pg=6041,7130894.

64 Col. G. W. Townsend, *Memorial Life of William McKinley* (publisher not listed, 1901), 193.

65 Ibid., 194

66 Ibid., 251

Chapter Twelve
Theodore Roosevelt: The Dawn of the American Century

1   United States Secret Service History, www.secretservice.gov/history.shtml.

2   The Secret Service began informal protection of President Cleveland in 1894, but only on a part-time basis. William McKinley also had official, part-time protection—but not on the day he was shot (www.secretservice.gov/history.shtml).

3   Seale, *The President's House,* 689.

4   US National Park Service, "The Roosevelt Pets," www.nps.gov/thrb/historyculture/the-roosevelt-pets.htm.

5   John Tyler and his two wives had fifteen children born between 1815 and 1860. One died before he became president, and seven were born after he left the White House.

6   Seale, *The White House,* 166.

7   Seale, *The President's House,* 650.

8   Edmund Morris, *Theodore Rex* (New York: Random House, 2001), 174.

9   Seale, *The President's House,* 659.

10 Monkman, 185.

11 Ferrell, "The Expanding White House," from *The White House,* Freidel and Pencak, eds. (Boston: Northeastern University Press, 1994), 108.

12 Leish, 85.

13 Seale, *The White House,* 168.

14 White House Historical Association, www.whha.org/whha_classroom/classroom_4-8-building.html.

15 The "Temporary" part of the name went away after about six months (Seale, *The President's House,* 690).

16 Willets, 69.

17 Seale, *The President's House,* 672.

18 Ibid., 690.

19 Ibid., 713.
20 Seale, *The White House*, 145.
21 Remnants of the Tiffany screens can be seen today across the street at St. John's Episcopal Church.
22 Monkman, 186.
23 Ibid., 192.
24 Ibid.
25 *White House History*, 124.
26 This shared interest aside, Theodore Roosevelt's "extreme distaste for Jefferson was well known" (Seale, *The President's House*, 673).
27 Seale, *The President's House*, 669.
28 Ibid., 671.
29 Ibid., 670.
30 Ibid., 672.
31 Ibid., 671.
32 Ibid., 669.
33 Ibid., 678–79.
34 Ibid., 679.
35 Ibid., 681.
36 Willets, 200–1.
37 Seale, *The President's House*, 651.
38 Michael Beschloss, "When T. R. Saw Lincoln," *New York Times*, May 21, 2014, www.nytimes.com/2014/05/22/upshot/when-tr-saw-lincoln.html.
39 During the Civil War, Mary and Abraham Lincoln had befriended and gone to church with Theodore Roosevelt's father (Beschloss, *New York Times*, May 21, 2014).
40 Willets, 48.
41 Monkman, 197.
42 Willets, 48–49.
43 Willets, 63.
44 Louis Auchincloss, *Theodore Roosevelt* (New York: Times Books, 2001), 41.
45 White House Historical Association, *The White House: An Historical Guide* (Washington, DC: White House Historical Association, 1991), 140.
46 Seale, *The President's House*, 691.
47 Ibid., 727.
48 Ibid.
49 Ibid.
50 Ibid.
51 Ibid., 687.
52 Ibid., 726.
53 James M. Goode, "The Theodore Roosevelt Years," from *White House History* (Washington, DC: White House Historical Association, 2004), 117.

Chapter Thirteen
Woodrow Wilson: The Secret Illness

1   A. Scott Berg, *Wilson* (New York: G. Putnam's Sons, 2013), 355.
2   Ibid.
3   Ibid., 358.
4   Boller, *Presidential Wives*, 219.
5   Berg, 6.
6   Miller Center, Edith Wilson, http://millercenter.org/president/wilson/essays/firstlady.
7   "Woodrow Wilson," *American Experience*, PBS, www.pbs.org/wgbh/amex/wilson/filmmore/fm_trans2.html.
8   Two of Wilson's daughters also married during his White House years: Jessie and Eleanor.
9   David Finn and Hillary Rodham Clinton, *20th Century American Sculpture in the White House Garden* (New York: Henry Abrams, Inc., 2000), 16.
10 Seale, *The White House*, 209.
11 Seale, *The President's House,* 800.
12 Ibid.
13 Monkman, 201.
14 Lenox Corporation, "Lenox History," www.lenox.com/index.cfm?ss=services&cat=about&dp=history.
15 Monkman, 201.
16 Ibid.
17 WhiteHousemuseum.org, "The Vermeil Room," www.whitehousemuseum.org/floor0/vermeil-room.htm.
18 Ibid.
19 Berg, 364.
20 "The Great War—Casualties and Deaths," www.pbs.org/greatwar/resources/casdeath_pop.html.
21 Roberts, 202–3.
22 Ibid., 203.
23 Russia had been an allied power until Vladimir Lenin, the Bolshevik leader, pulled Russia out of the war in 1917.
24 Prior to Wilson's testimony, the only sitting presidents who had testified before Congress were George Washington and Abraham Lincoln (US Senate archives).
25 Berg, 620.
26 Seale, *The President's House,* 830–32.
27 Boller, *Presidential Wives,* 226.
28 Wilson had been aware of his slipping memory for quite some time. He joked about his growing absentmindedness, saying he had a "leaky brain" (Berg, 569).
29 Seale, *The President's House,* 832.
30 Ibid., 832–33.
31 Ibid.
32 Phyllis Lee Levin, *Edith and Woodrow* (New York: Scribner, 2001), 337.

33 Berg, 642.
34 Levin, 338–39.
35 News conference by President John F. Kennedy, May 8, 1963, www.youtube.com/watch?v=GspxiLXt8CI.
36 Levin, 337.
37 Berg, 642.
38 Levin, 338.
39 Berg, 644.
40 Ibid., 643.
41 Rick Beyer, *The Greatest Presidential Stories Never Told* (New York: Collins, 2007), 149.
42 Levin, 341.
43 Boller, *Presidential Wives*, 226.
44 Ibid., 227.
45 James S. McCallops, *Edith Bolling Galt Wilson: The Unintended President* (Hauppauge, NY: Nova Publishers, 2003), 73.
46 Levin, 344.
47 Ibid., 352.
48 Ibid., 344.
49 Beyer, 148–49.
50 Ibid.
51 In the two months after his shooting, Garfield only performed one official act—signing an extradition order (John Milton Cooper Jr., "Disability in the White House: The Case of Woodrow Wilson," published in Freidel and Pencak's *The White House*, 75).
52 "Succession Confusion: When the President Is Incapacitated," *Los Angeles Times*, May 31, 1992.
53 Edmund Morris, *The Rise of Theodore Roosevelt* (New York: Random House, 1979), 780.
54 Nobel Foundation, *Nobel Lectures, 1901–1925* (Hackensack, NJ: World Scientific Publishing Co., 1999), 295.

Chapter Fourteen
Warren G. Harding: Scandals Galore

1 Samuel and Dorothy Rosenman, *Presidential Style* (New York: Harper & Row, 1976), 534.
2 Seale, *The President's House*, 837.
3 Ed Tant, "Harding Was Good Man but Bad President," *Athens* (GA) *Banner-Herald*, August 10, 2013.
4 Seale, *The President's House*, 848.
5 Ibid., 840.
6 Ibid.
7 Ibid.
8 Ibid., 841.

9   Rosenman and Rosenman, 525.

10   David Pietrusza, *1920: The Year of the Six Presidents* (New York: Basic Books, 2009), Chapter 14.

11   S. Joseph Krause, *Harding, His Presidency and Love Life Reappraised* (Bloomington, IN: Author Books, 2013), 102.

12   Rosenman and Rosenman, 528.

13   James D. Robenalt, *The Harding Affair: Love and Espionage during the Great War* (New York: Palgrave MacMillan, 2009), 41.

14   Carl Sferrazza Anthony, "A President of the Peephole," *Washington Post*, June 7, 1998.

15   Robenalt, 80.

16   Jordan Michael Smith, "The Letters That Warren G. Harding's Family Didn't Want You to See," *New York Times Magazine*, July 7, 2014.

17   Boller, *Presidential Wives*, 247–48.

18   Anthony, "A President of the Peephole," *Washington Post*, June 7, 1998.

19   Ibid.

20   Ibid.

21   Carl Sferrazza Anthony, "The Most Scandalous President," *American Heritage Magazine*, 1998, Vol. 49, issue 4, www.americanheritage.com/content/ most-scandalous-president?page=show.

22   Ibid.

23   Paul Duke, "Tales from the White House Coat Closet," *Washington Post*, March 1, 1998, C3.

24   Michael Kerrigan, *American Presidents: A Dark History* (New York: Metro Books, 2011), 140.

25   Mark Sullivan, *Our Times: The United States 1900–1925* (New York: Charles Scribner's Sons, 1937), vol. VI, 243–44.

26   WhiteHouseMuseum.org.

27   Miller Center, American President: A Reference Resource, Warren Gamaliel Harding Front Page (Charlottesville, VA).

28   Seale, *The President's House*, 842.

29   Ibid., 841.

30   Ibid., 842.

31   Associated Press, "Harding Lost Set of White House China at Poker," June 28, 1965.

32   Francis Russell, *The Shadow of Blooming Grove: Warren G. Harding in His Times* (Norwalk, CT: Easton Press, 1962).

33   Whitcomb and Whitcomb, 272.

34   Michael J. O'Neal, *America in the 1920s* (New York: Stonesong Press, 2006), 39.

35   Whitcomb and Whitcomb, 272.

Chapter Fifteen
Calvin Coolidge: The Roaring Twenties

1   White House Museum, www.whitehousemuseum.org/residence.htm.

2   David Greenberg, *Calvin Coolidge* (New York: Times Books, 2006), 67.

3 Seale, *The President's House*, 854.

4 Once Coolidge was woken up by a noise in his suite at the Willard. A fellow guest had broken in and was burglarizing the president. Startled to learn that it was Coolidge, the man explained that he didn't have enough money to return home. The president gave him $32, which he called a "loan" and sent the man on his way (Amity Shlaes, *Coolidge* [New York: HarperCollins, 2013], 259).

5 Richard Lederer, *Presidential Trivia* (Salt Lake City: Gibbs Smith, 2007), 51.

6 Peter Hannaford, *Presidential Retreats* (New York: Threshold Editions, 2012), 151.

7 Robert E. Gilbert, "Calvin Coolidge's Tragic Presidency: The Political Effects of Bereavement and Depression," *Journal of American Studies* 39, 2005, 91, http://bit .ly/12aFUrY.

8 Boller, *Presidential Anecdotes*, 244.

9 Lederer, 51.

10 O'Brien, 171.

11 Seale, *The President's House*, 866.

12 Seale, *The White House*, 211.

13 Seale, *The President's House*, 871.

14 Ibid., 872.

15 Ibid.

16 Ibid., 874.

17 Ibid., 875.

18 Ibid.

19 Seale, *The White House*, 212.

20 Seale, *The President's House*, 877.

21 Ibid.

22 Ibid.

23 Monkman, 206.

24 Ibid.

25 Seale, *The President's House*, 880.

26 Ibid., 883.

27 Ibid., 881.

28 Ibid., 883.

29 Seale, *The White House*, 214.

30 Ibid.

31 Roberts, 223.

32 Shlaes, 221.

33 Greenberg, 62.

34 Ibid., 63.

35 "A Million Persons Will Hear Coolidge's Voice When He Addresses Congress This Afternoon," *New York Times*, www.nytimes.com/learning/general/onthisday/ big/1206.html#article, December 6, 1923.

36 Shlaes, 272.

37 Ibid., 273.

38 Greenberg, 64.

39 Ibid., 65.
40 Robert Sobel, *Coolidge* (Washington, DC: Regnery, 1998), 369.
41 Shlaes, 381.
42 Sobel, 370.
43 Shlaes, 382.

Chapter Sixteen
Franklin D. Roosevelt: The Fireside Chats

1 "10 Things You May Not Know About the Roosevelts," www.history.com/news/10-things-you-may-not-know-about-the-roosevelts.
2 Amy La Follette Jensen, *The White House and Its Thirty-Four Families* (New York: McGraw-Hill, 1958), 235.
3 Whitcomb and Whitcomb, 300.
4 Ibid.
5 Ibid.
6 Ibid.
7 Ibid., 303.
8 Survey by the Siena College Research Institute in collaboration with C-SPAN and The White House Historical Association.
9 Roberts, 244.
10 Whitcomb and Whitcomb, 302.
11 Seale, *The President's House*, 926.
12 Ibid., 927.
13 Because Hickok's friendship with Mrs. Roosevelt compromised her objectivity as a reporter, she resigned her job at the AP and was hired—at the first lady's urging—at the Federal Emergency Relief Administration.
14 Hazel Rowley, *Franklin and Eleanor: An Extraordinary Marriage* (New York: Farrar, Straus and Giroux, 2010), 52.
15 Whitcomb and Whitcomb, 302.
16 Nick Taylor, "A Short History of the Great Depression," *New York Times*, http://topics.nytimes.com/top/reference/timestopics/subjects/g/great_depression_1930s/index.html.
17 After a fire roared through the West Wing in 1929, gutting the Oval Office, President Herbert Hoover used the rebuilding as an opportunity to install a central air-conditioning system, built by the Carrier Engineering Company. But Hoover neglected to install such a system in the neighboring mansion itself.
18 Seale, *The President's House*, 927.
19 Ibid., 923.
20 Ibid., 924.
21 Seale, *The White House*, 220.
22 Seale, *The President's House*, 925.
23 The indoor pool ended one of the more colorful chapters of presidential life: that of presidents heading to the nearby Potomac River for a brisk swim. John Quincy Adams, known for his early-morning dips in the nude, was once accosted by an

aggressive female reporter who sat on his clothes and wouldn't give them back until he answered her questions. The president, up to his neck, relented; Anne Royall's interview is believed to be the first newspaper interview with a sitting president ("Anne Royall Rock Gone," *New York Times*, August 21, 1913).

24 Seale, *The White House*, 221.
25 Ibid.
26 Ibid., 221–22.
27 Ibid., 223.
28 Seale, *The President's House*, 943.
29 Seale, *The White House*, 223.
30 Ibid.
31 WhiteHouseMuseum.org.
32 Ibid.
33 Matthew Pressman, "The Myth of FDR's Secret Disability," *Time*, July 12, 2013.
34 Franklin D. Roosevelt Presidential Library and Museum, www.fdrlibrary.marist.edu/facts/.
35 Stephen T. Early, *The Making of FDR* (Amherst, NY: Prometheus Books, 2008), 232.
36 Whitcomb and Whitcomb, 302.
37 Ibid., 314.
38 Ibid., 316.
39 Donald W. Whisenhunt, *President Herbert Hoover* (Hauppauge, NY: Nova Science Publishers, Inc., 2007), 70.
40 David Halberstam, *The Powers That Be* (New York: Alfred A. Knopf, 1979), 15.
41 Ibid., 16–17.
42 Frank Freidel, *Franklin D. Roosevelt* (Boston: Little, Brown and Company, 1990), 99.
43 Halberstam, 15.
44 Edward H. Kavinoly and Julian Par, eds., *My Friends* (Buffalo, NY: Foster & Stewart Publishing Corp., 1945), 8.
45 Telegram to the President, March 13, 1933 (Hyde Park, NY: Franklin D. Roosevelt Presidential Library and Museum).
46 John Steele Gordon, *An Empire of Wealth* (New York: HarperCollins Publishers, 2004), 332.
47 Amos Kiewe, *FDR's First Fireside Chat: Public Confidence and the Banking Crisis*, (College Station, TX: Texas A&M University Press, 2007), 118.
48 WillRogers.com, "Daily Papers," Telegram #2061.
49 Internal Revenue Service, "Statistics of Income for 1929" (Washington, DC: US Government Printing Office, 1931), 4.
50 Internal Revenue Service, "Statistics of Income for 1933" (Washington, DC: US Government Printing Office, 1935), 5.
51 RadioStratosphere.com, "Radio in the 1930s."
52 Halberstam, 15.

Chapter Seventeen
Harry Truman: "The Moon, the Stars, and All the Planets"

1 There have been questions as to whether Harding may have been poisoned by his wife, who was tired of is philandering. But there is no substantive evidence to support this.

2 David McCullough, *Truman* (New York: Simon & Schuster, 1992), 341.

3 Ibid., 342.

4 Ibid.

5 Ibid., 353.

6 Seale, *The President's House*, 1004.

7 Ibid., 1004–5.

8 Fires were nothing new to the White House. On Christmas Eve 1929, an electrical fire roared through the West Wing, gutting President Herbert Hoover's office.

9 Ibid., 1002.

10 Ibid., 1005.

11 Monkman, 218.

12 Seale, *The President's House*, 1005.

13 Harry S. Truman, edited by Margaret Truman, *Where the Buck Stops, The Personal and Private Writings of Harry S. Truman* (New York: Warner Books, 1989), 204.

14 Richard Rhodes, *The Making of the Atomic Bomb* (New York: Simon & Schuster, 1986), 617.

15 Truman, 204.

16 Ibid.

17 Einstein has gone down in history as the writer of the famous August 2, 1939 letter to Roosevelt, but he merely signed it. The letter was actually written by the Hungarian-born physicist Leo Szilard, who then persuaded the more famous Einstein (whose English was not good enough to have written such a letter) to sign it. The letter was then delivered to Roosevelt in person on October 11th by Alexander Sachs, who had worked on FDR's 1932 campaign and had served as an informal advisor ever since.

18 National World War II Museum, www.nationalww2museum.org/focus-on/iwo-jima-fact-sheet.pdf.

19 *American Experience*, PBS, www.pbs.org/wgbh/americanexperience/features/general-article/pacific-civilians-okinawa/.

20 Truman, 205.

21 www.nuclearfiles.org/menu/key-issues/nuclear-weapons/history/pre-cold-war/hiroshima-nagasaki/decision-drop-bomb-chronology.htm.

22 The full description, as noted by Brigadier General T. F. Farrell, is noteworthy: "The effects could well be called unprecedented, magnificent, beautiful, stupendous, and terrifying. The lighting effects beggared description. The whole country was lighted by a searing light with the intensity many times that of the midday sun. It was golden, purple, violet, gray, and blue. It lighted every peak, crevasse and ridge of the nearby mountain range with a clarity and beauty that cannot be described but must

be seen to be imagined" (www.nuclearfiles.org/menu/key-issues/nuclear-weapons/history/pre-cold-war/hiroshima-nagasaki/decision-drop-bomb-chronology.htm).

23 Rhodes, 673.

24 www.nuclearfiles.org/menu/key-issues/nuclear-weapons/history/pre-cold-war/hiroshima-nagasaki/decision-drop-bomb-chronology.htm.

25 Rhodes, 676.

26 Truman, 206.

27 McCullough, *Truman*, 392.

28 Ibid.

29 Brewster wrote to President Truman as well, arguing that the original purpose of the bomb was to get it before Hitler. "But with the threat of Germany removed, we must stop this project." Brewster advocated a demonstration of the bomb on a Japanese target, to be followed by the curtailing of material for future bombs. "The idea of the destruction of civilization is not melodramatic hysteria or crackpot raving. It is a very real and, I submit, almost inevitable result." Brewster went on to say "It would be better to take greater casualties now in conquering Japan than to bring upon the world the tragedy of unrestrained competitive production of this material. . . . In the name of the future of our country and of the peace of the world, I beg you, sir. . . ." It is not known whether President Truman actually read it. On June 3rd, the president scribbled in his diary that using an atomic bomb in Japan would cause death and destruction "beyond imagination."

30 Ibid., 394.

31 Truman, 206.

32 Rhodes, 734, 740–41.

33 The timing appears to be coincidental. During the Yalta Conference in February 1945, Soviet leader Josef Stalin had pledged to President Roosevelt and British prime minister Winston Churchill that he would declare war against Japan ninety days after the surrender of Nazi Germany. The Germans surrendered on May 8, 1945.

34 Ibid., 480.

35 Truman, 206.

36 Seale, *The President's House*, 1007.

37 Ibid., 1008–10.

38 TrumanLibrary.org, www.trumanlibrary.org/whistlestop/qq/ds2_1.htm.

39 Seale, *The President's House*, 1012.

40 *White House History*, 254–55.

41 Seale, *The White House*, 48.

42 Robert Klara, *The Hidden White House* (New York: Thomas Dunne Books, 2013), 33.

43 Truman, 372.

44 Rosenman and Rosenman, 432.

45 J. Robert Moskin, *Mr. Truman's War* (New York: Random House, 1996), 34.

46 Rosenman and Rosenman, 428.

47 The Secret Service wasn't thrilled with Truman's morning walks, during which the president would buy newspapers, shake hands with passersby, and even deposit checks at the bank. Agents even rigged traffic lights to turn green as he approached intersections. When Truman discovered this, he complained to agents that they were ruining his walks.

48 Klara, 25.

49 Ibid., 23.

50 Seale, *The President's House*, 1003.

51 McCullough, *Truman*, 556.

52 Margaret Truman, *Bess W. Truman* (New York: Macmillan Publishing Company, 1986), 294.

53 Seale, *The President's House*, 1025.

54 Klara, 37.

55 Seale, *The President's House*, 1026.

56 Ibid., 1025.

57 *White House History*, 256.

58 Seale, *The White House*, 238.

59 Klara, 66

60 Truman, *Bess W. Truman*, 329.

61 Klara, 67.

62 Truman, *Bess W. Truman*, 329.

63 Klara, 72–73.

64 Seale, *The President's House*, 1026.

65 Seale, *The White House*, 277.

66 That President Coolidge's third floor would remain seems ironic. Coolidge, sick of rain seeping into the private quarters in the second floor, had the third floor installed to help prevent this. But the sheer weight of the floor placed greater stress on the mansion.

67 Seale, *The White House*, 240.

68 Ibid, 243.

69 Ibid., 252.

70 Ibid.

71 McCullough, *Truman*, 877.

72 Klara, 157–58.

73 Ibid., 159.

74 Ibid., 161.

75 Truman's renovation has obviously been modernized and expanded over the years; today the White House bomb shelter is part of the President's Emergency Operations Center (PEOC), lying deep beneath the East Wing. This should not be confused with the Situation Room, which is located in the West Wing.

76 Seale, *The President's House*, 1033–34.

77 McCullough, *Truman*, 879.

78 Ibid., 880.

79 Klara, 73.

80 McCullough, *Truman*, 881.
81 Coincidentally the 1814–1818 rebuilding of the White House—starting with James and Dolley Madison fleeing on August 24, 1814, and ending with James Monroe officially moving back in on January 1, 1818—was 1,225 days.
82 Seale, *The White House*, 267.
83 McCullough, *Truman*, 885.
84 Seale, *The White House*, 267.
85 Ibid.
86 McCullough, *Truman*, 885.
87 Ibid., 886.
88 Seale, *The White House*, 261.

Chapter Eighteen
John F. Kennedy: The Blood Red Carpet

1 William Manchester, *The Death of a President* (New York: Harper & Row, 1967), 55.
2 President Kennedy seemed to enjoy his wife's fame more than she appeared to. "Nobody wonders what Lyndon and I wear," he joked on the morning of his assassination.
3 Doug Wead, *All the President's Children* (New York: Atria Books, 2003) 22.
4 Halberstam, 316.
5 Ibid., 385–86.
6 Donald Spoto, *Jacqueline Bouvier Kennedy Onassis: A Life* (New York: St. Martin's Press, 2000), 45.
7 Bill Adler, *The Eloquent Jacqueline Kennedy Onassis: A Portrait in Her Own Words* (New York: HarperCollins, 2004), 107.
8 Boller, *Presidential Wives*, 363.
9 Ibid.
10 Whitcomb and Whitcomb, 348.
11 Monkman, 234.
12 Ibid.
13 Ibid.
14 Ibid.
15 Ibid., 238
16 Ibid.
17 Ibid., 158.
18 "The Obamas and the Kennedys," *The Guardian*, September 9, 2003.
19 In addition to Eisenhower using the Resolute desk in his broadcast studio, many presidents used it in their private quarters on the second floor of the White House.
20 "Jackie Kennedy's Devotion to White House Revealed," *CBS News*, February 14, 2012.
21 James A. Abbott and Elaine M. Rice, *Designing Camelot: The Kennedy White House Restoration* (New York: Van Nostrand Reinhold, 1998), 44.
22 Boller, *Presidential Wives*, 354.

23 "A Tour of the White House with Mrs. John F. Kennedy," *CBS News*, February 14, 1962.
24 Monkman, 233.
25 Tom Wicker, *Dwight D. Eisenhower* (New York: Times Books, 2002), 109.
26 Tom Wicker, John W. Finney, Max Frankel, and E. W. Kenworthy, "C.I.A.: Maker of Policy, or Tool?", *New York Times,* April 25, 1966, http://ratical.org/ratville/JFK/Unspeakable/Item03.pdf.
27 John F. Kennedy Presidential Library & Museum, www.jfklibrary.org/JFK/JFK-Legacy/Situation-Room.aspx.
28 Michael Bohn, *Nerve Center* (Washington, DC: Brassey's, Inc., 2003), 23.
29 Ibid., 24.
30 Ibid., 32
31 John F. Kennedy Library and Museum, JFKLibrary.org.
32 Bohn, 34.
33 Ibid., 35.
34 Manchester, 16.
35 David Brinkley, *Brinkley's Beat: People, Places, and Events That Shaped My Time* (New York: Knopf Doubleday Publishing Group, 2003),196.
36 Manchester, 252.
37 Ibid., 465.
38 Jim Bishop, *The Day Kennedy Was Shot* (New York: Greenwich House, 1968), 409.
39 Manchester, 420.
40 US Capitol, Architect of the Capitol, "The Catafalque," www.aoc.gov/nations-stage/catafalque.
41 Sam Kashner, "A Clash of Camelots," *Vanity Fair*, October 2009, www.vanityfair.com/politics/features/2009/10/death-of-a-president200910.

Chapter Nineteen
Richard Nixon: The Enemy Within

1 David Greenberg, *Nixon's Shadow: The History of an Image* (New York: W. W. Norton & Company, 2003), 307.
2 Nixon won in a mega-landslide, winning 61 percent of the popular vote and 520 of 538 electoral votes.
3 David Greenberg, "Was Nixon Robbed?", *Slate*, October 16, 2000.
4 Kashner, "A Clash of Camelots," *Vanity Fair*, October 2009.
5 Roberts, 297.
6 Whitcomb and Whitcomb, 398.
7 "Pat Nixon and the Golden Age of the White House," Nixonfoundation.org.
8 Carl Sferrazza Anthony, *First Ladies: The Saga of the Presidents' Wives and Their Power; 1961–1990* (Volume II) (New York: William Morrow and Co., 1991), 188.
9 Anthony, *First Ladies*, 187.
10 Ibid.
11 "The Presidential Helicopter," nixonfoundation.org.
12 Anthony, *First Ladies*, 188.

13 "Pat Nixon and the Golden Age of the White House," www.nixonfoundation.org.
14 Robert Dallek, *Nixon and Kissinger* (New York: HarperCollins Publishers, 2007), 96.
15 Tom Scanlan, *Beautiful America's Washington, Part 3* (Woodburn, OR: Beautiful America Publishing Co., 2002), 75.
16 Dallek, 96.
17 Ibid., 99
18 Thomas J. Whalen, *JFK and His Enemies: A Portrait of Power* (Lanham, MD: Rowman & Littlefield, 2014), 13.
19 Helen Thomas, *Front Row at the White House: My Life and Times* (New York: Simon and Schuster, 1999), 125.
20 Jon Marshall, "Nixon Is Gone, But His Media Strategy Lives On," *The Atlantic,* August 4, 2014.
21 Douglas Brinkley and Luke A. Nichter, eds., *The Nixon Tapes* (New York: Houghton Mifflin Harcourt, 2014), 703.
22 Eugene L. Roberts Jr. and Douglas B. Ward, "The Press, Protestors, and Presidents," from *The White House,* edited by Frank Freidel and William Pencak (Boston: Northeastern University Press, 1994), 135.
23 Dallek, 97.
24 Ibid.
25 Ibid.

Chapter Twenty
Ronald Reagan: Lights, Camera, Action

1 www.whitehouse.gov/interactive-tour/family-theater.
2 Tim Sanford, "Cretors Anniversary Popcorn Machine Adorns White House Theater," *Vending Times*, Vol. 50, No. 9, September 2010.
3 "The Presidents," *American Experience*, PBS.org.
4 The only president with more prior executive experience than Reagan was Bill Clinton, who spent a dozen years as governor of Arkansas.
5 Whitcomb and Whitcomb, 423.
6 Lou Cannon, *President Reagan: The Role of a Lifetime* (New York: Simon & Schuster, 1991), 38.
7 David Burke, "WOC Radio Legacy Includes Ronald Reagan," *Quad-City Times*, September 14, 2014.
8 Cannon, 108.
9 Biography of Ronald Reagan, Virginia's Miller Center, http://millercenter.org/president/reagan/essays/biography/2.
10 Mark K. Updegrove, *Baptism by Fire: Eight Presidents Who Took Office in Times of Crisis* (London: Macmillan, 2009), 135.
11 Robert Schlesinger, *White House Ghosts* (New York: Simon & Schuster, 2008), 331.
12 Ronald Reagan Presidential Library, National Archives and Records Administration.

13 Like Warren and Flossie Harding, who privately flouted Prohibition during their brief White House tenure, the Carters refused to serve hard liquor in public, but privately were said to enjoy Bloody Marys—before attending church on Sunday.

14 Whitcomb and Whitcomb, 431.

15 Monkman, 259.

16 Whitcomb and Whitcomb, 431.

17 Ibid., 432.

18 Nancy Reagan, *My Turn* (New York: Random House, 1989), 29.

19 Ibid.

20 Ronald Reagan, *An American Life* (New York: Simon and Schuster, 1990), 250.

21 Ronald Reagan Presidential Library, National Archives and Records Administration.

22 James C. Humes, *The Wit & Wisdom of Ronald Reagan* (Washington, DC: Regnery Publishing, 2007).

23 Cannon, 57.

24 Ibid., 58.

25 Ibid., 61.

26 Ibid., 60.

27 "The Rise and Fall of Jim Crow," *American Experience*, PBS.

28 Roger Ebert, "The *Birth of a Nation* Movie Review," March 30, 2003.

29 Levin, 352.

30 Tevi Troy, *What Jefferson Read, Ike Watched and Obama Tweeted* (Washington, DC: Regnery Publishing, 2013), 119.

31 Ibid., 120.

32 Walt Disney Studios, *Walt Disney Treasures—Mickey Mouse in Black and White* (film), 2002.

33 Troy, 121.

34 Ibid., 125.

35 Mark White, *Kennedy: A Cultural History of an American Icon* (London: Bloomsbury Publishing, LLC, 2013), 64.

36 Manchester, 89–90.

37 Lyndon Baines Johnson Library, University of Texas.

38 Troy, 127.

39 Ibid.

40 Gerald R. Ford Library and Museum.

41 Tevi Troy, "What's Playing at the White House Movie Theater?", *Washingtonian* magazine, February 2011.

42 Interview with Roger Ebert, December 18, 1999, www.rogerebert.com/interviews/qanda-clinton-on-movies.

43 Ibid.

44 Whitehousemuseum.org.

45 Interview with Roger Ebert.

46 www.whitehousemuseum.org.

47 Interview with Katie Couric, September 23, 2008.

48   Troy, 130.

Chapter Twenty-One
Barack Obama: The bin Laden Raid

1   Carl Sferrazza Anthony, *America's First Families* (New York: Touchstone, 2000), 22.
2   Joshua Wolf Shenk, "Lincoln's Great Depression," *The Atlantic*, October 1, 2005.
3   While Willie was dying, the Lincolns' middle son, Tad, came down with the same illness and was confined to a nearby bedroom; the president and Mrs. Lincoln feared that they would lose him as well.
4   Donald, 336.
5   Ibid.
6   James L. Swanson, *Manhunt* (New York: HarperCollins, 2006), 154.
7   UCLA Newsroom, "Obama's Former Aide Shares Glimpses of Life with President," July 24, 2013.
8   The three other card players were his assistants Reggie Love and Marvin Nicholson, and White House photographer, Pete Souza (who, incidentally, was also President Reagan's personal photographer).
9   UCLA interview with Reggie Love.
10   The White House has never officially confirmed that the card game took place. Presidential spokesman Josh Earnest told me in 2015, "I wish Reggie hadn't said what he did" and refused to comment further, citing presidential privacy. Love indicated that the card game took place in the "private dining room," which usually refers to the second floor dining room. The dining room off the Oval Office is generally referred to as the "president's dining room" or the "Oval Office dining room."
11   Papers of John F. Kennedy: Presidential Papers, National Security Files, McGeorge Bundy Correspondence, Memos to the President, May 1961: 6–28.
12   Bohn, 26.
13   Ibid., 9.
14   Henry Kissinger, *White House Years* (Boston: Little, Brown, 1979), 315.
15   Avner Cohen, "The Last Nuclear Moment," *New York Times*, October 6, 2003.
16   Bohn, 115.
17   Ibid., 108.
18   Michael Bohn, "Former Staffers Remember the White House Situation Room on 9/11," McClatchy Newspapers, August 29, 2011.
19   Ibid.
20   Ibid.
21   The Civil War battle of Antietam—September 17, 1862—killed 3,650 (National Park Service data).
22   Nicholas Schmidle, "Getting bin Laden," *New Yorker*, August 8, 2011.

INDEX

About the Author

An award-winning, independent member of the White House press corps, and its most followed member on Twitter, **Paul Brandus** founded West Wing Reports in 2009 and provides reports for television, radio, and print outlets around the United States and overseas. A frequent speaker on presidential leadership and history and a columnist for MarketWatch, his career spans network television, Wall Street, and several years in Moscow, where he covered the collapse of the Soviet Union and its aftermath for NBC Radio, National Public Radio, and the Public Radio International's "Marketplace." He has traveled to fifty-three countries on five continents and has reported from, among other places, Iraq, Chechnya, China, and Guantanamo Bay, Cuba. He is a member of the White House Correspondents Association and a former board member of the Overseas Press Club of America.